The Mismeasure of the Self

The Mismeasure of the Self

A Study in Vice Epistemology

ALESSANDRA TANESINI

OXFORD
UNIVERSITY PRESS

Great Clarendon Street, Oxford, OX2 6DP,
United Kingdom

Oxford University Press is a department of the University of Oxford.
It furthers the University's objective of excellence in research, scholarship,
and education by publishing worldwide. Oxford is a registered trade mark of
Oxford University Press in the UK and in certain other countries

© Alessandra Tanesini 2021

The moral rights of the author have been asserted

First Edition published in 2021

Impression: 2

All rights reserved. No part of this publication may be reproduced, stored in
a retrieval system, or transmitted, in any form or by any means, without the
prior permission in writing of Oxford University Press, or as expressly permitted
by law, by licence or under terms agreed with the appropriate reprographics
rights organization. Enquiries concerning reproduction outside the scope of the
above should be sent to the Rights Department, Oxford University Press, at the
address above

You must not circulate this work in any other form
and you must impose this same condition on any acquirer

Published in the United States of America by Oxford University Press
198 Madison Avenue, New York, NY 10016, United States of America

British Library Cataloguing in Publication Data
Data available

Library of Congress Control Number: 2020948572

ISBN 978–0–19–885883–6

DOI:10.1093/oso/9780198858836.001.0001

Printed and bound by
CPI Group (UK) Ltd, Croydon, CR0 4YY

Links to third party websites are provided by Oxford in good faith and
for information only. Oxford disclaims any responsibility for the materials
contained in any third party website referenced in this work.

To M. Antonietta and Gaetano

Contents

Acknowledgements ix

1. The Measure and Mismeasure of the Self 1

PART I. THE PHILOSOPHY AND PSYCHOLOGY OF INTELLECTUAL VICE

2. Intellectual Virtues and Vices: Sensibilities, Thinking Styles, and Character Traits 21
3. Attitude Psychology and Virtue Epistemology: A New Framework 48

PART II. VIRTUES AND VICES OF INTELLECTUAL SELF-EVALUATION

4. Intellectual Humility, Proper Pride, and Proper Concern with Others' Esteem 73
5. *Superbia*, Arrogance, Servility, and Self-Abasement 96
6. Vanity, Narcissism, Timidity, and Fatalism 119

PART III. EPISTEMIC HARMS AND MORAL WRONGS

7. Harms and Wrongs 141
8. Wrongs, Responsibility, Blame, and Oppression 168
9. Teaching Intellectual Virtues, Changing Attitudes 193

References 205
Index 224

Acknowledgements

This book brings together several strands of research that I have pursued over the past five years. I have been helped in my thinking on these topics by a great number of people to whom I have a large debt of gratitude. Jon Webber introduced me to the topic of attitude psychology, and has offered comments on several chapters of this book. Heather Battaly, Quassim Cassam, and Ian James Kidd (aka the Vice Squad) have informed my thinking throughout, and put up with any intellectual vices I exhibited in my conversations with them. Paul Bloomfield, Brent Madison, Quassim Cassam, and Charlie Crerar have given invaluable feedback on drafts of the manuscript. Greg Maio has been extremely generous with his expertise about attitude psychology. His comments on Chapter 3 have saved me from making blunders. I am grateful to Michael P. Lynch for numerous conversations, and to Brad Hooker to help me think about admiration. Thanks also to Mark Alfano, Natalie Ashton, Michel Brady, Michael Croce, Christian Millar, Kristján Kristjánsson, Matthew Jenkins, Aidan McGlynn, Nancy Snow, Maria Silvia Vaccarezza, Jennifer Cole Wright, and to one further anonymous reader for Oxford University. I have delivered talks based on this material to numerous universities, thanks to all the organizers and the audiences for their valuable feedback.

Whilst none of the material included here has been published before, I have first aired many of the ideas defended in this book in various articles. The motivational account of vice presented in Chapter 2 is based on 'Epistemic Vice and Motivation'. *Metaphilosophy*, 49(3), (2018), 350–367. Chapter 3 is based on 'Attitude Psychology and Virtue Epistemology: A New Framework' in N. Ballantyne and D. Dunning (eds), *Reason, Bias, and Inquiry: New Perspectives from the Crossroads of Epistemology and Psychology*, Oxford University Press, forthcoming. Chapter 4 overlaps with research first discussed in 'Intellectual Humility as Attitude', *Philosophy and Phenomenological Research*, 96(2), (2018), 399–420 and 'Caring for Esteem and Intellectual Reputation: Some Epistemic Benefits and Harms', *Royal Institute of Philosophy Supplement*, 84 (2018), 47–67. Some of the ideas developed in 'Intellectual Servility and Timidity'. *Journal of Philosophical Research*, 43 (2018), 21–41 are revisited in Chapters 5, 6, and 7. Chapter 9 is based on 'Teaching Virtue: Changing Attitudes', *Logos & Episteme*, 7(4), (2016) 503–527 and 'Reducing Arrogance in Public Debate' in J. Arthur (ed.), *Virtues in the Public Sphere* (pp. 28–38). London: Routledge, 2019. I would like to express my gratitude to these journals and publishers for allowing me to borrow from my earlier work. Thanks also to Peter Momtchiloff and staff at Oxford University Press for their advice and assistance.

A Fellowship awarded by the Leverhulme Trust gave me the time to write this book. I thank the Trust for its support. Some of the research underpinning this book was carried out as part of the Changing Attitudes in Public Discourse Project, a subaward agreement supported by the University of Connecticut with funds provided by Grant No. 58942 from the John Templeton Foundation. Its contents are solely the responsibility of the author and do not necessarily represent the official views of UConn or the John Templeton Foundation. I also wish to thank Cardiff University for a period of study leave that helped me to tie up all the loose ends.

Finally, I would like to thank Bethan Bateman for her love and support over all these years but also for fostering in me courage and a spirit of adventure. This book is dedicated to my parents who have nurtured the intellectual virtues in me. Thank you for exemplifying inquisitiveness, creativity, and perseverance and for helping me to cultivate these traits.

1
The Measure and Mismeasure of the Self

1.1 The Measure and Mismeasure of the Self

We have all come across individuals who are remarkably poor judges of their own intellectual characters.[1] Some have a misplaced sense of confidence in their own abilities; others are exceedingly self-effacing to the point that they belittle their own achievements. Such misjudgments of self-assessment may be egregious or less severe; but they are very common. I suspect that, at least on a few occasions, we have been surprised to discover that we have made the same errors.

Having the measure of one's epistemic strengths and weaknesses is in ordinary circumstances a prerequisite for success in intellectual pursuits. Without an adequate appreciation of what one can achieve, what is beyond one's grasp, which methods are better suited to one's strengths, individuals are not able to set realistic goals or choose what is for them the best strategy to solve complex problems or acquire novel information. Without calibrated self-assessments individuals would also find it hard to understand where they need to improve and how to try to accomplish this task.

If those who have the measure of themselves are good judges of how to act to achieve their epistemic goals, many individuals fail in their aims because they do not make good evaluations of their intellectual strengths and weaknesses. Whilst sometimes misjudgments are the result of honest mistakes and other non-culpable shortcomings, oftentimes misjudgments flow from systematically biased thinking. My focus is on this second family of cases where motives, such as the desires to self-enhance or to get along, lead people to measure their intellectual abilities by the wrong unit. In what follows I briefly sketch four stances characteristic of individuals whose self-assessments are mis-calibrated. These stances are: fatalism, self-satisfaction, narcissistic self-infatuation, and self-abasement. Each of these will receive detailed treatment in Chapters 5 and 6.

Some people adopt a pessimistic and fatalistic stance towards their intellectual qualities. They judge many of their features to be weaknesses or limitations; they take a dim view of their abilities. Crucially, they adopt something akin to what Carol S. Dweck (2006) has dubbed a 'fixed mindset'. They believe that their capacities are fixed and thus that these cannot be improved through learning.

---

[1] Here, and throughout this book I use 'intellectual' and 'epistemic' interchangeably.

The Mismeasure of the Self: A Study in Vice Epistemology. Alessandra Tanesini, Oxford University Press (2021).
© Alessandra Tanesini. DOI: 10.1093/oso/9780198858836.003.0001

They judge themselves to be intellectually limited and resign themselves to these alleged shortcomings. Hence, these individuals shy away from challenges and do not even attempt to become more capable. They could choose to practise new skills or try to expand their breadth of knowledge; but as they judge that these activities are doomed to failure, they do not engage in them. Their approach to matters intellectual is likely to turn into a self-fulfilling prophecy since lack of practice will facilitate the atrophy of their intellectual skills. Further, one would expect this kind of fatalism about one's intellectual limitations to generate a sense of hopelessness and self-diffidence understood as a tendency not to trust oneself, one's views or intuitions.[2] In turn, a disposition to shy away from challenges and a propensity to lack in self-trust provide fertile ground for the inhibition of other character traits, such as curiosity, independence, adventurousness, and risk-taking, that are helpful when engaging in intellectual pursuits.

Other individuals adopt a self-satisfied stance towards what they regard as their intellectual strengths. They believe that a great number of their intellectual features are impressive. These individuals are also often averse to working towards improvement. They adopt this stance because they believe that they are already great and thus have no need to improve. Hence, their mindset is also fixed since they judge themselves to be naturally talented and thus capable of effortless success. Independently of whether some such individuals genuinely possess impressive skills or abilities, their self-complacency is likely to prove a hindrance to the successful pursuit of their intellectual goals. For instance, their smugness prevents them from trying to improve and from listening to views contrary to their own. Therefore, they end up being less knowledgeable and able than they would be were they not so self-satisfied. Further, one would expect their smug self-confidence to generate a tendency to trust oneself, one's views or intuition notwithstanding available counter-evidence. These propensities and dispositions are likely to promote other undesirable character traits such as closed-mindedness and dogmatism.[3]

These two kinds of orientation towards one's intellectual strengths and weaknesses generate what one may call distinctive 'thinking styles' respectively characterized by a lack of intellectual initiative and by hubristic complacency. Both styles in ordinary circumstances inhibit the successful pursuit of intellectual inquiry and of epistemic activities in general. The person who is fatalistic about her alleged limitations is likely not to engage in intellectual pursuits, and to desist at the first hurdle. Generally, the person who is self-satisfied lacks sensitivity to the evidential weight of critical opinions and thus runs a high risk of sticking to his views when he should revise them. Nevertheless, those who adopt these stances

---

[2] Medina (2013, pp. 41–42) refers to this trait as a tendency to ego-scepticism.
[3] There is a world of difference between assured self-confidence and smug self-complacency. It is only the latter that in my view has primarily negative epistemic consequences.

towards their intellectual qualities have, albeit superficially, a desire to know and understand. It is this desire that partially explains why the one is so downbeat and the other so smug. However, there are stances towards one's own intellectual strengths and weaknesses that seem predicated on a total disregard for truth, knowledge, or understanding. These are self-assessments that are wholly or primarily driven by considerations of self-presentation or impression management (Goffman, 1959). Individuals who adopt these stances engage in self-evaluations that are motivated by the desire to make a good impression on others.

Some people have a self-infatuated stance towards their intellectual qualities which they therefore assess as superlative without pausing to consider their true epistemic worth. This narcissistic attitude is a deepening of intellectual vanity. Those who are vain want to make a good impression. Consequently, they evaluate as strengths those qualities which promote others' good opinion of them as intellectual agents. They assess something as a limitation if, and to the extent to which, it has the potential to downgrade them in others' eyes. Vain individuals manage to sustain an overall positive assessment of their intellectual character but they achieve this fragile status by a constant effort to hide, downplay or rationalize away any potential shortcomings that may become visible to other people. Narcissism intensifies vanity because it entails denying that one may have any limitations; it turns inward the adoring gaze that those who are vain seek from others. Further, one would expect narcissists to be vainglorious and to have a callous disregard for the truth. Therefore, narcissism promotes epistemic insouciance understood as 'indifference or lack of concern with respect to whether... [one's] claims are adequately grounded in reality or the evidence' (Cassam, 2019, p. 79). In short, the narcissist is a bullshitter.[4]

Others have internalized the negative judgments and attitudes that the majority has directed towards them.[5] Consequently, they have become ashamed of their intellectual qualities which they perceive to be extremely limited. These individuals adopt a self-abasing and negative stance towards their intellectual abilities. This orientation towards their alleged limitations is closely related to a 'sense of looking at one's self through the eyes of others, of measuring one's soul by the tape of a world that looks on in amused contempt and pity' (Du Bois, 1990, p. 8). This measure of one's own intellectual worth in terms of the units of approval bestowed upon oneself by a despising or pitying community is a grave obstacle to the success of one's intellectual endeavours. Among its many negative aspects, one may

---

[4] For a canonical account of bullshit see Frankfurt (2005).

[5] This internalization is one of the damaging effects on subordinated individuals of systematic and unjust structures of discrimination. The existence of this phenomenon is one of the dominant themes of this book. The distorting effects of oppression and discrimination on the self-conception of those who are their target have been discussed in ethics by Bartky (1990), Card (1996), and especially Tessman (2005). In epistemology these themes are briefly mentioned by Medina (2013, pp. 41–42). Like Tessman (2005) I am aware that a focus on the character damage suffered by those who are oppressed runs the risk of appearing as an exercise in victim blaming. I return to this issue in Chapter 8.

include an excessively deferential and uncritical attitude towards the views held by one's detractors.

To recapitulate, fatalism, self-satisfaction, narcissistic infatuation, and self-abasement are stances that some individuals adopt towards themselves. These attitudes are the main focus of this book, which offers an account of the intellectual vices of self-appraisal, the motivations that generate them, and their widespread negative epistemic and moral effects.[6] These vices are exemplified by those who do not have the measure of their intellectual abilities because they assess their epistemic worth using the wrong unit of measurement. When people adopt one or more of these self-evaluations, they form assessments of their own strengths and limitations that are not well-calibrated.[7] Since these evaluations are crucial in the setting of realistic epistemic goals, in the choices of methods and strategies to adopt in inquiry and in the process of epistemic self-improvement, those whose self-assessments are thus misguided are unlikely in ordinary circumstances to excel in their epistemic pursuits.

Whilst one would expect those who adopt these attitudes towards the self to form a number of false beliefs about one's intellectual strengths and limitations, the deeper issue with these stances towards the intellectual worth of the self is that they are assessments calibrated to the wrong unit of measurement. Human beings generally evaluate their performance by comparing themselves to other people (Corcoran et al., 2011). These comparative assessments can be driven by different motivations which often bias the outcome. Thus, for instance, those who are motivated to self-enhance tend to compare themselves for how they differ from less capable individuals so as to find further confirmation of their excellence. I use the metaphor of measuring oneself by the wrong unit to describe this phenomenon of biased selection of the yardstick (as represented by the relative ability of another person or group) by which to evaluate one's own performance.

We should expect narcissistic and self-satisfied self-evaluations to be off the mark by underestimating shortcomings and overestimating strengths. However, in unusual circumstances, it is possible that such individuals may have impressive intellectual strengths and through sheer luck their self-assessments may prove to be largely accurate. Even self-evaluations that are true by luck are detrimental to a subject's ability to engage successfully in epistemic activities. The person with narcissistic tendencies, for example, is disposed to bullshit even though he holds true beliefs about his capacities. What makes his claims about the self, among other things, bullshit is that he does not care whether they are true. The person

---

[6] There might be other kinds of faulty intellectual self-appraisals. My focus is on some that are fairly widespread. Thanks to Paul Bloomfield for pressing this point.
[7] Not all these stances are mutually incompatible. A single individual may be both self-satisfied and a narcissist. Another may be both a fatalist and self-abasing.

who is a fatalist, but also possesses the intellectual limitations he attributes to himself, fails to improve because of his resigned attitude.

These evaluations towards the self for its epistemic worth are character flaws not primarily because they are themselves false or inaccurate but because they are guided by motivations that are irrelevant to epistemic assessments. These motivations drive their self-appraisals because they bias the selection of those to whom they compare themselves to and of the features they consider. In short, these self-evaluations are faulty because they are examples of motivated cognition irrespective of whether by sheer luck they produce an accurate verdict.[8]

The individual who is fatalistic about her intellectual abilities is ultimately interested in avoiding being challenged. She evaluates her intellectual features for their ability to confirm her resigned and pessimistic outlook on her epistemic worth by comparing herself to people who excel and seeking to find out how she differs from them. This person suffers from a sort of delusion, since if she were fully aware that her negative self-assessments flow from her pessimistic outlook that biases her selection of whom she compares herself to and of what she seeks to find out rather than supplying evidence to support it, she would feel rational pressure to change her opinion of herself. The person who adopts this stance measures her epistemic worth by a unit biased by her need for self-effacement even though she takes herself to be assessing her true limitations.

The individual who has a self-satisfied attitude to the self is ultimately interested in feeling good about himself. He evaluates his qualities for their contribution to his high sense of self-worth. This person is also somewhat deluded. If he were fully conscious that he rates highly an aspect of his character merely because this evaluation makes him feel good about himself, he would be unable to sustain the positive self-assessment. His positive attitude can enhance his self-esteem only if in some sense he believes that his attitude is well-founded. The person who adopts this stance measures his epistemic worth by a unit biased by his need for self-enhancement even though he takes himself to be assessing his true intellectual qualities.

The narcissistic person is in love with himself and does not care whether he is worthy of the adulation he heaps on himself. This person is, in some sense, less self-deceived than the arrogant and self-satisfied individual since as a fantasist he does not care at all whether he possesses the impressive features he attributes to himself. This person measures his epistemic worth by a unit biased by self-infatuation; he loves the most those things about himself that help him to love himself above all things. Finally, the person who adopts a self-humiliating or abasing stance may at some level be somewhat aware that his negative self-assessment is unwarranted. Nevertheless, he adopts it perhaps as a survival

---

[8] Motivated cognition is cognition driven by motives often unrelated to accuracy (Kunda, 1990).

strategy. Be that as it may this person measures his epistemic worth by a unit biased by his sense of shame. Thus, he comes to evaluate himself by the yardstick of a world that pities or despises him. That is, he compares himself to others by seeking to confirm the poor assessment of his abilities that is adopted by those who are prejudiced against him.

These examples illustrate some of the harms that beset individuals who lack good judgment about their epistemic worth. Having a well-calibrated sense of one's intellectual abilities and limitations is necessary for being a good inquirer or epistemic agent. Those whose self-evaluations are calibrated appraise their abilities by means of comparative assessments that are driven by the need to have an accurate account of strengths and weaknesses. These individuals do not let awareness of their achievements go to their heads. Even when their abilities are impressive, they do not suffer from the temptation to become smug or self-satisfied. These individuals are self-assured without being arrogant. Simultaneously, they do not let the awareness of their shortcomings, even when these are substantial, crush their self-confidence. They accept their limitations without being resigned to them. On the contrary, their hopeful outlook moves them to treat this knowledge as an incentive to tackle challenges and to improve.

These individuals' attitudes towards their own intellectual strengths and weaknesses facilitate the acquisition of knowledge and responsibly held belief in a number of ways. Firstly, they possess the self-confidence required to engage in intellectual pursuits such as challenging established views or trying to solve hard problems. Secondly, they are able to accept their limitations because they are neither resigned to them nor tempted to pretend that they do not exist. Thirdly, because they are not self-satisfied, they are open to learning from their critics. Fourthly, because they do not need their egos to be fanned, they are likely to find that others are willing to assist them in achieving their epistemic goals. Finally, barring bad luck, those who have the measure of their epistemic worth are also likely to have formed reliably true beliefs about their intellectual strengths and weaknesses. Since these beliefs guide goal setting, choices of methods or strategies to employ, individuals whose self-assessments are accurate are more likely to make the right choices. Their beliefs about what can or cannot be achieved are likely to be true; their choices about cognitive strategies to deploy given their own intellectual strengths and the nature of the task at hand are well-informed. In short, those who have the measure of their epistemic worth are excellent epistemic agents because they are in the best position to be successful in their epistemic activities.

They have attitudes that promote making the best of whatever cognitive abilities they have and of their potential for improvement in two related senses. First, they have attitudes that inhibit self-deception, promote self-belief, foster cooperation, and facilitate openness to multiple sources of information. Second, because, barring bad luck, they also have an accurate understanding of their strengths and weaknesses they are able to harness their capacities to their best use. So understood virtuous epistemic agents are not limited to those who are the most able and knowledgeable. Instead, the development of traits that promote making the most of one's epistemic faculties and skills is by itself a kind of intellectual excellence.

Importantly, those who have a calibrated evaluation of their epistemic worth have qualities that are helpful to other epistemic agents. Their willingness to listen to others' views is likely to promote self-confidence in team members who lack self-belief. Their lack of ego means that the epistemic community does not waste time and effort serving it. Because they are not show-offs, they do not deflect attention away from others who may thus be given an opportunity to shine or, at least, learn. In so far as they have an accurate conception of their strengths and weakness, these individuals are in a good position to know the roles within the team for which they are best suited. Importantly, their lack of ego makes it possible for them to choose that role should it prove to be peripheral. Further, because of their appreciation of their qualities, they are likely to have developed a sensibility for the occasions when they should speak up and demand the group's attention and for those in which they should shut up and take a back seat.

These individuals who have their own measure are rare. In Chapter 4 I offer an account of intellectual humility in these terms. There I argue that intellectually humble individuals appreciate their strengths and accept their limitations because their self-appraisals are not vitiated by egocentric biases. Humility is compatible with intellectual pride in those among one's qualities that meet the standards one has set for oneself. Intellectual humility is, instead, incompatible with self-humiliation and servility. Those who are humble are not afraid to demand the respect of others, since making such demands is part of the kind of self-respect that is integral to having a well-calibrated evaluation of one's own epistemic worth. Finally, since humility is incompatible with vanity, humble individuals do not wish to be recipients of undeserved admiration or reputation.

1.2 Vice Social Epistemology

Traditionally epistemologists have focused on positive notions such as knowledge, truth, justification, virtue, or method. This book, instead, contributes to a small but growing literature that is concerned with epistemically bad things such as ignorance, bias, and epistemic vice.[9] There are at least three reasons why

---

[9] For work on ignorance see Mills (2007); Tuana (2006). See also Le Morvan and Peels (2016) for an overview of definitions of ignorance. Good examples of work on the consequences for epistemology of the prevalence of cognitive biases are Alfano (2017); Olin and Doris (2014). For other work on epistemic vices see Battaly (2014, 2017); Cassam (2016, 2019); Kidd (2016, 2017b, 2019).

philosophical accounts of intellectual vices are long overdue. Firstly, we cannot simply presuppose that intellectual vices are the opposite of virtue. Hence, we cannot offer a theory of their nature and effects simply by reversing what we would say about virtues.[10] Secondly, since intellectual vices are often impediments to the successful pursuit of our intellectual goals, it is important to understand their nature, if we are to make effective proposals for their attenuation. Thirdly, intellectual vices such as carelessness, dogmatism, or arrogance are seemingly common, whilst intellectual virtues such as open-mindedness and meticulousness are rare. Their prevalence and negative influence on people's behaviour warrant making epistemic vices the object of philosophical attention.

This book is a contribution to autonomous, social vice epistemology with an ameliorative goal.[11] It is autonomous in the sense, articulated by Jason Baehr (2011, ch. 10) and pioneered by Christopher Hookway (2003b), of being largely unconcerned with traditional epistemological issues such as offering a definition of knowledge or supplying an answer to scepticism. Instead, in this book I focus on the nature of intellectual vices, on their effects on the successful pursuit of intellectual inquiry, and on the moral and epistemic harms which befall those who suffer from these failings and other members of epistemic communities who interact with these individuals. In this regard, I pursue a different course from that taken by the original proponents of virtue epistemology in both of its main incarnations. Many virtues reliabilists, following Sosa (2007, 2009), attempt to define knowledge in terms of virtue conceived as a reliable cognitive faculty such as vision or memory. Similarly, several virtue responsibilists, in the wake of Zagzebski (1996), think of knowledge as a matter of believing as the virtuous individual would. Instead, my starting point for thinking about vices (and virtues) is intellectual activity of the kind we pursue when we engage in inquiry (cf. Hookway, 2003b). The ends of this activity are epistemic, but they are not limited to the pursuit of truth, knowledge, or understanding. They include belief which is responsive to reasons and is therefore responsibly held, and the dissemination of information in ways that are readily accessible to many epistemic agents; they involve developing epistemic practices that are effective and just; they comprise promoting the development of the intellectual abilities of all epistemic agents to their full capacity.

Even though the objects of my investigation are vices and virtues that stem from appraisals of the self for its epistemic worth, the resulting account is social in at least three related but distinct ways. First, it is concerned with the effects that vices have on relations of epistemic dependence among epistemic agents. Second, it examines the social causes that are partly responsible for the formation of intellectual vices in individuals that are subject to systemic privilege or

---

[10] See Crerar (2017) for an apt description of this symmetry assumption.
[11] This roughly corresponds to what Roberts and Wood (2007) call 'regulative epistemology'.

subordination because of their group identities or because of the social roles they occupy. Third, the account itself relies on the findings of social psychology that is the branch of psychology concerned with the study of the effects of social interactions and social context on individuals' psychology.

The focus on the epistemic relations of dependence among epistemic agents is in my view crucial to vice epistemology once the nature of vices is properly understood. The distinction between self-regarding and other-regarding virtues is a staple of contemporary virtue ethics. Self-regarding virtues are those that are to the advantage of their possessors; whilst other-regarding virtues are primarily of benefit to other people (Von Wright, 1963, p. 153). This distinction is hard to sustain in the epistemic realm since often whatever makes an individual agent epistemically better off is also to the advantage of the epistemic community as a whole. Of course, it is possible that a community is prudentially harmed by the increased efficacy of a morally reprehensible agent with improved intellectual abilities. There may also be cases where the intellectual improvement of one individual leads to worse performance of the epistemic community as a whole. For instance, this would occur when a person improves his debating skills and thus succeeds in persuading a larger number of people, but his views—although plausible and well-evidenced—are nevertheless false. Nevertheless, it would seem that there are also many cases where individual progress enhances the epistemic standing of the community as a whole.

The close ties between the epistemic fate of individuals and that of the community to which they belong is even clearer with regard to intellectual vices.[12] Prejudices are to the epistemic detriment of those who harbour them since prejudicial beliefs are always irresponsibly held, but also of those who are targeted by prejudices, since they may, for example, see their testimonial credibility deflated in unwarranted and systematic ways.[13] I have already begun to detail how self-satisfied smugness and narcissism harm those who have these traits because they promote self-deception, dogmatism, or epistemic insouciance, but also other members of the community who are not taken seriously or are subjected to the bullshit expounded by the narcissist. In short, it is not possible to understand the nature of intellectual vices without understanding the harms they do to those who suffer from them but also their corrosive effects on the intellectual character and epistemic abilities of other members of the community. This is why vice epistemology is always social epistemology.

My approach is also social in another way. One of the characteristic objections of some feminists and critical race theorists to the virtue theoretical framework is

---

[12] That said, it might be the case that in non-ideal circumstances there are instances where individual epistemic vice happens to promote some epistemic good for the community (cf. Hookway, 2002, pp. 261–262; Kitcher, 1993).

[13] This phenomenon known as testimonial injustice was initially brought to the attention of larger philosophical audiences by Miranda Fricker in *Epistemic Injustice* (2007).

that its focus on the individual is to the detriment of a full appreciation of the social and systematic causes of oppression, discrimination, or subordination.[14] There is much to be said for this concern. A focus on the individual and especially on her shortcomings may cause us to lose sight of the power dynamics at play. Worse still it may serve as a justification for blaming the poor and the subordinated for their condition.[15] Nevertheless, as feminists (e.g. Bartky, 1990) and race theorists (e.g. Fanon, 1986) have long known, oppression, because it is internalized, damages the character of those who are oppressed. Mine is a study of the psychology of oppression with a focus on its capacity to damage the epistemic character of those who are subjected to it, but also of those who benefit from it.

Finally, and relatedly, the account of some intellectual vices provided here is social because it relies on the conceptual tools and findings supplied by social psychology. The turn to this discipline is the natural consequence of the hypothesis that vices as features of the psychology of individuals are formed largely, but not exclusively, in response to people's social interactions and to the social contexts individuals find themselves immersed in especially at an early age. This is the domain of study of social psychology, and for this reason, it is to this discipline I turn to understand the psychological bases of the vices that are the object of my investigation.

In addition to being an example of autonomous social epistemology my account of intellectual vices purports to be ameliorative. Hence, my approach is similar in spirit, although very different in practice, to that adopted by Michael Bishop and J. D. Trout's recommendation that epistemologists turn to ameliorative psychology to improve the epistemic prospects of human cognizers (Bishop & Trout, 2005). Even though I focus on different psychological theories, I use psychology—just like they do—to diagnose current widespread shortcomings in human intellectual activities but also to offer guidance about interventions that, given our best current understanding of human cognitive architecture, offer a realistic chance of addressing the biases to which we are prone by relying on the prompts to which we are most responsive. I also concur with Bishop and Trout that theories about ideal epistemic practices or forms of reasoning are of little use if our aim is to assist human beings, unless we have reasons to believe that attempting to approach these ideals is both humanly feasible and not counterproductive.[16] The concern with amelioration is one of the main motivations for focusing on vices rather than on virtues.

---

[14] This objection is often voiced in conversations rather than print but see Okin (1996).
[15] See Tessman (2005) for abundant examples where talk of character has been appropriated for these purposes.
[16] It could be counterproductive if improving one aspect of human cognitive activity leaving our other biases unchanged results in worse overall performance.

1.3 Intellectual Humility, Pride, Concern with Reputation, and Their Surrounding Vices

This book provides the first sustained philosophical account of eight vices opposed to intellectual humility and to the related virtues of intellectual pride and appropriate concern for one's intellectual reputation. I argue that these vices and virtues are best thought as based on clusters of attitudes.[17] Here, by attitude I mean a summary evaluation of an object, rather than something that, like a belief, is an orientation towards a propositional content (Maio & Haddock, 2015). This is the notion of attitude that is a central construct of social psychology and is fundamental to the framework developed in this book. In this section I explain some of the main features of these virtues and vices and describe the attitudes on which they are based. I postpone to Chapters 4–6 fuller characterizations of each virtue and vice together with justifications for the claims that these are based on specific clusters of attitudes serving characteristic functions.

The character virtues and vices that I am concerned with would also make an appearance in comprehensive lists of moral virtues and vices. Thus, for example, humility is not an exclusively epistemic virtue, and arrogance is not solely an intellectual vice. In this book I do not take a stance on the relation between moral and intellectual virtue and vices. However, my account of these intellectual character virtues and vices as based on summary evaluations for their epistemic worth of aspects of one's cognitive make-up such as skills, cognitive processes, faculties, and abilities would seem to indicate a plausible answer.[18] In some instances, intellectual virtues and vices would be clusters of attitudes that are part of those larger clusters that underpin the moral virtuous or vicious trait. Thus, for example, intellectual humility would involve those attitudes that summarize one's evaluations of one's own intellectual strengths and weaknesses; humility would comprise additional evaluations of strengths and weaknesses in other domains.[19]

My discussion of virtues and vices in this book often straddles epistemology and ethics. This is as a result of conscious decision. I am equally concerned with the epistemic harms that flow from moral vices as with the moral wrongs caused by epistemic vices. In this context I have not found strict adherence to a distinction between the moral and the epistemic dimension of virtue and vices to be particularly helpful. I have therefore often ignored it since in my view, contra Swank (2000), many intellectual character vices are not purely epistemic character

---

[17] I shall explain in Chapter 3 how attitudes are the causal bases of vices.
[18] In my view not all intellectual virtues and vices are character traits. Some are thinking styles and others are sensibilities (see Chapter 2). The relation between these and moral character vices is less clear.
[19] Alternatively, one could take ethics to have a larger remit than morality and to comprise everything that contributes to a good life. Given this conception of the ethical, all intellectual virtues and vices are examples of ethical virtuous and vices irrespective of their relation to morality. Thanks to Jonathan Webber for making me see this point.

traits since they often comprise elements such as emotional orientations that pertain to the moral domain.

In the table below the central column lists intellectual virtues whilst the columns on the left and right enumerate vices that oppose them. The top half of the table presents those virtues and vices that are concerned with the self-evaluation of a person's true intellectual strengths or actual good qualities. The bottom half details those virtues and vices that focus on genuine limitations or weaknesses. Intellectual humility straddles both because it includes two components: modesty about intellectual achievements and acceptance of intellectual limitations. The top and bottom rows list virtues and vices that are grounded on assessments respectively of strengths and limitations based on comparisons with the perceived strengths and limitations one attributes to selected individuals. Thus, for instance, pride is a cluster of positive evaluations of some intellectual features of oneself based on comparisons with the qualities one attributes to people whom one judges to be highly capable. The two middle rows enumerate virtues and vices which are based on evaluations that, whilst possibly derived from interpersonal comparisons, are primarily concerned with gaining an accurate assessment of one's abilities.

Haughtiness (Superbia) Positive attitudes about comparative performance biased by ego defensive motivations	Proper Pride Positive attitudes about performance driven by concerns for self-improvement	Servility Negative attitudes about comparative performance biased by social acceptance motivations
Arrogance Positive attitudes without focus on comparative performance biased by ego defensive motivations	Modesty about strengths Positive attitudes without focus on comparative performance driven by accuracy concerns	Self-Abasement Negative attitudes without focus on comparative performance biased by social acceptance motivation
	Humility	
Narcissism Positive attitudes without focus on comparative performance biased by social acceptance motivations	Acceptance of limitations Negative attitudes without focus on comparative performance driven by accuracy concerns	Fatalism Negative attitudes without focus on comparative performance biased by ego defensive motivations
Vanity Positive attitudes about comparative performance biased by social acceptance motivations	Proper concern for esteem Negative attitudes about performance driven by concerns for self-improvement	Timidity Negative attitudes about comparative performance biased by ego defensive motivations

At the centre of the table is the complex virtue of intellectual humility.[20] It comprises modesty about achievements and acceptance of limitations. It is based on positive attitudes towards some components of one's cognitive make-up, which are therefore evaluated as good qualities. But it is also based on some negative attitudes towards other elements of one's cognitive make-up, which are appraised as limitations.[21] These self-assessments are driven by motives of accuracy and are, therefore, not vitiated by egocentric biases. This virtue is accompanied by two further related intellectual virtues: pride in one's intellectual abilities and proper concern for one's intellectual reputation. Pride comprises positive self-assessments that are based primarily on comparisons with others that one judges to be high performing and thus one wishes to emulate. Proper concern for one's intellectual reputation involves caring that one is worthy of other people's esteem. It comprises negative self-evaluations that are based on interpersonal comparisons with others one judges to be high performing in the relevant domain. The person who is properly concerned with her reputation in the sense of meriting to be held in high esteem identifies her shortcomings by comparing herself to models she thinks are worthy of emulation. Hence, pride and concern for esteem are closely connected since they are both based on comparative assessments with exemplars. The virtue of pride involves a focus on achievements whilst that of concern with esteem comprises a focus on addressing shortcomings. Both are derived from interpersonal comparison driven by the motivation to improve.

Each of the eight epistemic vices flanking these virtues is a defective self-appraisal.[22] They are defective because they comprise evaluations that are biased by motivations unrelated to accuracy or self-improvement.[23] For example, *superbia* (haughtiness) is a positive assessment of many of one's own intellectual abilities because one estimates oneself to be better in this regard than other people,

---

[20] This table is a revised version of that published in my (2018e).
[21] As I have said above I do not take their reliability to be a defining features of virtue and vices. Instead, motives are crucial since these drive the formation and maintenance of those attitudes on which virtues and vices are based. Nevertheless, virtues are largely based on reliable self-appraisals and vices on assessments that are unreliable. This feature of virtues and vices is illustrated in the table since virtue involve positive assessments of strengths and negative assessments of weakness, whilst vices overestimate or underestimate strengths and weaknesses, or even mistake weaknesses for strengths and vice-versa.
[22] Even though I ultimately reject the description one might think of virtues as means that are opposed on one side by a vice of deficiency and on the other by a vice of excess.
[23] Motivations bias evaluations in two different ways. First, they lead agents to ask directional questions. Second, they create asymmetries of error costs. For instance, a person who is defensive about their self-esteem might be inclined to ask of objects whether they are a threat to the ego, rather than consider them under a different light. The asking of this question partly determines what is to be included as evidence when evaluating objects. Further, if one is defensive, mistaking a threat for something not threatening is more costly than the opposite. Thus, one sets a lower threshold of evidence required to believe that something is a threat, than to believe that it is not. See Kunda (1990) on directional questions and motivated cognition and Scott-Kakures (2000) on asymmetry of risks. I think of these as egocentric biases.

but where these appraisals are motivated by the need to feel good about oneself.[24] Arrogance proper is similar to *superbia* because it involves self-assessments biased by a desire for self-enhancement even though these evaluations are not as focused on comparative performance. Vanity is a positive self-assessment motivated by the need to be esteemed or accepted by members of a group to which one wishes to belong. Those who are vain end up having positive attitudes and thus treat as intellectual strengths or at least as good qualities features that contribute to them being held in high opinion by others irrespective of these qualities' real epistemic worth. Narcissism is, like vanity, driven by the desire to be liked, but it is not as focused on comparing oneself to others. These four vices comprise the vices of superiority.[25]

The same concerns with self-presentation and impression management that drive vanity are also at the core of the vice of intellectual servility. This vice, that involves thinking of oneself as being of lesser epistemic value than other people, is based on largely negative self-assessments of actual intellectual strengths biased by the need to be accepted by other members of the community. Intellectual self-abasement is a deepening of intellectual servility where one thinks of oneself as worthless. Intellectual fatalism is an aggravated version of intellectual timidity that occurs when a person has become so resigned to their alleged epistemic shortcomings that she no longer cares about comparisons with other people's levels of attainment.[26] These four vices comprise the vices of inferiority.

I explore the complex relations between these vices in several of this book's chapters. For now it suffices to say that vanity and *superbia* promote servility in others. The connections between vanity and servility are of particular interest since both are the outcome of an overwhelming desire for social acceptance. Vain individuals seek to be admired as high status members of the group, while those who are servile simply seek to belong to the community and are prepared to adopt the role of low status admirers of the dominant members in order to be accepted. Thus, servile individuals are ingratiators. In addition, *superbia* also promotes timidity in other individuals. Arrogance and timidity are closely connected since both are driven by defensiveness in response to an acute sensitivity to possible threats to one's self-worth. Those who suffer from *superbia* respond to this perceived danger by launching attacks to prop up their self-esteem. Those who are timid respond by fleeing the perceived danger and attempting to become inconspicuous. *Superbia* and timidity are, like vanity and servility, mutually supportive. Because individuals who are timid do not speak up, their silence

---

[24] In previous work I have named haughtiness the vice I describe here as superbia (Tanesini, 2016a). I am now convinced that this label does not quite capture the full range of postures, affects, and cognitions characteristic of this vice. I thus prefer the Latin term 'superbia' as a more fitting label.

[25] I borrow from Bell (2013) the label 'vices of superiority' to describe vices such as arrogance. Medina (2013) describes broadly the same traits as the vices of the privileged.

[26] This paragraph and the one preceding it are based on Tanesini (2018e).

buffers and supports the dismissive attitudes of those who suffer from *superbia*. In turn these superior attitudes intimidate those who are timid and thus promote their self-silencing. I discuss some of these circles of viciousness in Chapter 7 where I detail the harms and wrongs caused by the intellectual vices of superiority and inferiority.

1.4 Summary of the Book

The overall aim of this book is to offer detailed characterizations of the intellectual vices of self-evaluation, to highlight the epistemic harms and moral wrongs that flow from them, to explain their psychological bases and to suggest some interventions that inhibit vicious behaviour and promote intellectual virtue. To this end, in Chapter 2 I lay out the philosophical foundations of my approach. I argue that intellectual vices of self-evaluation are components of a defective epistemic agency. They are failures to monitor and control one's cognitive processes in a manner that is consonant with effective and responsible inquiry. These failures can ultimately be traced to motivations such as self-enhancement or impression management that bias epistemic activities. One of the distinctive features of my account is the adoption of a theoretical framework from social psychology. I explain my approach in Chapter 3 where I introduce the notions of attitude, of attitude strength and function. I also make an initial case in support of the view that the intellectual vices of self-evaluation are based on attitudes and their informational bases.

In Chapters 4–6 I develop my account of individual intellectual virtues and vices. Chapter 4 is dedicated to humility, pride, and proper concern for one's intellectual reputation. Chapter 5 provides accounts of the psychology of those vices opposed to modesty and pride. I argue that *superbia* is based on defensive attitudes that constitute a defensive form of high self-esteem; I also explain how *superbia* can deepen into arrogance. Servility opposes pride in the opposite direction of *superbia*. I argue that it is based on social-adjustive attitudes. These are attitudes motivated by the need for acceptance by one's elective social group. Finally, I show how servility can deepen into self-abasement. Chapter 6 is dedicated to those vices that oppose acceptance of limitations and proper concern for one's intellectual reputation. Both vanity and narcissism are based on social-adjustive attitudes. They result in failures to accept one's limitations or even, at least in the case of narcissism, to accept that one has any limitations. Antithetical to proper concern for others' esteem of oneself in the opposite direction from vanity is intellectual timidity which promotes, out of defensiveness, a propensity to avoid others' attention. In this chapter I also describe how timidity if left unchecked develops into a fatalistic stance towards one's alleged intellectual limitations.

In each of these chapters I describe the manifestations of these character virtues and vices in order to argue that the framework of attitudes explains why these cluster in characteristic ways. My accounts demonstrate that motivations and affects are central components of each of these traits. I show that each virtue and vice includes a characteristic motivation. Intellectual humility and its attendant virtues are driven by the need to make sense of the world. *Superbia*, arrogance, timidity, and fatalism are motivated by the need to defend one's sense of self-worth from real or imagined threats. Vanity, narcissism, servility, and self-abasement are biased by the propensity to be motivated by the need to be accepted by others.

Each of these motivations, understood as dispositions to be driven by a given kind of motive, is inflected by emotional dispositions that are fundamental to the virtues and vices of self-evaluation and that colour the intellectual lives of those who possess them. Genuinely humble individuals have a disposition to feel hopeful and optimistic. Those who are proud and care for being esteemed tend to experience feelings of self-love. The need to defend the ego from perceived threats gives rise to a disposition to fight or to flight. Aggressive self-defence is characteristic of *superbia* and arrogance. The characteristic emotional tendencies of these vices are respectively anger and contempt. Fearful self-defence is typical of timidity and fatalism whose characteristic emotional predispositions are fear and feelings of hopelessness. The need to be accepted by other people leads to a preoccupation with the impression one makes on them. This preoccupation can be expressed either through a tendency to seek others' attention or to try to ingratiate oneself to them. Attention-seeking behaviour is characteristic of vanity and narcissism whose characteristic emotional dispositions are spiteful envy (when one seeks to spoil, by denigrating them, those goods one envies) and morbid self-love. Ingratiating behaviour is also the trademark of those who are servile or suffer from self-abasement whose typical emotional orientations are shame-proneness and self-contempt.

Chapters 7–8 focus to the harmful consequences of these intellectual vices. Chapter 7 analyses the epistemic harms that flow from the intellectual vices opposed to humility and its attendant virtues. First, I show that these vices have numerous negative effects on cognition. They promote biased thinking directly or by way of fostering vicious thinking styles and sensibilities. Second, I examine the harms that these vices do to those who suffer from them. In particular I discuss their effects on intellectual self-trust and self-knowledge. Third, I explain the epistemic harms that these vices inflict on other epistemic agents. For example, the behaviour of vain and arrogant individuals promotes the development of timidity and servility in other people. Finally, I discuss the negative and positive effects of these vices on the epistemic community as a whole.

In Chapter 8 I analyse whether individuals are morally and epistemically responsible for their epistemic vices and the bad believing that flows from them.

I distinguish three forms of responsibility: attributability, answerability, and accountability. I argue that intellectual character vices are attributable to agents because they are part of who they are. I also defend the view that people are generally not answerable for their epistemic vices because agents do not reflectively endorse them, even though people are morally accountable for their vices when these reflect the quality of their regard for other people. Nevertheless, it is rarely morally appropriate to blame people for their vices since others frequently lack the required moral standing to hold them to account. In the same chapter I argue that people should however take responsibility for their intellectual vices and the bad believing that flows from them. Taking responsibility is essential if individuals are to address the damage done to self-respect by these vices.

In Chapter 9 I change gear, moving from diagnosis to intervention. Because of its focus on the social causes of the development of vices of superiority and inferiority in individuals, in this book I do not suggest that interventions targeting the character of individuals are the sole or even in the long term the best approach to the promotion of virtue. Nevertheless, such interventions are not ineffective and may in the short term be an essential complement to environmental solutions. In this chapter I focus on explicit education about virtue and on the exemplarist model favoured by Zagzebski (2010) and Han et al. (2017) among others. I argue that these approaches are, by themselves, largely ineffective. Instead, I propose an intervention employing self-affirmation techniques consisting in helping people to focus on their fundamental values and to reflect on what, in their view, makes them valuable (Haddock & Gebauer, 2011; Sherman & Cohen, 2002). These techniques are effective but can also serve as a propaedeutic to exposure to attainable exemplars.

PART I

THE PHILOSOPHY AND PSYCHOLOGY OF INTELLECTUAL VICE

2
Intellectual Virtues and Vices
Sensibilities, Thinking Styles, and Character Traits

This chapter supplies the philosophical foundations of my account of vices and virtues of intellectual self-appraisal. In my view these vices are impairments of epistemic agency caused by motivations, such as those of self-enhancement or impression management, that also bring other epistemically bad motives in their trail.[1] Such motivations bias epistemic evaluations of one's cognitive abilities, processes, and states.[2] These appraisals, in turn, have widespread negative influences on agents' epistemic conduct as a whole.

One of the most important aims of ameliorative epistemology is to offer guidance for the improvement of epistemic activities such as inquiry. Hence, my focus in this chapter and throughout the book is on epistemic activities, and on their epistemic evaluations, rather than on the properties of cognitive states such as knowledge or belief. I describe intellectual virtues and vices as among those psychological features of agents that are causally responsible for their epistemic conduct. Virtues contribute to being a good epistemic agent, whilst vices are characteristic of agents whose intellectual life does not go well. Epistemic virtues and vices of self-appraisal are a subset of epistemic virtues and vices in general. They are those vices that, because they bias individuals' self-evaluations, are responsible for agents' adopting unsuitable or ill-judged epistemic goals or for failing to appreciate the best means to their goals.

This chapter has three related aims. The first is to explain the nature of intellectual vices in general before explicating the specific features of the epistemic vices of self-appraisal. The second aim is to give an account of what makes intellectual vices vicious. I argue in favour of a motivational view. Vices are guided by motives to turn away from epistemic goods.[3] These motives often cannot be fully acknowledged by subjects since they are in tension with some of their

---

[1] Impression management is the motivation to influence how others perceive one in order to gain social acceptance (Goffman, 1959).
[2] I do not address here philosophical debates about the nature of motivational states and about the motivational power of reasons. My focus is on motives that are conative and affective states. However, I do not take a stance as to whether all motivational states are of these kinds.
[3] These motives are themselves derivative of other motivations that often concern ego-defence or impression management.

beliefs and other motivations. In these cases, individuals engage in delusive rationalizations of some of their actions and beliefs. The third goal is to lay out some key features of character vices to prepare the ground for Chapter 3 where I show that attitudes are the causal bases of intellectual character virtues and vices of self-appraisal.

This chapter consists of five sections. In Section 2.1 I highlight the contributions made by epistemic evaluations to epistemic activities such as inquiry, communication, teaching, or planning. These activities are carried out well, which is to say responsibly and effectively, only when agents' epistemic evaluations are correct. They go badly when these evaluations are off the mark. Section 2.2 provides an account of intellectual virtues and vices in general and of those of self-appraisal more specifically. I distinguish three kinds of psychological structures that might be virtuous or vicious: sensibilities, thinking styles, and character traits. Section 2.3 provides a characterization of epistemic agency to show that the intellectual vices of self-appraisal result in defects in the exercise of epistemic agency. Section 2.4 defends the motivational account of what makes intellectual vices vicious. Section 2.5 summarizes a list of key features of intellectual virtues and vices that have been highlighted in the preceding sections. In the next chapter I show that attitudes are the best candidates for the psychological states possessing these key features.

2.1 Epistemic Activities and Epistemic Evaluations

Ameliorative epistemology is concerned with understanding how agents pursue epistemic goals, such as asking good questions, becoming trustworthy, acquiring knowledge and understanding, or minimizing the number of false beliefs, and with developing practical guidance on how to become more effective in achieving these ends. Individuals pursue their epistemic goals effectively when they are usually successful in achieving them. They pursue them responsibly when they are responsive to reasons.[4] Once the point of doing epistemology is formulated in these terms, its focus shifts considerably. Finding necessary and sufficient conditions for knowledge or answering the sceptic are not among epistemology's most pressing concerns. Instead, the most important task for epistemology is to understand what people do when they engage in epistemic activities with a view to developing proposals to improve performance.[5] Hence, this approach in

---

[4] I owe the notion of responsible and effective inquiry to Hookway (2003a). Cassam (2019) offers a narrower interpretation of this notion.

[5] Hookway (2003a, 2003b) has pioneered a form of virtue epistemology that focuses on the virtues required to inquiry well.

epistemology focuses on such activities, and on the cognitive skills, abilities, and processes that are deployed when they are carried out.

Inquiry is something we do. It is a complex activity that requires time, effort, and commitment to carry out.[6] Broadly speaking, inquiry is an example of an epistemic activity. Other examples include teaching a class of students, engaging in a debate with a group of people, or building some experimental equipment. These are all instances of epistemic activities because they involve conduct aimed at goals that are primarily—or even exclusively—cognitive, including gaining knowledge and understanding or maximizing true belief.[7] Each of these activities comprises a range of smaller actions, which in turn may subsume even smaller tasks, contributing to common goals. Some of these actions are intentional and under the direct voluntary control of agents. For instance, as part of a sustained investigation, a researcher may decide to go through her calculations one more time to ensure that there are no errors. This is a process that she carries out deliberately and voluntarily. Others might be carried out automatically such as, for instance, sifting through emails, deleting or archiving those that require no response.

Epistemic activities are rife with evaluations. I define an epistemic evaluation as a ranking of a target object which is evaluated against a standard or norm that is epistemic. For example, to hold or to feel that a belief is certain is an epistemic evaluation of a belief. It appraises that belief against a norm that is epistemic since if the belief is (in an objective sense) certain, it is true. A positive evaluation of a belief against this standard can be expressed in a judgment that the belief is certain or a feeling of certainty whose target is the belief in question.

Epistemic evaluations guide and monitor agents' conduct in inquiry.[8] Epistemic evaluations belong to two families: cognitive evaluations that include first-order deliberations about the evidence and second-order (metacognitive) reflections about agents' cognitive states and processes; and affective evaluations that include feelings—like fear or excitement—determining patterns of salience in one's perceptual field and epistemic or metacognitive emotions and feelings about cognitive states and processes. These two different families of evaluations appraise their targets against epistemic standards. They are also instrumental in guiding epistemic activities by directing, starting, or halting them and in monitoring these activities by keeping them on track in the pursuit of the agent's epistemic goals.

Many of the epistemic actions that make up inquiry and other activities are themselves cognitive epistemic evaluations consisting of deliberations involving

---

[6] I use 'activity' here as a generic term that applies to actions directed at a goal as well as on-going activities done for their own sake.
[7] These goals are not always end states which if achieved terminate the activity. One may engage in an epistemic activity, such as reading philosophy, for the love of doing it. In these cases the agent's aim is to carry out the activity for its own sake.
[8] Proust (2008) labels these processes as self-probing when involved in the selection of viable strategies to achieve goals and as post-evaluation when they compare outcomes to goals to evaluate the success of the cognitive activities.

epistemic assessments of the evidence.[9] For instance, when an agent is trying to make her mind up, she engages in deliberation that might be wholly first-order and that consist in appraising several chunks of information. She is trying to evaluate the facts as she understands them to reach a conclusion. Evaluations of this kind include: estimating the reliability of some records; adjudicating between competing claims; assessing the weight of the evidence for some conclusion. These cognitive evaluations, that are the outcome of deliberations, guide other epistemic activities.

Some epistemic activities involve cognitive epistemic evaluations consisting of metacognitive (second-order) assessments of the epistemic standings of doxastic states, cognitive processes or agents' abilities. These might be prompted by impasses in deliberation, by doubts about one's intuitions or by feelings of error and uncertainty. They involve conscious reflection on epistemic conduct and its outputs. These activities include: reflecting on the reliability of a cognitive faculty; estimating the probability of success of a line of investigation; deciding whether one is likely to find the solution to a puzzle or whether one should consult a more experienced colleague. These reflective evaluations monitor first-order epistemic activities and contribute to guiding them. Both deliberative and reflective evaluations belong to the first family of cognitive evaluative activities since they crucially involve conscious processing that results in the formation of judgments or other cognitive states.

Epistemic activities are also frequently guided by affective epistemic evaluations (Hookway, 2003a). These are not themselves activities; they are states or events. This family of evaluations includes: feelings creating patterns of salience determining that some features of the environment are experienced as especially relevant to one's goals; and, episodic epistemic feelings of certainty, doubt, trustworthiness that are associated with specific psychological states, like beliefs, and processes such as making an inference.[10] Feelings of fear, for example, direct attention to some location in the visual field which is experienced as especially salient. By guiding attention, these feelings contribute to the regulation of epistemic activities such as observing, looking, listening, which are fundamental to inquiry. Affective states also guide epistemic conduct by supplying evaluative information about the agent's cognitive states and processes.[11] For instance, individuals continue to seek evidence, when they experience feelings of doubt

---

[9] That is, evaluations that monitor and guide epistemic activities are at times themselves activities.
[10] I say 'associated' because I do not take these feelings to be representations of beliefs or cognitive processes as certain. Instead, it is plausible that these feelings merely track some cues of these aspects of cognition. Since the feelings are accessible to consciousness they alert us of these otherwise unaccessed features of belief and of thinking. On some of these issues, see Arango-Muñoz and Michaelian (2014) and especially Dokic (2012). For opposing views on whether epistemic feelings might simply track rather than represent non-conscious processing see also Proust (2013) and Carruthers (2017).
[11] Feelings that determine salience alert us to features of the external environment whilst epistemic feelings track features of the subject's mental states and processes.

associated with a belief. They terminate inquiry when they feel certain of their answers. They revisit inferences when they lose confidence in them. They endorse conclusions when they are confident in their reasonings. These and other epistemic emotions or metacognitive feelings are widespread (Hookway, 2003a, 2008; Morton, 2010). We often experience them as gut feelings or intuitions. They monitor epistemic activities, including conscious deliberations, but also more habitual and semi-conscious processes. When one trusts one's emotions, they guide epistemic conduct. When one does not, one is prompted to engage in second-order reflection about one's own epistemic activities.

Epistemic activities can be performed well or badly. They are carried out well when agents make progress towards achieving their epistemic ends, and do not violate any of the epistemic norms that bind them. They are performed badly when norms are violated, or goals are frustrated. Epistemic evaluations are crucial determinants of good performance in inquiry. They guide activities aimed at achieving the agent's epistemic goals. Feelings determinative of salience, evaluations of the evidence, and of the fruitfulness of questions regulate our epistemic faculties in the service of the agent's epistemic goals. Evaluations also monitor progress towards achieving these goals. Inquiry is derailed when agents behave as if they were on track even though they are not, or vice-versa. Reflective evaluations and epistemic emotions serve these monitoring roles that contribute to guiding future epistemic conduct. They are partly responsible for terminating inquiries and for correcting previous activities so as to restore the effective pursuit of current cognitive goals.

Affective evaluations, in particular, serve distinctive roles in inquiry. First, they are shortcuts, saving time and cognitive effort (Hookway, 2003a, p. 87). It is easier and quicker to focus on some aspect of the visual field rather than to scan the whole environment. It is also more efficient to rely on feelings of certainty or doubt than always to reflect whether we can trust our opinions or whether the matter requires further investigation.[12] Second, affective evaluations motivate. Feelings of doubt motivate further investigation and direct attention. Epistemic feelings also drive us to persevere in our inquiries or to rest content with the current conclusions. Their motivational role is fundamental to commencing or halting epistemic activities.[13] Third, affective evaluations guide cognition including by pruning inferential

---

[12] Affective evaluations may be indispensable in this role, rather than functioning exclusively as convenient shortcuts, since it might not be possible, on pain of regress, to rely solely on deliberation to halt every inquiry. This point is defended by Hookway (2003a). The claim is plausible because, if every epistemic activity requires that one carries out epistemic evaluations, and epistemic evaluations are themselves activities, then they require prior evaluations to be carried out and so on ad infinitum. However, unlike at least some cognitive evaluations, affective evaluations are not activities since they are not tryings directed at achieving a goal (cf. Proust, 2008). They can, therefore, halt these regresses. I do not address this question here since what matters for my purposes is that human beings as a matter of fact rely on affective evaluations.

[13] I do not wish however to exclude that at times different cognitive states can provide the required motivation.

chains. They make it more likely that some things are considered and others are ignored. Feelings determinative of salience indicate which aspect of the scene is to be explored. Feelings of curiosity guide the person along some inferential paths, whilst others are ignored. Guidance here can be thought in terms of the allocation of different weights to individual branches in a decision tree. So understood affective evaluations generate patterns of salience by pruning decision trees in cognitive processing.[14] When these selection processes track epistemic standards, affective evaluations are an essential part of successful epistemic conduct.

One of the most distinctive features of the vices of intellectual self-evaluation discussed in this book is their intimate connection to affective epistemic evaluations that fail to track epistemic norms and standards. For example, arrogant individuals are often excessively confident in the correctness of their views and the excellence of their cognitive skills and capacities. People who are resigned to their alleged intellectual limitations seem to lack all confidence and are riven by overwhelming anxieties about their capacities. Decalibrated epistemic feelings are one of the trademarks of these intellectual vices.[15] While these affective states are among the manifestations of the vices, their presence also feeds into them and strengthens these aspects of character.

2.2 Faculties, Sensibilities, Thinking Styles, and Character Traits

Intellectual vices are heterogenous (Cassam, 2016, 2019). There are traits which are plausibly thought of as epistemic virtues or vices that are akin to sensibilities. These include the virtue of being observant and the vice of wilful inattention that opposes it (Hookway, 2003a). Other traits or tendencies that can be virtuous, vicious, or of mixed value are similar to thinking styles. These include a propensity to love and enjoy thinking, or to be closed-minded, a disposition to being prejudiced or dogmatic, a tendency always to play devil's advocate. Finally, intellectual virtue and vices can be character traits including intellectual generosity, courage, humility, arrogance, and servility. In this section I detail the main features of these three types of virtuous, vicious, and mixed traits.[16] I relate each type to characteristic

---

[14] Neil Levy (2015, p. 814) speculates that implicit attitudes might play a similar role in cognitive processing.
[15] They are decalibrated because they are not sensitive to the epistemic features of the situation. Instead, they are likely to track, at least partly, other factors concerning self-enhancement or the concern to make a good impression on relevant others. In my view feelings can thus be decalibrated because of the agent's motivations. Proust (2008) discusses the role of biased feedback in the decalibration of epistemic feelings.
[16] Hence, the account advanced here combines elements of zetetic accounts of virtues as dispositions to inquiry well with phronomic accounts of virtue as aspects of character driven by excellent motivations. For this distinction, see Axtell (2008). The notion of a mixed trait is due to Miller (2013, 2014).

patterns of epistemic evaluations and thus explain how these traits are effective in guiding epistemic activities in the right and wrong directions.

2.2.1 Sensibilities

Sensibilities are dispositions to use one's perceptual capacities in distinctive ways in the service of epistemic activities. Virtuous sensibilities are partly constituted by complex propensities to experience feelings that make some features of the environment appear as salient. They include the virtue of being observant (Hookway, 2003a). Vicious sensibilities are forms of insensitivity to what matters. They might be characterized by 'numbness' (Medina, 2016) or by strong but misdirected feelings that make some things appear as salient when they are not so. These include the vices of testimonial injustice (Fricker, 2007) and of wilful ignorance (Tuana, 2006). There are many other sensibilities that are neither virtuous nor vicious such as being observant when one is in a good mood.

Sensibilities play a role in guiding the use of perceptual capacities in epistemic activities.[17] I use the example of the epistemic sensibility of being observant to illustrate this point (cf. Hookway, 2003a). Visual perception is a cognitive capacity that takes visual stimuli among its inputs and produces visual perceptual beliefs as outputs. This capacity contributes positively to inquiry and other epistemic activities when it is reliable, but also fast, and capable of delivering outputs in a diverse range of circumstances.[18] Epistemic activities involving the use of vision go well only if vision is reliable. But reliability of perception is not sufficient to guarantee that observations are carried out well. Some people might have twenty-twenty vision but also possess a tendency to look at the wrong things given their specific goals in inquiry. Alternatively, they might have a tendency to be distracted and continuously flit through scattered features of the visual field. Individuals with these characteristics are unlikely to extract information useful to their endeavours through observation. Their failures are not the result of unreliable vision. Rather, they do not pay attention to what should be salient to them.

The person who is observant has reliable vision but he also experiences as salient those features of the visual field that are relevant to his epistemic aims. He directs visual attention to these aspects of the environment. By directing attention to them, and thus putting them at the centre of his visual field, he is able to take in more detail about these items since foveal vision has a higher degree of resolution than peripheral vision. Had those items remained at the periphery of his vision,

---

[17] It is possible that there might be sensibilities guiding the use of faculties other than perception.
[18] Virtue reliabilists describe cognitive faculties that are reliable as virtues because they are examples of excellence in cognition (cf. Greco, 2010; Sosa, 2007). I have no objections to their terminological choices. Instead, I think of my concerns as being orthogonal to theirs.

many of their features would have remained undetected. If this is right, being observant is the complex disposition to detect the salient aspects of the environment by experiencing feelings that direct one's attention towards these features (cf. Brady, 2013).

Salience is relative to the agent's epistemic goals. When a birdwatcher and a botanist look at a field, they might be trying to see different things. The birdwatcher might be interested in a nesting bird hidden in the undergrowth; the botanist might be searching for a rare plant. Being observant in both cases involves directing vision towards specific locations but these are different since the two agents are engaged in activities with different goals.

These examples illustrate that while vision itself is not an acquired ability the capacity to observe well is learnt. It takes much training for bird spotters, or for radiologists to learn to identify by sight the significant features of a bird or of an x-ray. Being observant understood as the disposition to direct vision to salient parts of the visual field is a skill. It is a kind of expertise acquired through training. Thinking of this epistemic virtue in these terms highlights its domain specificity. What it takes to be observant as a radiographer is not the same as what it takes to be good at identifying birds by sight. It might be true that some people might be better than others in general at noticing things. Nevertheless, being observant is, like most forms of expertise, domain-specific.

The development and preservation of skills requires a motivation to improve and the commitment to continue honing one's abilities. When the skills in question are intellectual the required motivation consists, at least partly, in the love or desire to acquire knowledge and understanding in the relevant domain.[19] Motivation also plays a key role in the development of intellectually vicious sensibilities. One may think of some forms of wilful ignorance along these lines. Some individuals become experts at not noticing some features of social reality. For example, some people are motivated to turn their attention away from facts about white privilege. They fail to observe the discriminatory nature of some behaviours; they profess utter ignorance about questions of race. Given the reality of racism, it takes effort to insulate oneself from the relevant facts. This effort involves the ability to direct one's attention away from them, so that one can claim in all honesty not to have noticed preferential treatment or discrimination.[20]

The motivations that lead to the cultivation of wilful ignorance are often hidden to the agents who develop this skill. They are effective in refining the ability to distract attention away from the relevant facts. In this way such agents are wishful

---

[19] For a discussion of the role of motivation for the development of moral expertise see Stichter (2016).

[20] For discussions of white ignorance and privilege see Mills (2007) and other contributions to Sullivan and Tuana (2007).

thinkers or prone to self-deception.[21] This is not to say that they necessarily possess contradictory beliefs about the reality of racism. Rather, perhaps unintentionally, their fear about being undeserving beneficiaries of privileges biases their cognition by directing their attention away from evidence of the existence of unfair advantage. We can think of these agents as experts at perceptual motivated believing in the domain of race and racism.[22] Their desire not to know the facts leads them either to avoid forming any opinion on these matters or to acquire false views.

These considerations help to distinguish virtuous from vicious sensibilities. A sensibility is epistemically virtuous only if (a) it is a skill that generally promotes the achievement of the subject's domain-specific epistemic goals, and (b) it is developed as a result of a general motivation to acquire epistemic goods. A sensibility is epistemically vicious only if (a) it systematically frustrates the achievement of some of the subject's domain-specific epistemic goals,[23] and (b) it is developed as a result of a motivation to turn away from epistemic goods.[24] So understood, vicious sensibilities do not need to have epistemically bad motives among their components since they are trained skilful perceptual responses to one's situation. Standing bad motivations, such as a chronic desire not to know, are instead causally responsible for the acquisition of these sensibilities.

This characterization of vicious sensibilities highlights their self-stultifying nature. Individuals who have developed them possess irreconcilable goals. Their perceptual activities are made intelligible by an appreciation of the fact that they are avoiding unpalatable truths, yet they engage in perceptual behaviour which they would rationalize as seeking to figure out the facts.

2.2.2 Thinking Styles

Thinking styles are complex dispositions to adopt some ways of thinking and to prefer them over their alternatives. They differ from sensibilities because they do not concern the use of our perceptual faculties. Some styles are plausibly epistemically virtuous such as a propensity to enjoy thinking and to be open to new ideas. Others are vicious; they include a prejudicial outlook and a tendency to seek

---

[21] I adopt a rather minimal sense of self-deception according to which a belief or an attitude about the self is deceptive when it is formed and preserved despite abundant counter-evidence, because of some directional motivation, and could not be acknowledged without creating a deep conflict between the subject's attitudes and doxastic states.

[22] On motivated believing see Scott-Kakures (2000) I return to this issue in Chapter 3 when discussing the role of motivated cognition in attitude formation.

[23] It frustrates the goals relevant to the acquisition of domain-specific knowledge but it facilitates achieving ignorance-related goals.

[24] The account of intellectual vices as obstacles to responsible and effective inquiry has been developed by Cassam (2015, 2019). I explain my motivational theory in Section 2.4 of this chapter.

certainty at all costs. More commonly thinking styles might turn out to be epistemically good in some circumstances but not in others. These mixed styles include a preference for working on one big thought (hedgehog) or on many smaller ideas (fox), but also a tendency to play devil's advocate.[25]

Thinking styles play a role in guiding the use of reasoning in epistemic activities.[26] I illustrate the point by way of the thinking style that flows from a high dispositional need for cognitive closure. The need for cognitive closure is a motivational element of cognition. It is the motive to seek certainties; that is, answers that are uniquely correct, unambiguous, and certain. It is often thought as a non-specific, rather than specific, need for closure since it is a motive to get any firm answer rather than a specific one (as in the case of wishful thinking). Instead, any answer will do provided that it is experienced as certain and clear-cut (Kruglanski, 2004). The need for cognitive closure is a situational factor because it increases when a person is under time-pressure or when error does not have serious consequences. However, there are also individual differences in the need for cognitive closure. Some individuals are dispositionally higher in their need for certainties than other people (Webster & Kruglanski, 1994).

The dispositional need for cognitive closure interacts with situational factors but also with subjects' confidence in their ability to achieve closure and their perception of their level of prior knowledge of the topic. When subjects high in dispositional need for closure also think that they are already well-informed and confident in their ability to gain closure, they manifest a tendency to freeze their existing views. They thus discount, rather than consider, any possible counter-evidence coming their way. Subjects who are confident in their ability to achieve closure, and have a high dispositional need for it, but perceive themselves to be poorly informed on the topic, have a tendency to seize on novel information, coming to a stable view prematurely. These tendencies to seize information when they think that they lack it, and to freeze or resist update when they have reached a view, are the most distinctive features of the need for cognitive closure in those people who are confident in their intellectual abilities (Kruglanski et al., 1993). These dispositions are likely to be the expression of mechanisms resulting in the exploration of a very limited range of alternative hypotheses. The need for closure closes the mind by making alternative views unattractive (Roets et al., 2015).

The high dispositional need for cognitive closure is responsible for prejudice against members of other ethnic groups and for dogmatic ways of thinking (Roets

---

[25] Cassam (2016, 2019) argues that some vices are thinking styles. He mentions wishful thinking and being a conspiracy theorist. The distinction between foxes and hedgehogs is due to Isaiah Berlin (2013).

[26] I am not assuming here that all reasoning involves the same kind of cognitive processes. Thinking does not need to be conscious but it involves transitions from information bearing states to other information bearing states driven by their contents. What I say about thinking styles here should be broadly compatible with the opposing positions held by Mercier and Sperber (2017) or by Kahneman (2012).

et al., 2015).²⁷ In this regard it is a good candidate for a vicious thinking style. People who suffer from this vice are not less able to follow rules of logic or to make inferences. Their inferential abilities are intact. However, these individuals are less inclined than others to explore possibilities and consider counter-evidence. To them, only a very narrow range of hypotheses and views feels salient.

Salience is recorded affectively as feelings of doubt, of error or of certainty. The need for closure motivates individuals to experience too soon the feeling of certainty that induces them to stop exploring alternatives. These epistemic feelings provide the signals that guide agents' epistemic activities. Feelings of doubt prompt individuals actively to seek further information; feelings of certainty halt investigations and offer resistance to opening the matter up for reconsideration. In sum, thinking styles are tendencies to prefer some ways of thinking to others. These preferred forms of thinking result from the monitoring and guidance of controlled cognitive processes partly by means of affective epistemic evaluations such as metacognitive feelings.

I have noted that the need for cognitive closure is a motivational element of cognition. It seems plausible that motivations play an equally crucial role in other thinking styles. The love of learning for instance might be partially a manifestation of a need for cognition (Cacioppo et al., 1996). A tendency to prefer conspiratorial explanation of events might be motivated by the narcissistic need for uniqueness (Imhoff & Lamberty, 2017).

These considerations lend some support to the view that thinking styles are partly the outcome of motivational influences on cognition. They include dispositions to experience episodic epistemic feelings in response to situations. These feelings guide the use of reasoning in inquiry, resulting in a marked preference for some ways of thinking over others. Thinking styles are virtuous only if (a) they are driven by motivations that are epistemically good and (b) generally promote the agent's epistemic goals.²⁸ They are vicious, rather than mixed, only if (a) they are driven by motivations to turn away from what is epistemically good, and (b) typically result in the frustration at least some of the agents' epistemic goals.²⁹ In the case of the need for cognitive closure the good that is discarded is the good of forming beliefs responsibly by considering rather than ignoring relevant evidence. This good is ignored in favour of the desire to settle quickly on an answer.³⁰ The need for cognitive closure also frustrates the achievement of some of the subject's epistemic goals. A person who suffers from it is likely to develop prejudiced views

---

[27] It is also associated with unstable self-esteem, see Jost et al. (2003).
[28] Good motivations are not sufficient since one must also be reliable or at least competent. See Baehr (2016) for the idea that intellectual virtue requires competence at the activities characteristic of the virtue.
[29] Such goals can also be frustrated by the presence of mere cognitive impairments rather than by vices.
[30] This is not to deny that settling quickly on an answer has some epistemic value. The problem here is the disregard for the epistemic value of evaluating the evidence before forming a belief.

even though in some sense they also aim to believe what is true. In this way, vicious thinking styles are, like vicious sensibilities, somewhat self-stultifying.

Thinking styles have causal effects on sensibilities. For example, the need for cognitive closure might promote a wilfully ignorant sensibility. It would be unsurprising if a propensity to want certainties, an intolerance of ambiguity, when combined with confidence in one's abilities, led to a tendency to direct attention away from inconvenient truths. The need for cognitive closure promotes a tunnel vision, if it is combined with fears about one's undeserved privileged status, such narrowing of focus might be directed towards those factors that assuage one's fears.

2.2.3 Character Traits

Epistemic character traits include complex dispositions to prefer some ways of conducting epistemic activities over others. Some of these dispositions are virtuous. Plausibly, open-mindedness, intellectual courage, and epistemic humility are virtuous character traits. Others, such as closed-mindedness, intellectual cowardice, and epistemic arrogance are vices. Many more are tendencies that prove epistemically beneficial in some circumstances but not in others. These might include being witty or being organized.

Intellectual character traits play a role in monitoring and guiding epistemic activities as a whole. They contribute to setting the proximate goals of these activities and to planning the means to achieve their ends. I illustrate these points by way of two examples: open-mindedness and intellectual arrogance. Open-mindedness is not a disposition to consider any possible viewpoint, or always to engage with any possible alternative to one's viewpoint.[31] The open-minded person is not someone who engages in endless rumination without ever making her mind up. Rather open-mindedness requires that one is willing to engage with relevant intellectual options.[32] This willingness is however not sufficient. It is also

---

[31] In this sense open-mindedness is the opposite of closed-mindedness which is defined by Battaly as 'an unwillingness or inability to engage seriously with relevant intellectual options' (2018b, p. 15). However, Battaly tends to lose sight of the fact that ignoring options that are not relevant is not a sign of closed-mindedness.

[32] Engagement, here, does not mean that one attempts to arrive at an independent assessment of all relevant alternatives. One might, for example, not have the skills required to scrutinize some counter-arguments. In these cases, open-mindedness might require that one seeks the opinion of experts and trusts their verdicts about the quality of arguments and counter-arguments. For these reasons, I disagree with Fantl's (2018) characterization of closed-mindedness partly as an unwillingness to reduce one's confidence in response to a counter argument one cannot fault. One might open-mindedly adopt this stance if one is no expert about the argument since one might not trust oneself to be able to evaluate it. Engagement with the argument in such case consists in seeking others' opinions about it. Fantl also argues in favour of closed-mindedness on the basis of the observation that a closed-mind might help not to lose knowledge one already possesses. Perhaps, but as Cassam notices in these cases one retains confidence without preserving the right to be confident (2019, pp. 114–116). If that is the

necessary that one is able to discriminate relevant from irrelevant options. So that one is able to engage with them, rather than simply willing to do so. Intellectual arrogance, instead, is partly a disposition to be supremely confident in the strength of one's intellectual abilities and the correctness of one's own views.[33]

These character traits guide our epistemic activities in at least two distinctive ways. First, they promote some forms of metacognitive thoughts and inhibit others. Second, they foster the development of some patterns of epistemic feelings and obstruct that of others. In these two ways, character traits contribute to the formation of different thinking styles. Consider open-mindedness, for instance. If open-mindedness is not be confused with the inability to make up one's mind, it must involve flexible and intelligent ways of seeking and evaluating alternative intellectual options. Thus, an agent must be able to sense when her opinion has been made less credible by an objection, she must be aware whether she has considered sufficient alternatives or consulted expert opinion, but she must also be able to halt her investigations and form a full and firm belief. To achieve this, human beings rely on a mix of epistemic feelings and meta-cognitive thoughts. Open-minded individuals trust their instincts, when that trust is well-placed. They explore alternatives or consult experts when they experience doubts about their views; they follows topics that excite them; they make up their minds when they feel certain of their conclusions.

There are times, however, when open-minded people know that they should not trust their feelings. They might, for instance, know that they tend to close their mind when tired or that they are subject to anchoring effects leading them to over- or under-estimate when guessing. In these cases, open-minded individuals might use reflection to override their feelings and preserve their ability to evaluate the range of hypotheses that they must assess before making up their mind. These considerations suggest that Riggs' (2010) account of open-mindedness is at least partly correct. He is right to conceive of open-mindedness as an attitude to the self, rather than to arguments and beliefs. This attitude, however, is not exclusively a belief in one's own fallibility, although it might well include this belief. Rather open-mindedness is the ability to evaluate and regulate one's epistemic activities so that only relevant alternatives are given due consideration. This ability is manifested in the development of patterns of epistemic feelings that guide one's epistemic activities. It is also manifested in the reflective ability to override these feelings in circumstances in which one knows or fear that they might be unreliable. Finally, it is expressed in the ability to rely on past experiences to train one's epistemic feelings so that they are better calibrated to the epistemic features of the

---

case closed-mindedness does not have much to recommend for itself. In Chapter 7 I also discuss Battaly's (2018a) arguments that in oppressive environments closed-mindedness can be a virtue.

[33] This is not a full characterization of this vice. I provide an account of it in Chapter 5.

situation (Dokic, 2012; Proust, 2008). These ways of evaluating one's own cognitions manifest what it really takes to think of oneself as fallible.

Intellectual arrogance is also an attitude to the self. It is manifested in a disposition to experience feelings of certainty about one's views that are fed by, and feed into, a feeling of self-certainty (Clarkson et al., 2009). These feelings of certainty, combined with high confidence in one's intellectual abilities, serve to promote a thinking style akin to the need for cognitive closure.[34] Further, those who are arrogant might be unable to change their behaviour by responding to transient feelings of doubt by way of reflection. Instead, they might be motivated to ignore these feelings and proceed regardless. Arrogance is often accompanied by this and other kinds of lack of self-control.[35]

There are motivational aspects to intellectual character virtues and vices. As I have shown above, it is plausible to take open-mindedness as an attitude to the self, acknowledging its general fallibility and its particular intellectual limitations.[36] It is also driven by a motivation to explore alternative and novel ways of thinking. Thus, epistemically good motivations are part of what drives individuals to develop patterns of affective and reflective evaluations of one's cognitive processing that facilitate the formulation of an appropriate range of alternative hypotheses and their evaluation on the basis of the available evidence. They also facilitate evaluation of the evidence in order to ascertain whether more must be sought. It is similarly plausible to take intellectual arrogance as an attitude to the self driven by the need to preserve a high opinion of oneself. Self-enhancement would thus be the chronic motivation that biases the affective and reflective self-evaluations of arrogant individuals.

If these considerations are on the right track, character virtues and vices comprise dispositions to form epistemic feelings and metacognitive thoughts that guide epistemic activities as a whole. These traits are virtuous only if they (a) are driven by motivations that are epistemically good because directed at what is intrinsically epistemically good, (b) systematically facilitate the agent's setting of epistemic goals that are commensurate to her abilities and that promote the attainment of epistemic goods, and (c) typically foster the achievement of the agent's epistemic goals.[37] They are vicious only if they (a) are driven by

---

[34] However, there might be some differences. Arrogant individuals might rarely experience the lack of confidence in one's prior opinions that is typical of the seizing tendency in the need for cognitive closure. Further, the need for closure is the need for any answer. Arrogance, on the other hand, is driven by a need for a specific closure. It is a need for self-enhancing answers. See Chapter 5.

[35] For example arrogant individuals are especially prone to anger see my (2018a) and Chapter 3.

[36] In this regard open-mindedness is an expression of intellectual humility. This closeness might explain why Leary et al. (2017) identify these two virtues.

[37] I am here presuming that virtues contribute to individual excellence. I think that this presumption is plausible with regard to the virtues and vices of self-appraisal. However, there are other intellectual virtues that contribute to making an agent excellent at promoting other people's epistemic flourishing (Byerly, 2020). That said, in those cases promoting others' epistemic success is one of the epistemic goals of the virtuous person.

motivations that are intrinsically bad because they involve turning away from what is epistemically good; (b) they also generally frustrate the agent's setting of epistemic goals that are commensurate to her abilities and promote the attainment of epistemic goods, and (c) typically hinder the achievement of the agent's epistemic goals.[38] I offer an argument for the view that intellectual character vices flow from epistemically bad motivations in Section 2.4 of this chapter.[39]

Character traits influence thinking styles and sensibilities. For example, although arrogance and the dispositional need for cognitive closure are different psychological phenomena, there might be connections between the two. It is possible that overtime arrogance might promote the cultivation of a thinking style that is aversive to nuanced answers, preferring instead clear-cut positions. The same mechanism might foster a dogmatic thinking style that is frozen because it is unwilling to give due consideration to information that is contrary to one's settled view. In addition, one might also speculate that arrogance fosters the sensibility of being wilfully ignorant about any facts that would force one to lower one's own high self-opinion. I return to these themes in Chapter 7, Section 7.1.

Both open-mindedness and arrogance partly consist in an appraisal of the self and of its intellectual abilities. In this book I leave it open that some character traits might not be so focused on self-appraisal. Nevertheless, as the two examples discussed here and those highlighted in Chapter 1 show, those vices and virtues that are related to humility can be characterized as being different kinds of self-evaluations.

2.3 Virtues, Vices, and Epistemic Agency

Sensibilities, thinking styles, and character traits are ways of exercising our epistemic agency. In this section I defend this claim. I also build on it to show that recent conceptions of epistemic virtues as corrections of natural vices are unduly restrictive. Talk of agency brings questions about responsibility in its trail. I begin to address these issues here, even though they receive more extensive treatment in Chapter 8. I conclude the section with a few considerations about the differences between vices, cognitive impairments, and mere eccentricities.

It is not my intention to weigh in on the complex disputes concerning epistemic agency.[40] Even opponents of the notion would concede that there are aspects of

---

[38] These three conditions distinguish vices from, for instance, cognitive impairments since the latter are not driven by motivations. I talk of generally frustrating goal setting and typically hindering their achievement to indicate that some vices might primarily frustrate goal setting whilst others might primarily hinder the achievement of goals.
[39] However, with the exception of those who are epistemically malevolent, individuals who suffer from intellectual vices rarely acknowledge their motivations. On malevolence, see Baehr (2010).
[40] See Kornblith (2012) and Ahlstrom-Vij (2013) for arguments raising doubts about the existence of epistemic agency and Olson (2015) for a defence.

our mental lives over which we have a significant degree of at least long-range voluntary control. Cognitive processes guided by sensibilities, thinking styles, and character traits are among these aspects. Consider first the case of sensibilities as domain-specific skills. I have argued that these are developed over-time through practice. Their acquisition requires the deployment of practical agency, sustained commitment, and deliberation. Thus, the view that people have some long-range voluntary control over the formation and maintenance of some sensibilities is fairly uncontroversial. Undoubtedly, each one of us has only developed some sensibilities and not others. Some people do not care for birdwatching; others pursue careers that do not require the ability to read x-rays. Either way, insofar as these interests are fundamental in the development of sensibilities that we could have cultivated, it makes sense to hold that whether we develop and sustain a given sensibility is something over which we have some control.

A proviso is, however, in order. Some people are denied the opportunity to undertake the kind of training required to possess many sophisticated sensibilities. For instance, unequal access to education might mean that a career as a radiographer is simply not an option for some. In these cases, a person has little control over whether she develops the relevant sensibility.

Sensibilities enable agents to have some control over their perceptual processing. Expertise involves having one's attention captured by locations in one's perceptual field that are relevant to one's epistemic goals but it also comprises the ability to direct voluntary attention, to focus on some aspects of the scene that have captured attention, to disregard others as distractors. In short, sensibilities as skills enable us to exercise some degree of control over perceptual processing and thus have some indirect influence over which perceptual beliefs we acquire and maintain. This control can facilitate the acquisition of relevant truths if it is part of the virtue of being observant; it can promote the avoidance of inconvenient truths when it is an element of the vice of wilful ignorance.

The degree to which we have control over the acquisition of thinking styles might be variable. Undoubtedly, many of these styles are akin to habits that one falls into, rather than skills one consciously or unconsciously cultivates. Be that as it may, it is possible to become aware that one has adopted a style. For instance, one may notice in oneself a tendency to play devil's advocate or a propensity to get bored quickly. However, it is possible that some character traits and sensibilities once set cannot be easily modified by individual efforts. I think that something like this is true of the vices of superiority and inferiority because once acquired they impair the ability to exercise control over one's cognitive processes. Thus, although one could have stopped oneself from developing these features, when they come to define who one is, they are exceedingly hard to change.

That said, not everyone is already set in their vicious ways. Provided that they are appropriately motivated, there are things that the majority can do to become less biased. This much is acknowledged even by critics of epistemic self-improvement (Ahlstrom-Vij, 2013, p. 279). Thus, at least to some degree, we can shape thinking styles. There are steps we can take to be less prone to some bad habits. Importantly, as the example of the need for cognitive closure illustrates, it might be more important to work on one's motivations rather than to attempt directly to correct one's biases.

Be that as it may, once agents have acquired thinking styles, having these gives them some control over their thinking processes. These styles involve dispositions to experience metacognitive feelings of certainty, doubt or error in response to given situations. These feelings, being conscious, alert the subject to features of their cognitive processing of which they would otherwise have no awareness. For example, feelings of doubt prompt the agent to continue to mull over the issue. Experiencing a feeling of certainty when an idea pops into one's head serves as a way of validating the product of a non-conscious cognitive process, which might have relied on heuristics. For example, one might feel certain that Munich is bigger than Essen without knowing why one thinks this. One might, of course, choose to doubt the intuition, but the feeling of certainty provides information that one's heuristic evaluation of this belief is that it is very likely to be true. In this way metacognitive feelings are indicators that allow subjects to monitor their thinking. Further, because these feelings motivate, they guide the subject's mental activity. Epistemic feelings are the means by which we exercise a degree of control over thought. They alert us about features of non-conscious processing so that we can react accordingly and they supply motivations to act by seeking further evidence or settling the issues. Whilst these feelings are not directly under our voluntary control, we can exercise some control over them, since we can deliberate whether to doubt or to endorse them.

Finally, character traits can be habituated or cultivated. Of course, this is not always possible. Children growing up in conditions of extreme deprivation, individuals that find themselves in very restricting circumstances have very limited opportunities to develop their character. Being forced to fight for one's own survival every day shapes people's character but this process of character formation is one over which the individuals themselves might have little control.

That said, once traits of character are formed, these dispositions give subjects some ability to monitor and control their epistemic activities as a whole. These traits recruit both epistemic feelings and reflection to monitor one's cognitive processing and to guide it. For example, the open-minded individual feels doubt about her current views when she encounters evidence that undermines them. This feeling of doubt alerts her to the need to re-consider and provides her with the motivation to engage in rational evaluation. Traits of character also supply the motivation to evaluate one's habits of thought and to appraise one's abilities to carry out the intellectual task at hand. However, some traits of character are responsible for poorly calibrated epistemic feelings of excessive certainty for instance. They are also associated with dispositions to experience directed emotions such as fear or anger that induce loss of self-control. In these ways, our character traits, for better or worse, shape how, and to what extent, we exercise control over our mental lives.

These considerations show that sensibilities, thinking styles and character traits are manifestations of epistemic agency because they are the complex dispositions by means of which we monitor and guide cognitive processing. It is because they are the means by which people exercise control over their mental lives that it makes sense to think of sensibilities, thinking styles, and character traits as virtues when they contribute to the agent's epistemic flourishing and as vices when they undermine it by impairing the subject's agentic abilities of self-monitoring and self-control.[41]

I have characterized virtues and vices as psychological features that guide the use of cognitive processes well by promoting the achievement of the subject's epistemic goals or badly because they frustrate the achievement of at least some of these goals. This description facilitates the distinction between vices and other intellectual impediments that are obstacles to effective and responsible inquiry without being vices. These include cognitive impairments and eccentricities.

Intellectual vices are manifestations of one's epistemic agency because they describe ways in which one exercises control over epistemic activities. These ways of regulating inquiry, however, are examples of agency that is impaired. Those who have intellectual vices are less sensitive to reasons, especially to reasons that might be contrary to their views, than it is desirable in an epistemic agent that is effective and responsible in her epistemic conduct. It is for this reason that intellectual vices, even though they reflect badly on those who possess them, also diminish these individuals' ability to be answerable for their vices and the bad believing that stems from them.[42]

Cognitive impairments are defects in the functioning of epistemic faculties. They include: poor eyesight or failing memory. These differ from vices because they are not manifestations of the subject's epistemic agency.[43] The person who is unreliable in this way is generally not to be blamed or criticized for these shortcomings. That said, sometimes she can take action to at least compensate for them. She can, for instance, buy a pair of spectacles. If so, she might be at fault for her omissions. Eccentricities are different from impairments. Often subjects have some control over them. For example, a person may be so superstitious that he never begins a new project on Friday the 13th. This feature is a part of the

---

[41] I take no position here on whether intellectual virtues constitute flourishing or are primarily means to achieve it. I am inclined to think that at least the motivations that are essential to virtue are partly constitutive of flourishing. An exploration of these difficult issues would take me beyond the scope of this book.
[42] I return to this issue in Chapter 8.
[43] More precisely, cognitive impairments are not attributable to agents because they are not part of their character that includes their commitments and cares. I elaborate this point in Chapter 8.

person's personality and, insofar as the superstitious belief is false, it is to the detriment of his ability to be effective in inquiry.[44] Unlike intellectual vices, however, quirks tend not to have far-reaching consequences. We think of localized superstition as an eccentricity, but if a person's superstitiousness is entrenched and so broad as to lead him to believe vast amounts of nonsense, we reclassify it as an intellectual vice.

The difference between quirks and vice is not exclusively a matter of how far-reaching their consequences are. In addition, there are motivational differences. The motives behind mere quirks might be heterogenous. Nevertheless, mere eccentricities are not motivated by needs to ignore the truth, to achieve certainty irrespectively of the evidence, or to believe whatever makes one feel great. It is this feature of vice that involves turning away from epistemic goods that distinguishes them from eccentricities.[45] These differences explain why cognitive impairments do not reflect badly on their possessors, whilst quirks might, but are not as bad as vices (cf. Cassam, 2019, esp. ch. 6).

There is a tendency in some recent work on epistemic virtue to construe virtue as a learnt or acquired corrective for natural vice. This approach is exemplified by Riggs' (2010) account of open-mindedness as in part a virtue of vigilance consisting in the ability to identify the situations in which one is more prone to bias and to act to counter-act this tendency. It is also illustrated by Roberts and West's (2015) description of virtue as a corrective for the natural epistemic defects highlighted by defenders of epistemic situationism (e.g., Olin & Doris, 2014). The account offered above shows why this approach to virtue is too restrictive. First, it mistakenly assumes that conscious reflection (second-order deliberation) is the primary or only means with which epistemic agents monitor and control their cognitive processing. Instead, as I highlighted above, epistemic feelings and attention often alert agents to what is salient relative to their circumstances and aims. These same indicators also motivate and guide the agent so as to facilitate the achievement of her cognitive goals.

Second, these same accounts end up providing a merely enkratic account of virtue. From their perspective, our natural cognitive endowments are both defective and rigid. We would thus be prone to epistemic temptations that divert us from epistemic goods. The role of virtue would be to enlist reflection in order to neutralise the workings of automatic processing. In my view, this conception of the human mind is mistaken. Epistemic virtue consists in the harnessing of our belief-forming mechanisms under the guidance of attention, epistemic feelings, and occasionally reflection. Each of these provide the kind of epistemic evaluations used

---

[44] Eccentricities are thus attributable to subjects who are liable to be criticized or praised for having them. I discuss attributability in Chapter 8.
[45] I have defended a motivational account of epistemic vice in Tanesini (2018c). I also detail this view in Section 2.4 of this chapter.

by agents to carry out their intended epistemic activities by using their cognitive faculties. In this way, epistemic virtues and vices make some ways of seeing, hearing, or thinking become spontaneous and intuitive. It is in this sense that they become a second nature (Fricker, 2007, pp. 97–98; McDowell, 1994, p. 84).

The account laid out so far of virtues and vices as ways in which we exercise epistemic agency over our cognitive processes helps to begin addressing questions of moral and epistemic responsibility. In this context it is helpful to distinguish responsibility for our epistemic activities and their outcomes from responsibility for possessing virtuous or vicious sensibilities, styles of thinking, and character traits.[46] It is a consequence of the view endorsed here that the beliefs, judgments, and opinions that individuals form and sustain as a result of the operation of their intellectual virtues and vices are attributable to them. These doxastic states reflect well or badly on agents because they are expressions of their intellectual character. Individuals often are also morally accountable for their bad believing because their beliefs reflect the poor quality of their motivations. For instance, the person who consistently fails to notice evidence of wrongdoing because she always looks away out of a desire to preserve her view of herself as a good and honest person is morally accountable for her false belief that all is well.

It is less clear whether and to what extent people are accountable for having the intellectual virtues and vices. These psychological qualities are often acquired in childhood. They are learnt, partly by imitation, from the adults that surround one. Children can also be easily indoctrinated and brainwashed. These considerations highlight that people might have little control over whether they acquire virtuous or vicious dispositions.[47] That said, people do not need to be saddled with their lot. As adults, agents sometimes are in a position to take responsibility for their character. An individual who, perhaps because of his upbringing, has become intellectually arrogant might be able to take responsibility for this trait and attempt to improve himself. Whilst this can be difficult to achieve, there is no reason to believe that one cannot make some changes in one's behaviour.[48]

2.4 Virtue, Vice, and Motivation

The accounts offered above of sensibilities, thinking styles, and character traits as exercises of epistemic agency highlight the important roles played by motivation

---

[46] Battaly (2016a) frames this distinction in terms of responsibility for possessing the virtue or vice as distinct from responsibility for exercising it.
[47] We should not conclude from these observations that people are not accountable for their vices, since, as I argue in Chapter 8, one might be accountable for qualities over which one has no voluntary control.
[48] I owe the distinction between attributing and taking responsibility to Card (1996).

in their formation and maintenance.[49] Motives and commitment are necessary to develop skills including sensibilities such as that of being observant. That is, motivations, even though they might not be components of sensibilities, have shaped their development to such an extent that reference to motivations can make intelligible the patterns of responses that characterize each sensibility. At least some thinking styles are driven by motivational states. This is the case, for instance, with the style characteristic of the need for cognitive closure. Finally, the view that intellectual character virtues have motivational components is plausible, even though controversial.[50] The discussion so far suggests that intellectual character vices, as well as virtues, have motivational components. This position is a minority view.[51] Although Battaly (2015, pp. 93–94) lists it among the possible contenders, she does not defend it in great detail. Cassam (2016) and Crerar (2017), however, have explicitly argued against it. In their view, motivation is not essential to intellectual character vice. It would even be perfectly possible for an intellectually vicious individual to have wholly good epistemic motivations. The main aim of this section is to explain and defend a motivational view of intellectual character vice and to show how adopting such a view helps addressing some difficulties with other accounts.[52]

Vice attributions, as Cassam (2015, p. 19) observes, are psychological explanations of belief and action that undermine that belief or action as lacking any rational grounds in its support. Cassam also notes that these attributions tend to be made from a third-personal perspective since one could not coherently see one's belief as stemming from intellectual vice without abandoning it. These observations seem exactly right. If, in a debate, one of the speakers accuses the other of being arrogant, the accuser is telling his opponent and their audience, that the opponent's beliefs are unwarranted because his believing them is explained by the fact that he is arrogant, rather than by any epistemic justification that he might have in their support. If this is right, coming to attribute an intellectual vice to oneself, would lead, on pain of irrationality, to seeing many of one's beliefs as being wholly undermined.

Cassam is an opponent of the motivational account of intellectual vice. Nevertheless, his observations about the nature of character vice attributions open the way to the development of such an account. To see why, one must first note that vice epistemology has operated to date with a very narrow

---

[49] My interest here lies with motivational accounts of intellectual character vices. I have no qualms with the view that reliabilist virtues do not have a motivational component. I agree with Zagzebski (1996) that character virtues have motivational components. A detailed comparison of her position with mine would be a distraction from my main task of defending the motivational account of vice.
[50] Battaly (2015) provides an excellent overview of the debate over the role of motivation.
[51] I have defended it in (Tanesini, 2018c). The arguments I supply in this section largely overlap with the considerations offered in that article.
[52] Thus, even if I believe that motivations typically play an important role in all kinds of intellectual vices, the motivational view that I defend here is restricted to character vices.

conception of motive. Once the diversity of roles that motives can play in the explanation of action and belief formation is appreciated, the motivational account of intellectual vice (including character vice) is shown to be superior to its rivals.

It is reasonably common place in the philosophy of action to distinguish between three kinds of explanations: justifications, rationalizations, and mere explanations. Actions are justified by supplying normative reasons in their favour. These are objective considerations that speak in support of the action. Actions are rationalized by providing the reasons that the agent takes to support her action.[53] Finally, actions can also be explained by invoking the psychological states that make their performance intelligible. I borrow from Alvarez (2016) an example of an action for which these explanations diverge to illustrate their distinctiveness.[54] Consider Othello's murder of Desdemona. There are no good reasons for this action. Therefore, the action cannot be justified. Othello's reason for his behaviour is that Desdemona is unfaithful. It is her alleged adultery that in Othello's view rationalizes his conduct. Finally, from an outside perspective, one can make Othello's behaviour intelligible by attributing to him the motive of jealousy. It is this motive that explains, without rationalizing, Othello's murder of his wife.

This example is analogous to explanations of the process of belief-formation in terms of evidence, justifications, and motivations.[55] Consider the example of a fictitious Galileo who believes that he is the smartest scientist in his research team. If Galileo's belief is off the mark, there might be no evidence in its support. Galileo's reasons for his belief are various. He thinks, for instance, that the team's successes are due to him and that his superior intelligence is the reason why people tend to be quiet around him or rarely contradict what he says. Galileo thus rationalizes his believing that he is superior by invoking these alleged facts as the epistemic justifications of his belief. These rationalisations can explain why Galileo believes as he does. From a third personal perspective, one can make sense of Galileo's believing that he is the smartest member of his team intelligible by invoking his arrogance. One may say that it is his arrogance that has led Galileo to believe in his superiority in the absence of evidence in support of this belief. It is also arrogance that has led him selectively to focus on some considerations that support this belief, and to fabricate other reasons that speak in favour of his intellectual superiority.

---

[53] These are the reasons that agents would spontaneously supply or would acknowledge if these are presented to them.

[54] In cases of rational activities the three explanations absorb each other. In those cases the considerations in favour of the action are the same as the considerations invoked by the agent to rationalize her behaviour. Further, these same considerations also make the action intelligible.

[55] I use 'justification' here in the unusual sense of referring to whatever one offers as a justification whether or not it offers epistemic support for the belief.

This tripartite explanation of belief formation clarifies the motivational role played by virtues and by vices. The person who open-mindedly engages with views alternative to her own probably would not rationalize her epistemic conduct in terms of her open-mindedness. Doing so would seem to be an exercise in moral grandstanding and would come across as arrogant. Instead, open-mindedness is the motivation that has guided her conduct and made her find reasons to engage with some views alternative to her own.[56] Her open-mindedness explains why she finds these views plausible or deserving of evaluation. Thus, both virtues and vices are best thought as the deep roots of epistemic conduct rather than as the conscious reasons used by agents to rationalize their views and conduct.

Nevertheless, both supporters and critics of motivational accounts of intellectual virtues and vices have mostly focused on the kind of motives that are available to agents to rationalize their behaviour. Consider, for instance, Crerar's description of Galileo as an arrogant scientist who is motivated to find the truth for its own sake (2017, p. 7). His arrogance causes him to form false beliefs about other people's abilities. Because he thinks that others are his intellectual inferiors, he does not give sufficient weight to their opinions. Hence, Galileo is disposed to dogmatism as well as arrogance. Crerar argues that the intelligibility of examples such as this one shows that intellectual vice is possible in the presence of wholly good epistemic motivations.[57]

It is not difficult to imagine that Galileo thinks he is intrinsically motivated by a desire for the truth. He might invoke this motive to rationalize his behaviour. He might tell himself that he does not listen to others' views because they could distract him away from his single-minded pursuit of the truth. Galileo, of course, does not think that he is arrogant. He could not conceive of himself as arrogant without undermining his belief in his own intellectual superiority. Further, if Galileo came to see himself as arrogant, he would begin to re-describe his past conduct in new ways. He would not rationalize his tendency to discount other people's view as motivated by a single-minded pursuit of the truth, but as explained by his arrogance. In short, he would come to think that contrary to what he thought he was not really motivated by a desire for truth but by a desire for dominance. He would re-assess his earlier rationalizations as delusive.

Similarly from a third personal viewpoint, if one accepts the explanation of Galileo's beliefs and treatment of other people as stemming out of his arrogance, one is bound to find this explanation as undermining the description of Galileo as

---

[56] Here and throughout I distinguish between motives as episodic states that are among the causes of practical and epistemic activities and motivations. The latter are dispositions to have motives of a given sort. For instance, a person might act in a given occasion out of fear. She might, however, also be a fearful person. If so, she is someone who is disposed to feel fear. In this case, fear is a motive whilst fearfulness is a motivation. A similar distinction is also adopted by Zagzebski (1996, pp. 131–132).

[57] Cassam (2019) also offers what is essentially the same example of an intellectually vicious person whose epistemic motivations are wholly good. See Tanesini (2018c) for a defence of the motivational account against a wider range of counterexamples.

motivated by a desire to find the truth for its own sake. One can make sense of Galileo seeking the truth when such behaviour fans his arrogance. But being prepared to follow the truth wherever it takes requires that one is willing to learn some unpalatable truths about oneself. This willingness, as a trademark of intellectual humility, is at odds with arrogance. From this outside perspective, one is hard pressed to describe Galileo as both arrogant and truly intrinsically motivated by the truth. Instead, it makes more sense to think of Galileo as someone who has adopted the persona of a truth seeker. Ultimately, however, this rationalization is in the service of the desire for domination that is part and parcel of his arrogance.

Galileo's self-redescription does not need to be wholly confabulatory. He might have acquired a genuine concern for the truth. He might have also developed skills. Hence, he might in some domain of inquiry be observant. He might be a good reasoner whose thinking style is at least partially successful. Even so, Galileo's motivations are at best mixed. His concern for the truth could be wholly instrumental. Representing himself as someone who cares for the truth is ultimately just a means for self-enhancement.[58] In addition, the desire for domination is plausibly manifested in a range of intrinsically bad epistemic motives some of which are non-instrumentally had. The person who wishes to be intellectually superior or dominate others is bound to see other people's successes as an obstacle. He must thus desire to see them fail. His oppositions to others' epistemic success is unlikely to be wholly instrumental since arrogance often entails a delight in, and enjoyment of, seeing others failing. Further, pleasure in others' epistemic failure is an intrinsically bad epistemic motivation. It is also an inextricable feature of the kind of arrogance characterized by a desire for self-enhancement through the domination of other people.

To summarize, when we accept that some motivations make actions and belief intelligible, do not rationalize it, and further cannot be endorsed without undermining the rationality of the action or belief that flows from them, it becomes possible to understand the motivational core of intellectual character vice. When an agent's conduct and beliefs are correctly understood as stemming from vice, and thus as something for which there are no good reasons, the agent's rationalizations cannot be fully consonant with the true motives at the root of their beliefs and behaviours since these motivations undermine the rationality of those beliefs or behaviours. These true motives are the motivations characteristic of the character vice responsible for the agent's conduct and views. Since these motivations if acknowledged would undermine the rationality of the belief or conduct by the agent's own lights, the subject is likely to re-describe his motivations to rationalize his activities. This is why vices are stealthy (Cassam, 2015). It is hard for

---

[58] But it is also possible that his motivations are mixed so that he cares both for self-enhancement and intrinsically for the truth. After all, it is wholly possible to have desires that cannot be co-realized.

individuals to discover their intellectual vices since they have usually developed over time ways to rationalize their behaviour to cover up the mechanisms that are in fact responsible for it. Individuals who are intellectually vicious are therefore prone to something akin to self-deception.

The view that character vices have unendorsable motivational components also explains how intellectual vices negatively affect information processing. If intellectual character vices must include motivations that cannot be acknowledged, then these vices are causally responsible for widespread wishful thinking and self-deception about any issues that threatens to expose the motivated nature of the agent's beliefs.[59]

One might object to my motivational account that there are character vices which appear to have no specific motivational component.[60] Cassam (2019, p. 16) singles out stupidity as foolishness as one such vice. I do not find this example convincing because there are different kinds of foolishness, each of which plausibly has a distinctive epistemically bad motivation. Some people's foolishness is an expression of snobbery that is motivated by a desire to belong to the epistemic elite irrespective of merit. Others' stupidity is really gullibility characterized by the epistemic bad motivation to believe what people say irrespective of the evidence.[61] For sure, even if I am right about foolishness, it is possible that there might be another character vice that lacks a distinctive motivation. If so, the burden of proof is on the opponent to describe this character vice and show that it has no characteristic motivational component.[62] The more general argument about the psychology of vice presented in this section strongly suggests that there are no character vices without distinctive motivations.

We are now in a position to see what makes intellectual vices vicious. Sensibilities are shaped by motivations to turn away from, ignore, and avoid epistemic goods. These same motivations drive thinking styles and are components of character traits. Vices are vicious because of their tight connections to intrinsically bad epistemic motivations.[63] In addition, and as a side effect, vices are also vicious because of their self-stultifying and self-deceptive nature. Individuals

---

[59] I return to this topic in Chapter 7.

[60] I restrict my attention to character vices because we do not have a pre-theoretical understanding of thinking styles. I have identified these as resulting from various dispositional needs which serves as motivations. Those who deny that thinking styles have motivational components are simply using another theoretical conception. Any disagreement between the two can only be addressed by comparing their explanatory power rather than by considering hypothetical cases. I also do not consider sensibilities since these do not have motivations as components even though motivations are causally responsible for their development.

[61] 'Stupidity' could also refer to lack of intelligence. This kind of stupidity lacks any motivational component. It is however also not a vice but a cognitive impairment.

[62] One might claim that character vices have numerous possible motivations rather than a single characteristic one. The difference between this view and mine focuses on how thinly to individuate character vices. I do not pursue this issue here. Thanks to Paul Bloomfield for raising it.

[63] In Chapter 7 I argue that character vices are also vicious because they include dispositions to experience emotions such as spiteful envy that are responsible for morally bad behaviours.

who suffer from these psychological features do not usually embrace them. On the contrary, they tend to rationalize away their presence. When this happens individuals are trapped in a kind of motivated irrationality since they possess motivations that pull them in different and irreconcilable directions.

2.5 Some Trademarks of Intellectual Virtue and Vices

In the next chapter I present the social psychological framework that I adopt in my account of intellectual humility and of the vices that oppose it. This is an approach that is based on the notion of attitude conceived as summary evaluation of a target object. In that chapter I defend the view that attitudes are the causal bases of the intellectual vices of self-appraisal. I conclude this chapter by listing briefly some of the qualities of intellectual virtues and vices that have been unveiled in the discussion provided in this chapter. These qualities receive more detailed consideration in Chapter 3 where I show how these can be explained using the vocabulary attitudes.

1. Virtues and vices are **aspects of a person's character**. Qualities like being observant, being prone to wishful thinking, being courageous or perseverant contribute to defining who people are (Annas, 2011, p. 9; Miller, 2013).
2. Virtues and vices are **stable over time and consistent across situations**. That is, they are psychological qualities that are predictive of behaviour across a broad range of situations and over extended periods of time (Miller, 2014). This cross-situational consistency and temporal stability is characteristic of sensibilities and thinking styles as well as traditional character traits. However, the stability that is characteristic of some vices might be apparent only at a high level of abstraction. For instance, the servile individual consistently acts in a deferential manner. But, what counts as being deferential might depend on the opinions held by those to whom the servile person defers.
3. Virtues and perhaps some vices, are **intelligent** because they are flexible and are responsive to reason (Annas, 2011; Snow, 2010).[64] These points are often couched in the vocabulary of skill. This terminological choice is especially apt with regard to virtuous sensibilities, but it is not wholly out of place when discussing thinking styles. Be that as it may, behaviour and beliefs stemming from virtue frequently involve picking out patterns as salient or important given the agent's goals. This is often achieved by recruiting attention to guide the use of cognitive faculties such as perception.

---

[64] I take this feature to comprise what Baehr (2016) calls competence and judgment.

4. Virtues and vices have **motivational components**. The view has been defended by Zagzebski (1996) with regard to intellectual character virtues which in her opinion all share the ultimate motive of love for cognitive contact with reality.[65] If the view defended above is correct, motivations, as dispositions to possess characteristic motives, are also an intrinsic part of intellectual character vices. These motivations include a standing desire to defend the ego against putative threats or to gain social acceptance.
5. Virtues and vices have **emotional elements**, or at least have characteristic emotions associated with them (Baehr, 2016; Zagzebski, 1996). In my view each of the epistemic vices that I address in this book is closely linked to a disposition to experience a characteristic aversive emotion such as anger, shame, spite, or envy. The tendency to experience a wide range of situations as warranting these emotional responses colours the whole intellectual lives of those who suffer from these vices. The character vices and virtues of self-appraisal are also involved in monitoring and guiding cognition by way of their close association with metacognitive feelings of doubt, confidence, certainty, or error.

Claims 1 to 5 are relatively uncontroversial. In Chapter 3 I assume that any plausible account of the psychological states that are the causal bases of intellectual virtues and vices must explain why they possess the features detailed in these statements. The main aim of that chapter is to show that a theory based on the findings of attitude psychology is well-placed to supply such an account.

---

[65] Other supporters of the view that intellectual virtues have motivational components are Baehr (2016) and Montmarquet (1993).

3
Attitude Psychology and Virtue Epistemology
A New Framework

Virtue ethicists and epistemologists have generally presumed that virtue and vices are real psychological states or traits amenable to empirical study.[1] There is, however, no agreement on the psychological constructs that may play this role.[2] In this chapter I introduce the apparatus of attitude psychology that, in my view, supplies a theoretical framework suitable to understand those intellectual vices which in Chapter 2 I have described as defects in epistemic agency. The approach throws light on the affective, motivational and cognitive dimensions of the vices which are under scrutiny in this book. This chapter has two aims: the first is to introduce and explain some concepts from social psychology that are central to the framework adopted here. The second is to provide some considerations in support of thinking that attitudes are the causal bases of intellectual character virtue and vices of self-appraisal.[3] Whilst the arguments presented in this chapter are intended to make this claim at least plausible, I consider them to be preliminary. In my opinion the strongest evidence in favour of this account consists in its ability to explain the deep connections between the differing manifestations of each individual intellectual vice. For instance, as I show in Chapter 5 the account can explain why anger is a typical manifestation of *superbia*. It is this ability to make sense of the underlying psychological roots of each vice that is the strongest form of support for the approach presented here.

The chapter consists of two sections. In the first I explain the social psychological notion of an attitude and describe its principal features. These are: object, content, structure, function and four dimensions of strength: accessibility,

---

[1] There are exceptions: most notably, Julia Driver (2001, 2016).
[2] Some have argued that they are units of the Cognitive Affective Personality System (Snow, 2010). More recently, advances have been made adopting the so called Whole Trait Theory (Snow et al., 2019). See Miller (2013) for an overview. In addition some have argued that humans do not possess the kind of robust global character trait required by virtue (Alfano, 2012; Doris, 2002; Harman, 2000). This objection is known as the situationist challenge. Its sting has been rather undermined by the question marks now hanging over the validity of some of the empirical research on which it was based (Alfano, 2018). I briefly address it in Section 3.2.2.
[3] I suspect that the approach generalizes to all character virtues and vices, but I do not defend this claim here. For an account of some moral character virtues in terms of attitudes, see Webber (2015) and Rees and Webber (2014).

extremity, centrality, and certainty. In the second section I defend the claim that intellectual virtue and vices of self-evaluation are based on attitudes. I identify attitudes together with their informational bases or contents as the mental states that ground the broad dispositions that are constitutive of these virtues and vices. I defend this identification by highlighting that attitudes possess many of the characteristic features of character traits discussed in Chapter 2. Adopting the attitude framework supplies a unified explanation of why virtues and vices exhibit these properties.

3.1 Introducing Attitudes

Attitude is the central construct of social psychology.[4] Attitudes are akin to likes or dislikes of things. As such they are not propositional attitudes, like belief, of the kind familiar to philosophers. The purpose of this section is to explain those features of attitudes that are central to the account offered in this book. I detail the concepts of attitude object, content, structure, and function and I discuss four dimensions of attitude strength: accessibility, extremity, centrality, and certainty. In the next section I return to these features of attitudes to defend my view that attitudes are the causal bases of the virtues and vices with which this book is concerned.[5]

Attitudes are summary evaluations or appraisals of objects that are their targets. For example, I dislike liquorice in its refined form. This dislike, which is manifested in aversive behaviour towards liquorice, is a negative attitude. The thought of liquorice, or any encounter with it, triggers negative feelings and emotions; it induces a gagging reflex, prompts negative memories, and makes me want to avert my eyes and move away from the stuff which, in some sense, I regard as disgusting. My attitude, thus, is rather extreme. It is also very accessible since the mere thought of liquorice is sufficient to activate the negative reaction. The attitude, however, is not very central to my self-conception; liquorice does not loom large in my life. I suspect that this attitude was formed early in my childhood when I was very unwell after eating some large amount terracattù (silver coated liquorice pellets). I must have associated sickness with liquorice and the association has stuck, although its extremity has weakened over time as I have come to realize that liquorice is harmless. My attitude was initially formed to serve the need to avoid feeling sick, it persists satisfying the same need even though it is

---

[4] Some of the material covered in this and the next section partly overlaps with my discussion of the issues in (Tanesini, forthcoming).

[5] In Section 3.2 I explain what I mean when I say that virtues and vices are based on attitudes. Briefly, attitudes are the causal bases responsible, together with the relevant situational factors (e.g., triggering conditions), for the manifestations of the disposition.

itself partly responsible for the unpleasant feelings and reflexes that it is the attitude's function to avoid.

Social psychologists' concept of an attitude is an attempt to capture and render clearer a notion that is in common parlance. We often talk of people's attitudes to political parties, to values, to groups, and branded products. These attitudes are evaluations of their objects. Hence, we may describe a person's attitude towards an item as positive, negative, or as ambivalent. Psychologists capture this thought by thinking of attitudes as psychological states consisting of an association between one or more valences, understood as positive or negative affects, and a representation of the object that is the target of the attitude.[6] My negative attitude to liquorice, for example, is an association between a negative affect or valence and a representation of liquorice. In my mind the activation of the representation of liquorice, which can be caused by a chance encounter or a passing thought, triggers the negative affect. Thus, my attitude is an associative state because it is a pairing of two psychological states—the representation of an object and a valence or affect—which is in part acquired because of the strong hedonistic disvalue of my initial encounter with liquorice pellets and a history of pairing liquorice with negative affect.

Attitudes are said to be constructs because they cannot be observed. However, attitudes can be measured and they have been shown to be predictive of behaviour in a range of circumstances (Maio & Haddock, 2015, pp. 67–78). Hence, there are good reasons to think that attitudes have psychological reality. We may, therefore, ask why we have them. A plausible answer is that attitudes function as cognitive shortcuts. They record the outcome of our overall evaluations of objects. We are thus saved the effort and time that it takes to assess afresh how we feel and think about those things that frequently cross our paths. For instance, creatures that do not need to revaluate whether snakes are good or bad (in some regard) every time they see one nearby, but treat them immediately as dangerous, are at an advantage over animals that reassess serpents every time they come face to face with them.[7]

Whilst all human beings have attitudes towards a vast number of things, attitudes differ from person to person. These differences range along several dimensions. Some may have positive attitudes to a person, whilst others' attitude towards the same individual may be ambivalent or negative. Attitudes vary in strength, can serve different needs, they can also be based primarily on affective or doxastic evaluations of objects. The study of attitudes, therefore, offers some

---

[6] I do not mean to imply here that the association is primarily based on, or caused by, affect. Rather the association has the import of being an evaluation because it is the association of the representation of an object with something positive and/or something negative. These positive and negative states are affects.

[7] If this is right, attitudes are stored in memory rather than assembled on the hoof. Although most psychologists think of attitudes in this way, the view is not uncontroversial (Maio & Haddock, 2015, pp. 48–49).

insight into the psychology of individual differences. In this regard, it differs from much cognitive psychology and from some studies of social cognition that focus instead on commonalities. Hence, the psychology of attitudes may help to reveal the processes that explain why some people are better epistemic agents than others.

3.1.1 Object, Content, Structure

The *object* of an attitude is what the attitude appraises. The notion of an object is understood formally to range over absolutely anything. It includes universals, such as umbrellas in general; concrete particulars, like my umbrella; values, for example, equality; specific people and even social groups. Basically, everything that can be experienced or thought about can be the object of an attitude (Banaji & Heiphetz, 2010; Maio & Haddock, 2015). Even propositions can figure as objects of attitudes since they may invoke affective responses. In these limiting cases the attitude is directed towards the proposition as an object rather than as an articulated content.

The *content* of an attitude is the informational basis from which the attitude is derived. The attitude itself is the result of weighing up all the positive and negative considerations relevant to its target object.[8] These considerations speaking for or against the object are the informational content of the attitude which the attitude itself summarizes. The attitude, then, is a cognitive shortcut because it helps us know what we think and how we feel about an object without having to reconsider every time what we know about it (Banaji & Heiphetz, 2010; Fazio & Olson, 2007).

The contents of attitudes comprise components of three different kinds. These are: cognitive elements that include evaluative knowledge and beliefs about the relevant object; affective elements comprising the feelings and emotions one experiences about it; behavioural elements consisting of memories of one's past behavioural responses to the object as well as one's current behavioural dispositions towards it (Maio & Haddock, 2015, pp. 29–32). For example, my negative attitude to liquorice is based on my evaluative belief that it stains the tongue when ingested, my feelings of disgust, memories of retching after eating it. The informational bases of attitudes change as we acquire novel information and make new experiences. These changes prompt re-evaluations of the target object and thus revisions of the attitudes themselves. Attitude change is thus responsive, albeit patchily, to reasons. It would seem, therefore, that, even though the attitudes themselves are associative states, the processes that lead to their formation include inferences as well as traditional associative processes such as conditioning (Maio

---

[8] Thus attitudes are psychological states that are distinct from those that constitute their bases. Attitudes are the outputs of cognitive processes of weighting up or summarizing that take the attitude contents as their inputs.

& Haddock, 2015, pp. 196–198). I return to these issues in Chapter 7 when I discuss the role of attitudes in motivated cognition.

Oftentimes attitudes are neither wholly positive nor wholly negative. Instead, they comprise both negative and positive affects. These attitudes are said to be ambivalent. The existence of such attitudes has prompted psychologists to reconsider how we weigh up positive and negative considerations when forming attitudes. Contrary to initial theories, experimental evidence indicates that positive considerations do not always inhibit negative ones (or vice versa). Hence, recent accounts attribute to some attitudes more than one dimension of appraisal. That is, when evaluating objects we first aggregate positive and negative factors separately. Psychologists represent this two-dimensional structure by identifying the valence of the attitude as a point on a Cartesian coordinate where one axis represents degrees of positivity and the other degrees of negativity (Maio & Haddock, 2015, p. 40). Attitudes, therefore, can be the summary of evaluative information which is unidimensional and thus represented by a point along a line from high levels of negativity to high levels of positivity or bidimensional and thus represented by a point in a Cartesian plane. Psychologists refer to this feature of attitudes as their *structure*.

The idea that we can be ambivalent about some things seems right. For example, many people, and especially women, have ambivalent attitudes to chocolate. They feel both very positive and very negative about it. Positivity stems from its hedonistic reward value; eating chocolate can be immensely pleasurable. However, if one is concerned about weight, and the health implications of the refined sugar contained in much of the chocolate that is available in shops, one is likely to harbour negative evaluative beliefs about the implications of eating chocolate for one's health and weight. When one is ambivalent about something, negative and positive considerations and affects do not cancel each other but coexist alongside each other. It is this feature of ambivalent attitudes that psychologists try to capture when they attribute to some attitudes a two-dimensional structure.

Three further points about ambivalent attitudes are also worth mentioning in order to fill in the picture. First, attitudes that are ambivalent are more susceptible to situational influences and thus less predictive of behaviour (Maio & Haddock, 2015, p. 41). This is not surprising since, depending on which features of the object are particularly salient on a given occasion, either the representations of positive or negative aspects of the object may be activated (Bell & Esses, 2002).[9] Ambivalent attitudes can lead to very positive or very negative responses to the

---

[9] There is a difference between the ambivalence of attitudes which prompt one to react positively to an object in one situation and negatively in another, and the kind of ambivalence that is felt by the subject and that leads to indecision in every situation (Maio & Haddock, 2015, p. 41). It is the first kind known as 'potential ambivalence' that I am discussing here.

object because one is swayed by situational factors. Second, the coexistence in ambivalent attitudes of negative and positive factors indicates that although the attitude summarizes its content, both this informational basis and the way in which it is organized are important factors in the prediction of behaviour. Thus, attitudes as global evaluations do not replace the contents that they summarize. When one explains the influence of attitudes on behaviour, one must also consider the attitude's content and structure as further factors.[10] Third, and relatedly, ambivalent attitudes are less accessible than attitudes that are unidimensional (Maio & Haddock, 2015, p. 48). That is, the attitude as a whole is less likely to be triggered quickly when one encounters the target object. Presumably, it is this weaker accessibility that explains the ambivalent attitudes susceptibility to situational factors.[11]

3.1.2 Function

Attitudes are acquired, revised, or maintained to satisfy human needs (Maio & Olson, 2000b). These needs individuate the function or functions served by attitudes. These functions are not elements or components of attitudes. Rather, the notion of attitude function offers a method for classifying attitudes that consists in sorting them by the needs that the attitude contributes to satisfying or the motives that are instrumental in its formation and maintenance. Because of difficulties with measurement and taxonomy, the functional approach to attitudes had been dormant before being more recently revived. This approach is of special significance to understand the roles of attitudes in epistemic activities. Whilst there is no consensus on how attitudes are revised in the light of novel information, all the dominant models predict that people process more deeply persuasive messages that are relevant to the function served by their pre-existing attitudes about that object. That is, they predict function matching effects. For example, the Elaboration Likelihood Model (ELM) (Petty & Cacioppo, 1986) predicts that people are more likely to scrutinize more deeply arguments that speak to their motives for holding a given attitude than those who are not similarly relevant. For example, if a teenager's positive attitude to the latest iPhone serves the need to be accepted by her peers, she will pay more attention to messages about whether these phones are 'must haves', then to messages about whether they are value for money. Similarly, the Heuristics Systematic Model (HSM) holds that individuals when they are highly motivated process messages that are relevant to that motivation

---

[10] This is further evidence that attitudes and their contents are distinct psychological states.
[11] This is a complex matter, however. Each of the two evaluations that comprise the two dimensions of the attitudes might be highly accessible. Nevertheless, the attitude as a whole might be more weakly accessible because it takes time to aggregate the two unidimensional attitudes.

more systematically but in a biased manner, than they would if their motivation were low (Chen et al., 1999).[12] In short, people pay more attention to messages, intended to persuade them to change their mind, that speak to the needs that their attitudes serve to satisfy. That said, deeper elaboration or systematic consideration can be biased. Hence, one should not conclude, from the fact that we scrutinize arguments that speak to our needs, that such scrutiny yields less biased or more reliable conclusions, than the quick and dirty reliance on heuristics. Attitude function is therefore an important aspect of the psychology of attitude if we are concerned with the role of attitudes in argumentation and reasoning.[13]

There are several taxonomies of attitude functions currently in use. Although these are different, there are significant overlaps between them. Broadly speaking, six functions have gained widespread acceptance. These are: object appraisal, knowledge, instrumental, ego-defensive, social adjustive, and value-expressive. The object appraisal function is defined as the function shared by all attitudes to appraise their objects (Fazio, 2000). It is also characterized as the combination of knowledge and instrumental functions. I largely set the appraisal function aside in this book to focus on one of its constituents. This is the knowledge function (Katz, 1960). Attitudes serve this function whenever they are formed and revised to satisfy the need to make sense of the world. If one cashes out function in motivational terms (cf. Marsh & Julka, 2000), attitudes serving a knowledge function are those whose formation and revision is guided by the motivation to have an accurate account of the target object. That is, attitudes serving the knowledge function are the outcome of cognitive processes of evaluation based on the attitude content and driven by accuracy motives.[14]

Instrumental attitudes are those that serve the need to satisfy preferences and to avoid what one disfavours. Adopting the account that sees attitude function as derivative of motivation, we can define instrumental attitudes as those that are formed, revised, and sustained by evaluating objects for their utility. That is, since attitudes summarize the considerations for and against the given object on the basis of the person's affects, evaluative beliefs, and behavioural tendencies towards it, the motives incorporated in the notion of attitude function provide the questions that guide the evaluation of the attitude object. We can think of motives,

---

[12] High motivation (e.g., to the defend the ego) is said to raise the threshold of the amount of evidence required to feel confident in beliefs and thus leads to more systematic processing of information that is relevant to one's motivations and impacts on one's current opinions.

[13] In his pioneering work on attitudes and virtue, Jonathan Webber (2015) ignores this aspect of attitudes. In his view, function does not play a distinctive explanatory role. I disagree. The best way of accounting for attitude change in the context of persuasion is to explain some of the results as function matching effects.

[14] There is no consensus as to whether attitude function is derived from the content or whether it should be understood as closely related to the motivations and goals leading an individual to form and revise her attitudes. For a summary of the evidence in support of the latter approach see Maio and Haddock (2015, p. 263).

therefore, as having a role in the formulation of the hypothesis about the object that a subject is going to assess.

For example, the instrumental motivation leads a subject implicitly to interrogate the object for its utility. The agent subconsciously asks himself 'Does this thing get me what I want?'. This directional question determines which among the evaluative beliefs, affects, and behavioural dispositions about the object are relevant to the set question. In this way motives influence the selection of the evidence (i.e., informational basis) that is considered when appraising this object (Kunda, 1990).

To make this point vivid, imagine the case of a person who has a positive attitude, serving an instrumental function, towards taxis. Taxis are a reliable and quick way to reach one's destination. This belief, combined with positive past experiences, and a tendency to use taxis when away from home, might be part of the attitude content summarized by the attitude itself. The same person, however, might also have other evaluative beliefs about taxis. For instance, that it is often impossible to tell whether the upholstery is clean. Conceivably, this belief could count as a consideration against using taxis. But, if the individual in question does not care for cleanliness, the belief that taxis often have dirty seats will not be considered when weighing up one's attitude to taxis. In short, the motives for forming and maintaining the attitudes contribute to selecting which attitude relevant beliefs, affects, and behavioural tendencies are part of the base to be weighed up when forming and sustaining the attitude.

Motives also influence attitude formation, maintenance, or change in more profound ways. In addition to playing a role in hypothesis formulation, they also contribute to the evaluation of the evidence thus selected. To see this consider that the costs associated with error vary depending on a number of things including pragmatic considerations. It seems quite rational to put more effort in making sure that one gets it right when the cost of a mistake is high than when it is low. So in cases where it does not much matter whether one is wrong, it is sensible to set the threshold of evidence for belief as lower than the threshold required when errors are costly. Motives are an important determinant of costs, and thus indirectly determine the required evidential thresholds for belief (Scott-Kakures, 2000).[15]

These points are best grasped by considering two attitude functions that loom large in this book. These are the functions of ego-defence and social-adjustment. Ego-defensive attitudes are those that evaluate objects for their capacity to pose a threat to the self. Social-adjustive attitudes appraise objects in relation to their role in promoting or inhibiting social acceptance (Maio et al., 2004; Maio & Haddock, 2004; Maio & Olson, 2000a, 2000b). For example, a person's negative attitude to a political rival might serve an ego-defensive function since one appraises rivals negatively, and hence dislikes them, because one takes them to be a threat to one's

---

[15] Supporters of the Heuristics Systematic Model label the same point as the 'sufficiency principle' (Chen et al., 1999).

success. Similarly, teenagers harbour positive attitudes towards some branded product (e.g., the latest iPhone) serving a social adjustive function because evaluating these goods positively, and thus seeking to own them, helps to be part of the in-group.

The motivations of ego-defence and social-adjustment bias the evaluative processes that lead to the development of attitudes (Maio & Haddock, 2015, pp. 61–62 and 65; Watt et al., 2008). Motives contribute to the hypothesis that is formulated when forming an attitude about an object. That is, they set directional questions which determine the evidence to be included in the informational basis (content) of the attitude. Ego-defensive motives lead subjects to appraise objects by implicitly asking the question: 'Is this thing (person) a threat to how I see myself?'. Hence, motives bias the selection of the evidence to be considered when appraising an object. Further, motives also contribute to the determination of an assessment of the costs associated with making a mistake. The evaluation of the object for its threat potential becomes, for those who are suitably motivated, more important than other dimensions of appraisal. Thus, one would expect these subjects to process more extensively threat-related considerations than evidence of another sort. Most importantly, the costs associated with mistaking a threat for something non-threatening (false negatives) are higher than those associated with mistaking a non-threatening thing for a threat (false positive). This motive-induced asymmetry of error costs sets the evidential thresholds at different levels. Much more evidence is required to believe that something is not a threat than is necessary to feel confident in the belief that it is a threat (Haddock & Gebauer, 2011, p. 280).

Generally, people are also habitually motivated to seek social acceptance, to preserve good personal relationships, and to fit in society. This need may be so dominant in some people that they evaluate any person or object for its potential to promote or to hinder one's social image. Social adjustive motives lead subjects to appraise objects by asking the question: 'Is this thing (person) an obstacle to my fitting in?'. In addition to making considerations of social acceptance in general more salient so that they attract more attention, social adjustive motives also set asymmetries in the costs associated with errors.[16] Mistaking something that hinders social acceptance for something that does not (false negative) is a bigger danger than making the opposite mistake (false positive). For example, befriending by mistake someone who turns out to be an outcast is costlier to one's reputation than not befriending someone who is a member of the in-crowd. Powerless individuals whose attitudes serve a social adjustive function thus develop attitudes that are in line with what they perceive are the views shared in their social group in order to avoid costly mistakes. They are conformists whose attitudes track the value that society puts on things. They also engage in extensive

---

[16] This is the function matching effect which is predicted by both the Elaboration Likelihood and Heuristic Systematic models.

self-monitoring to make their attitudes match what they think is socially expected of them in a given situation (Watt et al., 2008).[17]

The final function served by attitudes that I discuss in this book is to express one's values (Maio & Haddock, 2004; Maio & Olson, 2000a). The object of value-expressive attitudes does not need to be itself a value. For example, I have a positive attitude towards my walking boots. In part this attitude is generated by the role played by these boots in facilitating the promotion of values such as autonomy, freedom, and awe. The boots remind me of the great outdoors and facilitate exploring it. Hence, my attitude satisfies the need to give expression to a set of values which I hold dear.

Psychologists talk of goal pursuit, motivation, and need satisfaction interchangeably when discussing attitude function. This approach seems unwarranted since not every activity is pursued as a means to a goal distinct from it. Thus, for example, if we have a positive attitude towards reading because we love doing it, we do not engage in this activity for any further end which is distinct from it. The activity itself is its own end. Thus, there is no need whose satisfaction causes the activity to stop. We pursue reading for its own sake; our motive is the love of reading. If this is right, it may be preferable to think of attitude function in motivational terms in order to avoid assuming that all activity involves the pursuit of a goal distinct from the activity in itself. For this reason in what follows, I understand attitude function in terms of motives although for convenience sake, I will help myself to the vocabulary of need satisfaction and goal pursuit.

There is a potential ambiguity in talking about the functions served by attitudes. For example, a person who is motivated to seek social acceptance may develop a negative attitude towards features of the self, such as her Afro-textured hair, because of society-wide prejudice. She has learnt to dislike her hair, because she has noted in the past that this aspect of her appearance has been an obstacle to being accepted by those whose acceptance she seeks. In addition, however, this person may also develop a dislike of Afro-textured hair because possessing this negative attitude and expressing it in public also promotes social acceptance and thus fulfils her motive. Thus, attitudes serve their functions in two related ways. First, they promote further behaviours aimed at the satisfaction of a specific need. Second, the possession of the attitude itself can facilitate the fulfilment of that need. I shall return to this feature of attitudes in Chapter 5 where, for example, I discuss how positive but defensive attitudes towards one's abilities and skills fulfil the need to feel good about oneself.

Each attitude may serve more than one function. Hence, for example, the positive attitude to reading in the person who loves it plausibly serves both

---

[17] Relatively powerful individuals who are moved by considerations of social acceptance might develop a tendency to perceive others as obstacles and be envious of their successes. I discuss the relations between vanity and envy in Chapter 6.

knowledge and value expressive functions. In addition, ambivalent attitudes often serve different functions. A person could have a negative attitude to chocolate to serve the need for social acceptance since indulgent eating is frowned upon, and a positive attitude because of the pleasure it brings (Maio & Olson, 2000a, pp. 429–430).

3.1.3 Strength

Strength is another feature of attitudes that, like function, moderates their influence on thinking and behaviour and their susceptibility to rational persuasion. Social psychologists use the term to refer to a number of distinct aspects of attitudes that often appear to be somewhat unrelated. Nevertheless because they all capture some dimension of strength, it is not uncommon for some of these to be aggregated into one measure of strength.[18] In this book I am concerned with four dimensions of strength: accessibility, extremity, centrality, and certainty.

Attitude strength conceived as accessibility is a measure of the strength of the association between the components of the attitude: the representation of the object and one or more valences (Fazio, 2000). This strength of association is operationalized as a latency measure. That is to say, experimenters measure how quickly subjects respond to questions related to the attitude. The speed of response is also taken to imply that the activation of the representation of the object reliably triggers the activation of the valence (Fazio et al., 1986). Hence, accessible attitudes are more likely to be activated by the presentation of the object than less accessible attitudes. In this book 'attitude strength' is used exclusively to refer to accessibility.

In the psychological literature, however, the expression is also used to refer to other features of attitudes. One of these is attitude extremity. An attitude is said to be strong in the sense of extreme when it is either very positive or very negative. For example, a person who strongly likes a politician is said to have an extreme attitude about said individual. My negative attitude to liquorice is similarly extreme. For my purposes, keeping attitude extremity and attitude accessibility distinct is especially important since these two dimensions of attitudes have different effects on information processing. Individuals whose attitudes on a topic are extreme are less interested than those whose attitudes are strong along other dimensions in reading more stuff that is relevant to that topic (Brannon et al., 2007). Attitude extremity thus seems to be related to a high dispositional need for cognitive closure and to closed-mindedness in general.

---

[18] Psychologists are lumpers in comparisons to philosophers' predilection for conceptual distinctions.

Attitude centrality is a third measure of attitude strength. It refers to attitudes that are important to the person because they are close to one's self-defining values and commitments (Clarkson et al., 2009; Zunick et al., 2017). Attitudes that serve a value-expressive function are usually strong; it is plausible to assume that their high accessibility must in part be thought as a consequence of their centrality.

Finally, 'strength' is at times used to indicate attitude certainty which refers to a subject's confidence in her attitudes. Certainty, however, is ambiguous between two different notions that are not always kept distinct in the relevant literature. Certainty could be understood as confidence in the correctness of one's views. Alternatively, it could be thought as clarity that a given statement reflects one's attitude. Thus, certainty may measure how confident a person is that her view is right or the extent to which she is confident that an assertion expresses her attitude (Petrocelli et al., 2007). These two notions easily come apart since a person may be not very confident that her views are correct but have no doubt about what they are.

Attitude certainty is often described as a metacognitive feature of attitudes (Tormala & Rucker, 2007). It is best thought as a judgment or belief about one's level of confidence that one's attitude is correct or appropriate. Hence, measures of attitude certainty concern beliefs rather than epistemic feelings. However, these cognitive states are evidentially based on epistemic feelings of certainty and uncertainty (Petty et al., 2007; Smith et al., 2008).

3.1.4 Measurement

Issues concerning the measurement of attitudes loom large in the psychological literature. This is a topic of some importance for my purposes since measuring attitudes and how they change is crucial to assessing the efficacy of interventions designed to inhibit intellectually vicious behaviour. There are two main kinds of attitude measurement. These are: explicit and implicit measures. Attitudes are measured explicitly—that is, directly—by means of questionnaires and self-reports often recording degrees of agreement or disagreement with a statement as ranked in a Likert scale (Maio & Haddock, 2015, pp. 10–14).[19] Attitudes are measured implicitly—that is, indirectly—by measuring speed and accuracy of response in implicit association tests (IATs) or after evaluative priming or by other indirect measures where the subject is not aware of what is being measured (Maio & Haddock, 2015, pp. 14–21).[20]

---

[19] The scale may, for instance, be from 1 to 5 where 1 indicates strong disagreement, 3 neither agreement nor disagreement, and 5 strong agreement.
[20] In Evaluative Priming subjects are first presented with a picture of an object on a computer screen. This is the object of the attitude one is interested in measuring. After this priming stimulus, subjects are immediately presented with a word. This is an adjective which is either good ('delicious') or bad

Explicit and implicit measures of attitudes frequently dissociate. It is possible to have a positive attitude towards a thing when the attitude is measured directly but to have a negative attitude to the same thing when it is measured indirectly (or vice-versa).[21] This fact has prompted some researchers to conclude that the constructs being measured in each case are different.[22] Alternative viewpoints, however, are equally prominent. According to an influential account known as Mode (Motivation and Opportunity DEterminants of behaviour) developed by Russell Fazio (1990) explicit measures account for the influence of attitudes in deliberative processes when subjects are motivated to reflect on their attitudes and are given the opportunity to do so. Implicit measures would instead reflect the influence of attitudes on behaviour when subjects are not motivated to reflect or when, because of time pressure, they do not have the opportunity to do so. In these cases, if attitudes are highly accessible, they have a direct influence on behaviour that is not mediated by reflection on the specifics of the situation one finds oneself in. The MODE model, thus, postulates that there is only one kind of attitude and two kinds of cognitive processing. Explicit measures of attitudes would reflect their role in deliberative processing, whilst implicit measure would register the implications of attitudes in automatic processing.[23]

('disgusting'). After seeing the word, subjects have to press a key as quickly as possible to indicate if the adjective is good or bad. This procedure is repeated several times. Depending on whether subjects are faster at classifying good adjectives as good or bad adjective as bad, one can infer that the subject's attitude to the prime is positive or negative. The effect occurs because processing information about an item should facilitate processing of other items that are similar (e.g., also good) and inhibit the processing of items that are dissimilar (Fazio et al., 1995). In Implicit Association Tests (IATs) response latency (speed) is also measured. There are various versions of the test but, broadly speaking, the test measures associations by measuring how fast and accurate one is in pressing the keyboard key for, say, female when presented with the word for a humanities discipline and the key for male when presented with the name of a science, rather than the other way round. If one is faster when the pairings are man/science, woman/humanities than the other way round, one is shown to associate men with science and women with the humanities (Greenwald et al., 1998).

[21] Importantly, however, dissociation tends to occur only when the attitudes concern objects that induce responses that subjects are inclined not to endorse. Thus, there are no dissociations in attitudes to uncontroversial objects such as flowers or umbrellas. In addition the correlation between different indirect measures of the same attitude is low in some cases. This is true, for example, for attitudes to the self (Bosson et al., 2000). It is plausible that these measures may tap into different components of the attitude's content. That said, there are other reviews that support the convergence and predictive validity of different implicit measures, see Cunningham et al. (2001).

[22] The Associative and Evaluative Process Model (APE) developed by Gawronski and Bodenhausen (2006) posits that there are two kinds of attitudes: implicit attitudes that are associative and explicit attitudes that are propositional. Gawronski and Bodenhausen appear to make claims about the structure of the attitudes merely on the basis of the nature of the cognitive processes in which they are involved. However as Brownstein (2016) notes Gawronski and Bodenhausen make illicit inferences from the nature of the processes in which attitudes are involved to the nature of attitudes themselves. They fail to notice that propositionally contentful states can figure in associative processes.

[23] It is also sometimes thought that attitudes as implicitly measured are not accessible to consciousness. Although philosophers tend to assume that this is the case, the claim is—to say the least—controversial. See Hahn et al. (2014) for evidence of awareness of implicitly measured attitudes.

In what follows I avoid as much as possible commitment to the details of any particular account of the relation between attitudes as implicitly and explicitly measured.[24] The only aspect of this debate that is crucial to my position is the firmly established fact that implicit and explicit measures of attitudes to the same object can dissociate. I return to the point in Chapter 5 where I propose that arrogance, *superbia*, servility, and self-abasement are characterized by discrepant attitudes to the self-concept as measured explicitly and implicitly.

3.2 Intellectual Virtues and Vices as Based on Attitudes

The claim that attitudes are the causal bases of intellectual character virtue and vices of self-evaluation is one of the main theses defended in this book. To my mind, the best argument for this claim is given by the fruitfulness of interpreting vice and virtue through the lenses of attitude psychology.[25] In this section, however, I wish to mount an initial and more general defence of the framework. I argue that attitudes possess many of the features that are traditionally attributed to these character traits.

In the final section of Chapter 2 I have highlighted five characteristic features of intellectual virtues and vices.[26] These are: (1) they are components of a person's character; (2) they are causally responsible for behaviour that is stable over time and consistent across situations; (3) they are intelligent, often involve skills, and direct attention; (4) they are closely related to, or comprise, a motivational component; (5) they have affective elements or are closely connected to feelings and emotions. In what follows I first show that attitudes can explain why virtues and vices have these five features, before considering a further quality of virtues and vices—namely, their apparent dispositional nature—that seems to be at odds with a framework based on psychological states such as attitudes.

---

[24] But, because I frame the issue in terms of measurement, as is common among psychologists I place less emphasis on the issues of automaticity and accessibility to awareness that, because of their focus on moral responsibility, often dominate philosophical accounts of implicit bias or attitudes (cf. Brownstein, 2016).

[25] Another advantage of this framework lies in its ability to address some worries about the individuation of character vices. Roberts and Wood (2007) provide a very fine-grained taxonomy. Others, e.g. Battaly (2014), work with a fairly coarse-grained classification. The attitudinal framework can identify some stable clusters of attitudes and their informational bases as vices (or virtues) that subsume other narrower vices (and virtues) that are based on distinct sub-clusters. Thus, for instance, arrogance, but also narcissism, are vices that subsume the narrower vice of domination, understood as the vice of trying to dominate another's agency in the service of one's self-importance (Roberts & West, 2017).

[26] These features are not sufficient to characterize something as a virtue or a vice. Other kinds of psychological qualities share these characteristics without being virtues or vices. For instance, dispositions to be neat and tidy, or to be lively and enthusiastic (Annas, 2011, p. 101). One difference between these character traits and virtues or vices is that they do not have a direct impact on the moral or epistemic standing of the people who have them (cf. Miller, 2014, ch. 1).

3.2.1 Character

Character virtues and vices, but also sensibilities and thinking styles, are deep features of individuals because they define who they are, or what they are like. Virtues and vices can also express the deeply held commitments and values of individuals (Annas, 2011; Miller, 2013) who may not be fully aware of what these are. Some attitudes, although not all, are defining of a person's character and identity. These comprise attitudes that are highly accessible and that subjects think are central to them as persons. But they also include attitudes to the self. For instance, people who have defensive attitudes to the self, and react defensively in many circumstances, could be said to have defensiveness as an aspect of their personality or character. In particular, I argue in Chapter 5, intellectual arrogance is a character trait that is based on some defensive attitudes towards the self. Further, attitudes that serve a value-expressive function identify a person's values and commitments when these are defining of the self. These can also be plausibly considered to be part of a person's character. For instance, for some people egalitarian values are deeply important. These values may have led them to form attitudes about career choice, donating to some charities, and political affiliation. These people may work in the third sector, be left leaning, and donate a percentage of their salary every month. It seems plausible to think of the attitudes that are at the root of these behaviours as being part of an individual's self-concept and thus of her character.

3.2.2 Stability and Cross-Situational Consistency

Virtue and vices conceived as sensibilities, thinking styles or character traits, are powerful levers of behaviour. Their influence on conduct is not sporadic but constant. Intuitively, virtuous behaviour must be stable over time and consistent across situations. For example, an individual is not genuinely courageous unless she consistently acts bravely over a period of time and in a varied range of circumstances that require courage such as confronting an aggressor or saving a child from a fire.[27]

These considerations about temporal stability and cross-situational consistency do not easily transpose to all vices. Some intellectual character vices such as arrogance, some thinking styles, like high need for cognitive closure, and sensibilities such a disposition to wilful ignorance, exhibit these features. For instance, the arrogant individual feels consistently superior to others. He is also boastful and aggressive. Other intellectual vices are expressed in conduct that is predictably

---

[27] Different virtues might require different degrees of consistency and stability. Alfano (2013, pp. 31–32) makes this point by distinguishing high-fidelity from low-fidelity virtues.

inconsistent and lacks stability over time. People who suffer from these vices are, so to speak, stably and consistently inconsistent and lacking in stability. For example, servile individuals have few stable beliefs and do not always behave consistently across situations. Some conduct exhibits consistency. For instance, the obsequious person has a propensity to belittle her abilities and to ingratiate herself to others. However, her servility is also precisely manifested in behaviours that vary in accordance with her situation. She believes what powerful others claim, and this varies depending on whom holds sway on her on a given occasion. There is consistency even in this kind servile behaviour but this consistency can only be captured in descriptions made at a higher level of abstraction.

Attitudes can be powerful determinants of behaviour. Both explicit and implicit attitudes have predictive validity. However, these predictions are obtained using paradigms that require a high degree of correspondence between measures of attitude and behaviour. Thus for instance, both would be measured roughly at the same time and in the same context. The target object of attitude and behaviour should also be closely matched so that if the attitude measured is about, for instance, a specific politician, the behaviour predicted should concern specifically that politician rather than politicians in general (cf. Maio & Haddock, 2015, p. 69). In the absence of these constraints attitudes in general are poor predictors of behaviour. Therefore, one may conclude that they are unsuitable candidates for being the psychological bases of virtues or vices. This conclusion is, however, premature because there is a large variation in the power of attitudes to determine behaviour. First, attitudes that are strong, and consistent with a person's beliefs, tend to lead to behaviour that matches the attitude (Fazio, 2000; Maio & Haddock, 2015, pp. 73–74). Second, attitudes that are central to the person and serve the function of expressing her values are also important determinant of behaviour (Maio & Haddock, 2015, p. 73; Watt et al., 2008).

In addition, there are individual differences. Some individuals are high self-monitors, they tend to assess frequently whether they fit the situation they are in (Snyder, 1974). Unsurprisingly, their attitudes are poor predictors of their behaviour, since they tend to match what they do to what they think is required in their situation (Chen et al., 1996; Lakin et al., 2003). However, individuals who have defensive self-esteem (people who measure high in self-esteem as explicitly measured, but low in implicit measures) behave in ways that are predicted by their attitudes (Haddock & Gebauer, 2011).[28] Attitudes are also better predictors of behaviour in individuals who are high in need for cognition (that is, who desire and enjoy effortful cognitive activity) compared to those who do not have this need to the same extent (Cacioppo & Petty, 1982; Cacioppo et al., 1986). These individual differences are plausibly related to the function of attitudes. Individuals

---

[28] In Chapter 5 I identify this cluster of attitudes as the psychological basis of arrogance and especially *superbia*.

whose high self-esteem is defensive generally possess attitudes whose function is ego-defensive (Baumeister et al., 1996), high self-monitors possess attitudes whose function is usually socially-adjustive (Watt et al., 2008). Further, the need for cognition—conceived as enjoyment of cognitive activity—is closely related to the possession of attitudes serving knowledge function since it increases responsiveness to the cognitive features of persuasive messages (Maio & Haddock, 2007, p. 577). In all of these cases, attitudes are predictive of behaviour which is stable over the long term and, when it is described at the appropriate level of abstraction, consistent across situations.

Hence, attitude psychology supplies the materials to answer the situationist challenges to virtue ethics and epistemology (Alfano, 2012; Doris, 2002).[29] Many individuals, perhaps the majority, have attitudes that are predictive of behaviour only in a narrow range of situational circumstances. Others, however, have attitudes that demonstrate the required stability and consistency to qualify as grounding global and robust character traits.

3.2.3 Intelligence, Skill, and Attention

Virtues, and perhaps some vices, are intelligent because they are flexible, involve skills, and are responsive to reasons (Annas, 2011; Snow, 2010). Given that attitudes are only patchily reason-responsive they may be thought to be ill-suited as the causal bases of virtue. This point fails to take into account that attitude are in general susceptible to change following arguments of good quality (Maio & Haddock, 2015).[30] Also to the point, it is worth noting that attitudes vary greatly in their responsiveness to reasons. Attitudes whose function is to serve knowledge are likely to be more responsive to reason and more successful in guiding activities which lead to the formation of true beliefs (Watt et al., 2008, p. 196). Attitudes serving different functions are more likely to be involved in biased or motivated cognition. For instance, individuals who are very defensive are better than others at detecting a threat when it is actually present. However, they are also biased as they often represent non-threatening situations as threats (Haddock & Gebauer, 2011). Be that as it may, attitudes, together with their contents, are sufficiently sensitive to reasons to rationalise actions and to figure, in combination with

---

[29] Questions have been raised about the validity of the empirical results on which situationists have based their challenge to virtue ethics and epistemology. In the wake of this replication crisis Alfano has largely retracted his earlier objections to virtue epistemology (Alfano, 2018).

[30] Psychologists are more interested in non-rational influences on attitudes. Thus, they tend to highlight examples where message quality is less effective than other properties in leading to persuasion. But even in these examples, quality counts for something. See for instance figure 5.1 of Maio and Haddock (2015, p. 118) and compare it with the characterization of this result offered on the preceding page.

behavioural intentions of planned intelligent activity, among their causal antecedents (Maio & Haddock, 2015, p. 85).

Some virtue and vices are sensibilities. They are dispositions to pick out patterns of salience by directing attention to relevant features of the environment. In addition, as I indicated in Chapter 2, character virtues and vices are associated with the development and continuation of a range of sensibilities. A similar point has been highlighted by Bommarito who argues that several virtues are partly virtues of attention. Modesty, in particular, would require not paying particular attention to, or making especially salient in one's thinking, one's own good features (Bommarito, 2013). The person who is modest about her achievements is not ignorant of what they are; she does not underestimate them, but she does not give to her strengths pride of place in her thinking. She directs her attention away from them.[31] These considerations can be generalized. The generous person is able to detect opportunities for generous behaviour; the person who is inquisitive asks good questions because she is sensitive to patterns of salience in inquiry. Closed-minded individuals may experience as salient the shortcomings of views opposed to their own, and be prone to neglect the evidence in their favour. Therefore, some character virtues and vices are related to sensibilities that recruit visual attention and direct it towards some features of the situation perceived as salient and away from others experienced as unimportant. Since strong attitudes are an important influence on attention, these considerations point to a link between virtues, vices, and attitudes. In particular, attitudes play a crucial role in the selection of the information to which we pay attention and of what we instead ignore (Maio & Haddock, 2015, pp. 56–60).

3.2.4 Motivations

I defended a motivational account of vice in chapter two. I argued that vice attributions are explanations of behaviour that make it intelligible while undermining its rationality. These attributions ultimately invoke motivations that the subject cannot fully acknowledge. This inability fully to avow one's motivations leads to rationalizations of behaviours that are not wholly confabulatory but that are nevertheless evidence of self-deceptive tendencies.

Attitudes, when these are classified functionally, are well-suited to explain these phenomena. Attitude functions are often understood in motivational terms (Maio & Haddock, 2015, pp. 262–265). The formation and preservation of attitudes is influenced by motives that are deployed when selecting the elements of the

---

[31] In Chapter 4 I argue against this claim. I agree with Bommarito, however, that humility like other character virtues and vices shapes our perceptual sensibilities.

attitude contents. Motives also bias the evaluation of this content by establishing asymmetries of costs associated with errors. When forming attitudes, subjects evaluate which considerations are relevant to the appraisal of the object in terms of their relevance to the goal one is motivated to pursue. For example, if a person's goal is to feel good about himself, he is motivated to defend his ego against any threats to his positive self-view. Such person ends up evaluating objects for their potential to be threats to self-esteem or to promote self-enhancement. He bases his attitudes only on information that is relevant to these concerns. Further, because of the high costs of mistaking a threat for something that is not threatening (false negative), his appraisals are defensive and indicative of hypervigilance. These evaluations are summarized in his attitudes that, therefore, serve an ego-defensive function.[32] Hence, attitude function is closely related to dispositions to possess characteristic motives. These are standing motivations of which the subject is usually not fully aware.

3.2.5 Affect and Emotions

Character virtues and vices are often thought not just as dispositions to act but also to feel (Hursthouse, 2001, ch. 5). Thus, for example, the charitable person engages in charitable activities but she also experiences pity and feelings of sympathy. Similar considerations can be advanced with regard to vices. Intellectual vanity, for instance, is closely associated with a disposition to envy others' intellectual successes. The intellectually vain individual is tuned in to every indication of other people's opinion of his intellectual stature. He perceives others' achievements as extremely salient and as a bad thing; he is acutely aware of others' acknowledgement of his own successes. The discussion in Chapter 2 has highlighted the centrality of feelings and emotions to virtues and vices. I have argued that sensibilities and thinking styles recruit epistemic feelings to monitor and guide epistemic activities. The considerations above suggest that, in addition, several character virtues and vices dispose those who have them to experience a range of characteristic emotions. I have already indicated that vain individuals are prone to spiteful envy because they seek to denigrate those goods that they envy but cannot achieve. In Chapters 5 and 6 I suggest that anger and contempt are typical manifestations of *superbia* and arrogance, shame-proneness of servility and self-abasement, morbid self-love of narcissism, fear of timidity, and hopelessness of fatalism. These emotional propensities can colour the whole cognitive life of those who possess these vices. For example, fearful people experience the world as scary. Even when they do not experience occurrent fear about something in particular,

[32] See Chapter 5, where I argue that arrogance is based on ego-defensive attitudes, for more details.

these individuals feel vulnerable. This is a background way of experiencing one's situation that is akin to what Ratcliffe (2008) has called existential feelings.

These features of virtues and vices can be accommodated if these psychological qualities are based on attitudes. Attitudes have affective states among their contents. That is, emotions are components of attitude contents. Virtues and vices have characteristic emotional manifestations, because emotions are elements of the contents of the attitudes on which these psychological features are based. Further, attitude certainty (or attitude doubt) are features of attitudes. These metacognitive dimensions of attitudes have as their evidential bases epistemic feelings of certainty, conviction, and doubt that are recruited by thinking styles and character traits, conceived as clusters of attitudes together with their informational bases, in the service of monitoring and guiding epistemic activities (Petty et al., 2007).

3.2.6 States and Dispositions

It might be objected to the argument developed so far that attitudes cannot be the bases of virtues and vices because attitudes are psychological states, whilst virtue and vices in the form of sensibilities, thinking styles, and character traits are dispositions. There are several initially plausible answers to this objection. First, one may deny that every virtue or vice is naturally understood as a disposition which is manifested when the circumstances trigger it. Some virtues, such as generosity, require that one attempts to bring about the circumstances that would make generosity appropriate. Others virtues, such as integrity, perseverance, or humility, require continuous exercise (Rees & Webber, 2014; Webber, 2015). The same holds true of a vast range of vices. Laziness and arrogance do not appear to have triggering circumstances. The person who is lazy is indolent in most circumstances. Similarly, whilst arrogance may be more evident on some occasions, the arrogant individual inflects her whole conduct with arrogance. Therefore, it is at least not obviously true that virtues and vices are dispositions.[33] Hence, one may plausibly conclude that neither attitudes nor virtues and vices are dispositions, thus removing this obstacle to their identification.

Second, and conversely, it has been suggested from various fronts that attitudes are, like virtues and some vices, traits. In psychology Ajzen (2005) thinks of attitudes as dispositions. In his view, attitudes are traits because they are dispositions to

---

[33] At least if these are understood as having manifestations and stimulus conditions. Jonathan Webber has pointed out in conversation that he thinks that virtues are dispositions but that the latter are powers. So his argument that some virtues have no triggering circumstances should not be read as supporting the conclusion that they are not dispositions.

evaluate and then to judge, act, and feel, on the basis of that evaluation.[34] More recently, Eduard Machery (2016) has also offered a dispositional account of implicit attitudes. If attitudes are dispositions, then they are the same kind of entity as character traits like virtues and vices. Again, consideration of ontological status would be no barrier to their identification.

I suspect that in psychology at least the classification of attitudes as dispositions is actually a confusing way of adopting a reductivist stance toward dispositions themselves. That is, Ajzen's view, for instance, is that attitudes are what explains the truth of dispositions which he identifies as relevant lists of conditionals whose antecedents describe triggering situations, and whose consequents describe the resulting behaviours. Hence, he surmises that attitudes and evaluative dispositions are the same thing.

I am also suspicious of Machery's arguments in favour of the dispositional nature of attitudes. In his view an attitude is a disposition that supervenes on the cluster of psychological states that constitutes the attitude's content. Machery's defends his dispositional account of attitudes by arguing that it can explain some facts about implicit attitudes. For instance, they are easily manipulable and subject to situational factors. They are also poor predictors of behaviour and exhibit poor inter-measure correlation. These observations lead him to conclude that attitudes are just dispositions whose causal bases are the contents of the attitude. Machery's argument is not wholly convincing since even if one grants that implicit measures of attitudes often tap into different aspects of their contents, it does not follow that the attitudes themselves are not also causally efficacious. Machery effectively claims that attitudes are mere dispositions whose causal bases wholly consist in those contents upon which they supervene.

In my opinion Machery's position cannot fully account for the effects of persuasive messages on attitudes. In particular, it cannot easily explain the well-established function matching effects that I outlined in Section 3.1.2. These effects show that motivations are crucially important to understand which kinds of message subjects process deeply and which instead are considered only superficially. These effects cannot be predicted on the basis of attitude contents' alone. There would thus seem to be more to the attitudes than their contents.[35]

Finally, one may grant that attitudes are states whilst virtues and vices are dispositions, while arguing that the former are among the causal bases upon which the latter supervene. This view bears some relation to Machery's. He claims that attitudes are type-identical to traits as dispositions whose causal bases are the mental states such as beliefs, affects and desires that constitute

---

[34] Philosophers sometimes claim that character traits unlike other personality traits have an evaluative dimension (Timpe, 2008). If this is right, the identification with attitudes would appear especially apt.

[35] Machery could perhaps respond that attitudes supervene on their contents and on the subject's motivations.

the attitude content. The view under consideration here holds that attitudes including their contents are mental states which constitute the causal bases of traits as dispositions.

The causal basis of a disposition is the property or properties that are causally responsible for the behaviour that manifests the disposition. For example, the molecular structure of sugar is the causal basis of its solubility because it causes sugar to dissolve when it is put in a solvent (given some background conditions). Thus, to say that attitudes are among the causal bases of traits is to say that attitudes (and their contents) are causally responsible for the manifestation of the relevant dispositions.[36] Thus, for instance, the attitudes underpinning arrogance as a character trait are among the causes of arrogant behaviour.

This view can predict the empirical results mentioned by Machery but it can also explain the function matching effects of persuasive messages. For this reason, this is the position I adopt in this book. Thus, when I say that virtues and vices are based on attitudes and their content, my claim is to be read as asserting that attitudes are causally responsible for the behaviour that constitutes the manifestation of a virtue or vice.

---

[36] I do not wish to enter here the debate about the metaphysical relation that holds between dispositions and their causal bases. One can think of it as a matter of token-identity or of supervenience.

PART II
VIRTUES AND VICES OF INTELLECTUAL SELF-EVALUATION

4
Intellectual Humility, Proper Pride, and Proper Concern with Others' Esteem

Intellectual humility is, in my view, based on a cluster of strong attitudes (together with their informational bases) towards the self and elements of the subject's cognitive make-up that are driven by knowledge and value-expressive motivations appraising the self and its features for their strengths and weaknesses.[1] Humility itself might be thought as the combination of two other intellectual virtues: modesty about achievements and acceptance of one's shortcomings. These two components of humility are conceptually distinct but psychologically associated so that modest people generally are also disposed to accept their limitations and vice-versa. Two further virtues, that are expressions of intellectual self-esteem, have important connections to intellectual humility. These are: pride about one's intellectual strengths and a proper concern for the esteem with which one is held by others.

This chapter provides accounts of these virtues of intellectual self-appraisal that see them as based on strong attitudes serving knowledge and value-expressive functions. The main difference between humility (as comprising of modesty and of acceptance of limitations) on the one hand, and pride and concern for esteem on the other, lies in the nature of social comparisons on which they are based. Humility relies on appraisals of the worth of one's qualities that might be gauged by comparing oneself to other people and which are driven by a concern for accuracy. For instance, one might evaluate one's mathematical abilities by comparing one's performance to that of classmates in order to achieve an accurate appraisal of one's abilities. Both pride and the desire to be esteemed, instead, involve assessments of one's own qualities that are motivated by the desire to improve and rely on comparing one's abilities to those of others one takes to be high performers in the relevant domain. Therefore, pride and the desire to be esteemed are also closely connected to the motivation to achieve and to have one's achievements recognized by other members of the epistemic community.

---

[1] I use the expressions 'cognitive make-up' broadly to include any of a subject's cognitive states, processes or capacities. Intellectual humility can be thought as the disposition to behave and feel in characteristic ways in relevant circumstances. The attitudes and their contents are the causal bases of the disposition. I do not take a stance about the ontological status of dispositions. The material discussed in this chapter and especially in Sections 4.1 and 4.2 partly overlaps with the account I offered in (2018d).

The Mismeasure of the Self: A Study in Vice Epistemology. Alessandra Tanesini, Oxford University Press (2021).
© Alessandra Tanesini. DOI: 10.1093/oso/9780198858836.003.0004

The main aims of this chapter are to offer these accounts and to defend them against some objections and rival theories.

The chapter consists of four sections. The first is dedicated to intellectual modesty. After a brief characterization of the typical manifestations of this trait, I show that it does not require ignorance of one's own intellectual good qualities. Instead, modesty is rooted in strong positive evaluations, driven by knowledge and value-expressive motivations, of some of one's cognitive capacities, skills, character traits or thinking styles. The second section describes acceptance of one's own intellectual shortcomings as a component of humility which is distinct from modesty. I argue that accepting one's limitations is an attitude of freely acknowledging their existence. Accepting one's limitations is not the same thing as knowing what they are. Not being in denial about the extent of one's shortcomings is also not sufficient for being fully accepting of them. One may know one's limitations and not be in denial but nevertheless wish to hide them from other people's scrutiny. In my view, acceptance of limitations is based on strong negative attitudes, serving knowledge and value-expressive functions, towards aspects of one's cognitive make-up. The third and fourth sections are respectively dedicated to pride and to concern with being esteemed by others. I characterize these psychological qualities and defend their identification as virtues. I argue that pride and concern for being esteemed consist in attitudes that largely overlap with modesty and acceptance of limitations even though they partly differ in motivations and in the evaluative beliefs that are included in their contents or informational bases.

4.1 The Modesty Dimension of Humility

The characteristic manifestations of humility in general and more specifically of intellectual humility are surprisingly heterogeneous. They include: being realistic about one's abilities; not seeking the limelight; being quietly assertive rather than arrogant or boastful; not bragging; being a team player; generously acknowledging other people's intellectual achievements and being forgiving of their shortcomings; being open to the possibility that one is wrong; being able to acknowledge openly one's errors even when doing so might damage one's interests. We can classify these manifestations of intellectual humility by noting that they are, or presuppose, evaluations of intellectual strengths or weaknesses of the self or of other people.

Philosophical accounts of this virtue tend to focus on one of these aspects of humility to the detriment of the others. Views of humility as modesty concentrate on the evaluation of intellectual strengths but neglect appraisals of limitations. Characteristic of this approach are a family of views that identifies humility with the disposition to underestimate one's self-worth, and thus to misjudge or to be ignorant about one's own good features (Driver, 1989, 1999).[2] Modest individuals would be those who genuinely fail to appreciate their abilities and their successes. Related to Driver's position are a range of views that identify modesty with dispositions not to dwell on, pay attention to, or take delight in, one's own successes (Bommarito, 2013; Garcia, 2006). What these views have in common is a conception of modesty as a virtue of self-appraisal that consists either in not knowing the extents of one's strengths or in not taking pleasure in, or enjoy, one's successes. Because these positions require that modest individuals are ignorant of, or otherwise ignore, their strengths, they are best thought as ignorance-based accounts of the modesty dimension of humility.[3]

These accounts, even when interpreted as directed exclusively at modesty, face insurmountable difficulties. First, it is extremely implausible that an intellectual virtue might require ignorance or the possession of false beliefs about the self.[4] Second, ignorance or underestimation of one's intellectual strengths is not necessary for modesty. One can imagine a brilliant, and humble, scientist who is fully aware of her abilities and her track-record of success. She is humble because she does not boast or brag. She is neither falsely modest nor self-aggrandising. If this is right, one might be humble, and know one's intellectual strengths and successes. It seems also plausible that one might be proud of these, and thus take pleasure in them, without lacking in humility. Since we can make sense of a kind of pride that is compatible with modesty, humility cannot require that one ignores or does not enjoy personal success. Third, ignorance or underestimation of strengths is not sufficient for modesty. As Driver also notes, the person who belittles her own abilities is self-abasing; she is not humble.

It is worth noting that modesty is even compatible with the overestimation of one's strengths or successes. A humble scientist might overestimate the importance of her discovery which in hindsight might be revealed to be less significant than initially thought. Similarly, an individual might be a fool and consistently believe others' overestimation of her abilities without thereby being arrogant. These examples strongly indicate that there is no conceptual connection between modesty and the absence of an overestimation of one's intellectual strengths. That said, one might also agree that as a matter of fact modest people do not usually overestimate their good qualities.

---

[2] Driver acknowledges that underestimation of one's strengths is a characteristic of modesty alone rather than of humility (1989, p. 378, n. 5). However, humility is not in her view very dissimilar from modesty.

[3] I also include in this family the view of humility as being the opposite of the vices of pride defended by (Roberts & Wood, 2003, 2007). Their view differs from others by taking humility to be characterized by an absence of concern for the things that preoccupy the person who is vain or self-aggrandizing (Roberts, 2016, pp. 65–67). In addition, however, they also claim that the intellectually humble person shows a concern for epistemic goods.

[4] This is not to deny that ignorance can on occasion have some instrumental epistemic value.

These problems with ignorance-based accounts of intellectual modesty might suggest that this virtue is not primarily one of self-assessment, but that it is instead a trait focused on other people. Priest (2017), for instance, has argued that intellectual humility is an interpersonal virtue that consists in treating other epistemic agents with respect qua epistemic agents. Therefore, the humble person takes other people's views seriously; she does not dismiss their criticisms; she acknowledges that she might be able to learn from them and so forth. I agree with Priest that intellectually humble individuals are typically respectful of other people and show concern for their epistemic needs. But I disagree with her view that these respectful attitudes and concerns define intellectual humility.

Priest's view is that intellectual humility is ultimately driven by a concern for other people's intellect (2017, p. 477). In this regard her view is similar to Wilson's account of modesty as a virtue of kindness consisting in a disposition to 'present [one's] accomplishments/positive attributes in a way that is sensitive to the potential negative impact on the well-being of others, where this disposition stems from a concern for that well-being' (Wilson, 2016, p. 78). Thus, intellectual humility as modesty would involve a disposition to describe one's successes and strengths to others in a way that is especially mindful of their interests.

In the social domain there might be a kind of modesty as politeness that is displayed by the person who, because she does not wish to hurt others' feelings, shows immense tact when discussing her accomplishments. In this regard, modesty in the intellectual domain is rather different. It is least possible, even if perhaps rare, for a person to be humble without demonstrating much concern for others' intellect and needs. This person could be exacting, without being disrespectful, in her criticism of other people. Thus, a scientist can acquire a reputation for humility, single-mindedness, and bluntness. One might think of her as driven by her love of truth. She is humble because she is not self-serving; she is single-minded because of her exclusive focus on the task; she is blunt because she adopts the same high standards for herself and for others, while she is not afraid to be candid about her views. Humility requires a commitment to truth and to assessing one's own abilities by its standard, but in principle at least it need not involve a high focus on others' needs.[5] Humility, however, is incompatible with disrespectful behaviour towards other people. But this is because this behaviour, by being for instance dismissive, is often at variance with what the truth demands.

I would, however, expect intellectual modesty to be usually accompanied by interpersonal virtues of treating other people generously. Humble individuals do

---

[5] Priest considers the objection that her view reduces humility to a kind of politeness. She denies that this is the case on the grounds that politeness is compatible with a fake concern for others, while humility requires a genuine concern. My objection, is different. In my view, intellectual humility is motivated by love of truth. However, I agree with Priest and with Nadelhoffer and Wright (2017) that in ordinary cases the humble person shows concern for the needs and interests of others.

not have a self-inflated concept of their self-worth; they primarily care for the truth, they have no incentives to deny to others credit for their successes. Further, their love of truth might actually give them reasons to be especially supportive of other people's epistemic endeavours, since this generosity might promote reciprocity.[6]

It should also be noted that there is some truth to the claims made by Garcia (2006) and Bommarito (2013) that intellectual humility entails a lack of focus on the self. Intellectual humility requires that one's ego is not invested in being right. The humble person does not focus on the self in the sense that she is not defensive about her beliefs. But this lack of self-involvement does not require that one does not pay attention to oneself. It does not require ignorance of one's abilities. It is compatible with taking pleasure in one's successes, provided that one cares about them for their epistemic value, rather than primarily because of their boost to one's self-esteem. This lack of ego-investment finds its expressions in self-evaluations of one's strengths that are not vitiated by egocentric biases. The humble individual, therefore, does not measure her good features using standards that are relative to a need for self-enhancement or to gain social acceptance.

These points are important because there is building psychological evidence linking humility to low self-focus (Nadelhoffer & Wright, 2017). However, in the empirical literature this notion does not involve a lowering of self-assessment or even a lack of concern for the self. Instead, it is possessed by individuals who are not self-centred or self-obsessed. These are people who do not put themselves at the centre of their perspective by evaluating everything and everyone exclusively in terms of their impact on oneself. Hence, these people do not endlessly ruminate about potential threats to the self. They are self-confident without being defensive.

The account of intellectual modesty as based on a cluster of strong attitudes towards one's intellectual capacities, skills and other elements of one's cognitive make-up that serve knowledge and value-expressive functions explains the features of modesty highlighted so far. First, humility is compatible with knowing one's strengths, underestimating or even overestimating them. Even so, we would anticipate that modest individuals are usually accurate in their self-estimates. This is what we would expect if modesty is based on attitudes serving knowledge functions since these summarize evaluations that are driven by the motivation to be accurate. These attitudes are, therefore, generally reliable, even though in some cases they are not.[7] If a person has formed her attitudes in biased environments,

---

[6] There is some empirical evidence that gratitude mediates (that is, explains) why intellectual humility predicts prosocial values and behaviours such as behaving generously or altruistically (Krumrei-Mancuso, 2017).

[7] Attitudes cannot, strictly speaking, be reliable or unreliable since they are preferences. However, one's attitude towards elements of one's cognitive make-up can be more or less consonant with their actual properties. Thus, attitudes are reliable in a loose sense if one prefers one's strengths and prefers them to a degree that is proportional to their strength while disliking weaknesses in proportion to their weakness.

her appraisals of her strengths might be inaccurate. She might underestimate or overestimate them depending on the nature of the false information that figures in the bases of her attitudes.

Second, intellectual modesty is compatible with experiencing episodic feelings of pride. If modesty is a matter of self-assessment that is driven by the need for knowledge, one might, based on an honest—rather than self-serving—assessment, feel proud of what one has achieved. Modesty and pride (as a character trait rather an episodic emotion) are based on overlapping clusters of strong attitudes driven by the knowledge and value-expressive motives. These attitudes share much of their informational bases including evaluative beliefs about one's cognitive skills, intellectual track record, and abilities. Pride, as I explain below, is derived from informational bases that are heavily reliant on comparisons with other people's qualities. Further, pride involves a desire to achieve that is not an essential component of modesty. Despite their differences, these traits are compatible. This is not surprising if, as I contend, they are based on overlapping psychological states.

Third, intellectual modesty is an assessment of one's strengths which is driven by a love of the truth for its own sake. Hence, modest self-assessments are not self-serving. The modest individual is not defensive; he is not invested in being right. Instead, he only cares that he gets it right. By contrasting ego-defensive with knowledge and value-expressive motivations, the account of modesty as attitude explains the lack of defensiveness in the self-assessment made by modest individuals. It also explains their commitment to truth for its own sake. Modest people prefer those aspects of their cognitive make-up that help them make sense of reality, and find that these preferences are also expressive of their values. Hence, they are committed to the value of truth, knowledge, and understanding.

The account of modesty as grounded in clusters of attitudes and their informational bases explains variation in modesty. It is possible for people to be modest about some aspects of the self, without being equally modest about other features. This variation is explained in terms of specific attitudes about individual elements of one's cognitive make-up. All the attitudes directed at elements of one's cognitive make-up of the fully modest person serve a knowledge and value-expressive functions. Some are positive because they are directed at (what she takes to be) her good features, other are negative directed at her perceived weaknesses. People who are modest in some regard but not others have attitudes directed at elements of their cognitive make-up serving different functions. Some are driven by knowledge and value-expressive motives. These constitute modest self-assessments. Other attitudes might serve different motives. They embody the dimensions along which these individuals are lacking in modesty. Intuitively, people can also be more or less modest in another sense. They can be fully or only partly modest about a specific aspect of their cognitive make-up. They are fully modest, if they are always modest about it. If their modesty waivers, they are only partly modest. The attitude account also explains this kind of variation in terms of attitude strength understood as accessibility (Fazio, 2000).[8]

4.2 Humility as Acceptance of One's Own Limitations

There is more to humility than modesty about strengths and successes, one must also be open about weaknesses and failures without being resigned to them. Humble individuals are aware of human limitations in general but also of their own specific shortcomings. This acknowledgement of limitations is manifested in a tendency to acknowledge one's own mistakes, to be open about the possibility that one might be wrong, and to accept criticisms with equanimity and without resentment. In this regard, intellectual humility is closely related to open-mindedness.[9] Acknowledgement of limitations is also manifested through an optimistic attitude towards self-improvement. In this regard, intellectual humility is closely linked to a hopeful disposition.[10]

This dimension of intellectual humility is the focus of another family of accounts of this virtue that take it to consist, at least partly, in knowing one's own intellectual weaknesses. This idea is the core of knowledge-based accounts of humility. These include Snow's (1995) view of humility as possessing an accurate assessment of one's own limitations; Hazlett's (2012) higher-order account of humility as proper assessment of the epistemic statuses of one's first-order beliefs, and Church's (2016) view that humility consists in tracking accurately what one justifiably takes to be the epistemic status of one's beliefs. Whitcomb et al.'s (2017) limitation-owning account might also belong to this family if, as I suspect, its authors identify the 'owning' of limitations with their acknowledgment in the sense of not being in denial about their existence. However, if 'owning' is thought as a disposition to own up to the existence of one's own limitations, even in contexts where such openness might harm one's self interest, then these authors' view of this dimension of humility is close to the one that I endorse. We still differ, however, since I think that attitudes to one's shortcomings are only one dimension of humility. Instead, they think that the focus on limitations captures the whole story.[11]

---

[8] See Chapter 3, Section 1.3.
[9] For empirical work identifying open-mindedness as an element of humility see Alfano et al. (2017) and Leary et al. (2017).
[10] See Cobb (2019) for an exploration of some of the connections between intellectual humility and hope. I discuss hopelessness in Section 4.1 of Chapter 6.
[11] We also disagree about the role of motivation. In their view, a person could consistently behave as the intellectual humble person would even though their desire for epistemic goods is only instrumental. For them, such a person behaves humbly, even though she does not possess the virtue. They suggest a student who is ultimately motivated by a desire for good grades rather than the love of knowledge might be an example of such a person. I argue instead that it is not plausible that the humble behaviour

I have indicated that acceptance of limitations is owning up to them, being open to correction and optimistic about its success, rather than knowing that one has limitations and taking this knowledge into account when evaluating one's beliefs. Knowledge of one's own actual limitations is not necessary for adopting an attitude of acceptance of limitations (actual or presumed). An individual might have mistaken opinions of her weaknesses, she might be poor at tracking the epistemic statuses of her beliefs without lacking in humility. Her false self-assessments might be caused by cognitive impairments or by misleading evidence in her possession. Either way, they do not prevent her from owning up to whatever limitations she thinks she has.

Conversely, one might be aware of one's limitations and use that knowledge to cover them up. A person might be very good at tracking the epistemic statuses of her beliefs. This person is in several ways a good epistemic agent. However, she lacks in humility if she is not open about her shortcomings. Acceptance of limitations, therefore, should not be identified with the possession of reliably formed beliefs about one's skills, abilities, and the epistemic features of one's first-order beliefs. Instead, it is best conceived as a cluster of attitudes towards these elements of one's cognitive make-up that are motivated by the desire to acquire accurate self-assessments. In short, the motive to form accurate self-assessment is one fundamental aspect of humility; the ability to arrive at self-assessment that are in fact accurate is not. In addition, one must be open about one's shortcomings and realistically optimistic about one's ability to address them. The knowledge motivation, and the desire to express one's commitment to epistemic values such as truth, explain why one does not hide one's perceived weaknesses from others.

Acceptance of limitations, especially in individuals who are not self-centred, could induce negative moods. This might explain why humility has in the past been classified as a sad passion (cf. Soyarslan, 2018). It seems at least possible for a person to own up to her limitations and as a result to become resigned to them and fall into a state of despair. The person who is in some sense humble but without hope cannot strive to improve because she sees such endeavour as pointless. Such hopeless intellectual humility is to my mind closer to resigned fatalism rather than to genuine humility. It is also not a virtue. Firstly, the conviction that learning is beyond one's grasp undermines the motivation to seek the truth that is characteristic of all epistemic virtues (Zagzebski, 1996). Secondly, we have reason to believe that many intellectual limitations can with effort be reduced or overcome. Hence, a resigned attitude to them is a manifestation of an inaccurate assessment of one's intellectual weaknesses. If these considerations are correct, only acceptance of limitations that is accompanied by a

of such a person would exhibit the required cross-situational consistency (Tanesini, 2018d, pp. 406–408).

hopeful attitude is virtuous (Cobb, 2019). Hope, when well-calibrated, supplies the necessary optimism that one's limitations can be addressed.[12]

I have already indicated why both modesty about achievements and acceptance of one's own shortcomings are part of humility. Two examples should help to see that in principle they can come apart. These considerations together show that humility is not a single virtue, but a cluster of two conceptually distinct virtues. Its dual nature explains why the literature contains so many seemingly unrelated accounts.

Some people are modest about their achievements without accepting their limitations. This tendency is exemplified by individuals who rigidly identify with some orthodoxy that might be religious or political in nature. These people might not think of themselves as intellectually special and be very modest about their individual achievements. They might even exhibit their modesty in their choice of clothing and their general demeanour. However, their uncritical adherence to an ideology causes them to be dogmatic. They do not admit to any errors or to the possibility that their views might be mistaken. They are therefore not accepting of their intellectual limitations.

Conversely, there are people who have a very high opinion of their own intellectual abilities but are, nevertheless, open to criticism. These individuals might come across as 'cocky'. They are certainly not modest about their achievements. However, they are also serious about figuring out issues. They might enjoying debating. These people might demonstrate an ability to listen and to treat challenges seriously. At least when these come from those which they consider to be their peers.[13] They are, therefore, accepting that they might be mistaken.

These examples show that modesty and acceptance of limitations are conceptually distinct. It seems likely however that they are psychologically connected. The cultivation of modesty should lead one when reflecting about achievements to appreciate their limits and thus to develop the disposition to accept one's own limitations. Similarly, acceptance of limitations, when this is accompanied by a desire to improve rather than a resignation to their fixity, should stimulate awareness of one's existing strengths as well as one's general capacity for self-improvement. Thus, one would expect modesty about achievements to promote acceptance of one's limitations. Similarly, one would expect that owning up to one's limitations would facilitate modesty about achievements.

If the above is correct, then acceptance of limitations is also to be explained as based on strong negative attitudes towards aspects of one's cognitive make up.

---

[12] Hope itself is not always virtuous since it might, on the one hand, be unrealistic or, on the other, insufficiently optimistic. See Snow (2013) for an account of hope as an intellectual virtue that supplies energy to all inquiries.

[13] Of course, these people might think that only few others are their intellectual equals. They are also likely to be mistaken in this regard.

These attitudes are formed out of the needs to acquire knowledge and to express the values to which one is committed. The attitudes are negative because they are evaluations of their objects that treat them as hindering the satisfaction of the needs that have motivated the formation of the attitudes. An example should help to clarify these points. Suppose that I have a negative attitude towards my mathematical ability. Such attitude is a dislike of this feature of the self. If the attitude is formed and sustained by the knowledge motivation, the attitude registers the assessment that my mathematical ability has served me poorly when attempting to acquire knowledge. This assessment is emotionally laden. It generally also includes a behavioural tendency not to rely on this ability.[14] The attitude might, of course, be inaccurate especially if its informational basis is misleading. For instance, if I inhabit an epistemically hostile environment, I might have acquired negative but misleading feedback about my ability to do math. Even in these circumstances, provided that my attitude is driven by the knowledge motivation, it is the basis of acceptance of intellectual limitations.

In addition, if this negative attitude also serves a value-expressive function, it indicates one's commitment to truth and knowledge. That is, the person evaluates negatively her mathematical abilities because one appraises them as being an obstacle to making good on one's commitments. Possession of this commitment, when combined with a desire to improve, is crucial to raise performance. Further, as the level of one's performance increases, one acquires new evidence of one's abilities. This new evidence should prompt attitude change. In reality, matters might not go as smoothly. Nevertheless, attitudes serving the knowledge function tend to be the most sensitive to the quality of evidence (Watt et al., 2008, p. 196).[15] Thus, one would expect them to update rationally in a more systematic way than attitudes of other kinds. Attitudes serving a value-expressive function, however, are especially resistant to change (Maio & Haddock, 2015, pp. 120–121). That said, attitudes might respond differently to persuasive messages if the values that motivate them are themselves epistemic. To my knowledge, this possibility has received no attention in psychology. Hence, it is wholly possible, that the attitudes that are, in my view, the causal bases of the virtue of humility are among the most reason-responsive kinds of attitude.

Explaining the acceptance of one's own limitations in terms of negative attitudes accounts for many of the characteristic manifestations of this virtue. It explains why knowing one's shortcomings is neither necessary nor sufficient for humility, even though the humble person typically possesses an accurate measure

---

[14] This is why humility must include a hopeful attitude to avoid the risk of becoming resigned to one's own limitations.

[15] This is what we would predict since the motive to be accurate guides the selection and evaluation of the information on which to base the attitude. This avoids creating asymmetry of error costs. For evidence that intellectually humble people are attuned to the strength of arguments and thus tend to be accurate in their assessments see Leary et al. (2017).

of her strengths and weaknesses. What matters is the motivation to seek knowledge, rather than the ability to achieve it. It explains why humble individuals are open about their weaknesses. The motive to seek knowledge and the commitment to epistemic values are inconsistent with hiding the nature and extent of one's shortcomings from oneself but also from other people. In addition, the account in terms of attitudes explains why acceptance of limitations involves being open about their existence while adopting an optimistic outlook about one's ability to address these shortcomings. Attitudes serving a knowledge function are associated with a high dispositional need for cognition that consists in finding cognitive activity pleasurable and should thus combat tendencies to the adoption of a fixed mindset characteristic of resignation.[16] Finally, since attitudes are closely related to emotions, this account can help to explain the feelings and experiences associated with humility. When one has negative attitudes towards parts of the self, one might feel humble and experience doubts about some of one's views. These feelings and emotions also regulate one's epistemic conduct.

There are three kinds of intellectual virtues and vices: sensibilities, thinking styles, and character traits. Intellectual humility as modesty and acceptance of limitations is a character trait that promotes the development of some thinking styles and sensibilities. For example, it promotes the open-minded thinking style that is associated with high dispositional need for cognition understood as the enjoyment of cognitive effort (Cacioppo & Petty, 1982; Cacioppo et al., 1996). In addition, given the connections between humility and generosity, one would expect humility to promote a sensibility of empathetic concern for the needs of other people. Various recent studies have shown that feelings of humility are positively associated with taking oneself to be similar to other people and thus with feeling empathetically concerned about their well-being (Ashton-James & Tracy, 2012; Nadelhoffer & Wright, 2017). These findings can be accommodated within the attitudinal framework. Since humility is based on attitudes shaped by the motivation to be accurate one would expect these to promote enjoyment of thinking in the service of discovering the truth. One would also predict the association with believing that one is similar to other people since often these judgments are accurate. In addition, if people exhibiting humility are guided by accuracy motives one would expect them also to develop virtuous perceptual sensibilities provided that they do not suffer from perceptual impairments.

The possession of a character trait entails that its motivational and emotional components are habitual. The humble person has a disposition to feel humbled by her limitations but hopeful that they can be overcome. She is equally humble in the face of a range of achievements and successes exhibited by other people.

---

[16] See Cacioppo and Petty (1982); Cacioppo et al. (1996) on the need for cognition. The positive correlation with humility has been supported by Leary et al. (2017). The study of a fixed mindset is due to Dweck (2006).

She is also chronically motivated to seek knowledge in a variety of situations. These tendencies to experience emotions and to possess motives guide her attention to aspects of her situation that become salient to her. This attentiveness when habituated is tantamount to the acquisition of a sensibility to be aware of other people's epistemic successes and contributions to shared endeavours and of their epistemic needs. Intellectually humble subjects are good team players partly because humility promotes a sensibility to detect other people's intellectual achievements and their epistemic needs.

4.3 Intellectual Pride

There is a kind of person who is reasonably described as proud but who is not arrogant. What makes the description apt is not directly linked to how often or how strongly they experience pride in their achievements. On the contrary, proud individuals might be especially susceptible to shame, if they think they have failed to meet those standards they have set for themselves.[17] What is distinctive of proud individuals is that they care that they have achievements to their name. In this regard pride is related to a kind of high self-esteem. The latter is a positive attitude to oneself based partly on the belief that one can take credit for several accomplishments. Proud people have this kind of high self-esteem when they think that they have achieved several successes. In this section, I offer an account of intellectual pride as a character trait based on attitudes towards one's perceived achievements.[18] I also defend the view that it is an intellectual virtue.

Much philosophical and psychological research on pride concerns the emotion of pride rather than the character trait (Ashton-James & Tracy, 2012; Brady, 2017; Taylor, 1985). This episodic pride is a positive emotion focused on the self that takes as its intentional object a quality or a thing that is associated to the self. It differs from other positive emotions of self-assessment, such as being pleased about some aspect of the self, in that pride in addition requires that being associated with this quality or object also enhances the worth of the self (Brady, 2017, p. 15). Alternatively, one may hold that pride necessitates that the quality or thing of which one is proud must be valuable and something for which one can

---

[17] I owe to Kristjánsson (2001) the insight that pride as a character trait is a disposition to experience both shame and pride as episodic emotions. He sees this character trait as one component of Aristotle's megalopsychia. For discussion of shame as a response to the realization that one's desires are not worthy of one, see Tessman (2005, p. 24). Deonna et al. (2011) also argue for the positive role of shame in self-improvement. I argue in Chapter 5 that shame can take different forms but it is often also a reaction to the thought that one has failed to meet standards to which society expects one to measure up.

[18] In Tanesini (2018d) at times I confuse pride as desire to achieve and satisfaction in one's accomplishments with the virtue of demanding the esteem that is properly due to one. In this chapter I distinguish these two virtues.

take credit (Morgan-Knapp, 2019).[19] Thus, for example, one might experience pride when one finally solves a difficult puzzle that has occupied one for some time.

People can experience emotions of pride without being proud individuals. Conversely, someone might be a proud person and, because of it, feel that they have very little to be proud about. Pride in this second sense is a disposition to evaluate oneself by some standards and to be especially exacting in applying these standards to oneself. A person who is proud in this sense is not smug or self-aggrandising. On the contrary, she is a person who is not prone to self-serving biases. This person, however, also desires to achieve. In this regard, she differs from the modest person who is not particularly motivated to have accomplishments to her name. In short, the proud individual is ambitious; the modest person is not resigned to alleged shortcoming but she might not be driven by the desire for success. In addition, a proud person is also assertive. She claims entitlement to what she is owed. She is not someone who puts up with treatment that is not befitting her self-worth. Pride in this sense is a character trait that is closely associated to dignity, integrity, and self-respect (Kristjánsson, 2001; Morton, 2017). For this reason self-love is a characteristic emotion associated with pride but also with concern for being esteemed. I understand self-love as the emotional manifestation of valuing oneself as an agent. Such valuing includes being committed to 'make of oneself and one's life something good and worthy of oneself' (Dillon, forthcoming, p. 9 in MS).

This kind of pride has its epistemic equivalent. The intellectually proud individual judges herself exactly by high epistemic standards. She does not cut herself much slack. She is also intellectually ambitious because she is driven to add more and better accomplishments to her name.[20] However, she is not motivated to think of any success as an achievement just because it is hers. She does not experience pride for successes for which she cannot take credit or that are not, in her eyes, genuinely valuable. The same person is prone to feel shame when she falls short of her intellectual standards. She is dismayed with herself if, for example, she discovers that she has been careless in her epistemic activities.

Pride, as a character trait, thus comprises the dispositions to feel the twin emotions of pride and shame about some features of one's cognitive make-up and about one's intellectual activities. These are: the disposition to feel pride about those aspects of the self that are genuine achievements and to feel proud about

---

[19] This characterization only applies to pride about achievements. There are other forms of pride: vicarious pride in the achievement of others who are associated to the self (e.g., pride in the achievements of one's grandmother); and identity pride that is pride in one's group identity even though one can take no credit for belonging to that group (e.g., black pride). I ignore them here. In my view, identity pride is a corrective to redress the risks of shame-proneness that beset individuals belonging to subordinated social groups. See Chapter 5.

[20] In this regard the authentically proud person differs from the individual whose pride is hubristic and does not strive to improve. The latter but not the former exhibits complacent self-satisfaction.

them in proportion to their worth; and the disposition to feel shame about those aspects of the self that are failures. However, there is more to pride than dispositions to emote. The intellectually proud individual is ambitious and assertive without being arrogant. Her ambition is manifested in her striving to improve herself and accomplish more. Her assertiveness is manifested in her willingness to speak with authority, when she thinks that she can make a genuine contribution to a debate. She can be confident in her abilities. It is this confidence that, when present, enables her to claim entitlement to the epistemic goods and resources that are due to her. These include: claiming speaking time for oneself, presenting oneself as an expert, sending one's work for publication to the best journals.[21]

Feelings of confidence are not the same as feelings of pride. It is appropriate to feel confident in our intellectual abilities even when, as in the case of cognitive faculties, their strength is not something for which we can take credit. One might be confident in one's eyesight because of its reliability, but it would be inappropriate to be proud of one's 20/20 vision. It is however fitting to be proud of one's sensibilities such as being observant, for example. Feelings of pride play a role in identifying some aspects of the self as especially worthwhile and thus in reinforcing their development. In addition to ambition, fearlessness, confidence, and assertiveness, the intellectually proud person is above all not servile. She is not prepared to subscribe to views that are not her own because doing so would make life easier. She also does not put up with being bullied or shouted down.

The description offered above identifies a character trait for which the term 'pride' is appropriate. Unfortunately, however, the term in English is multiply ambiguous. I have already discussed the difference between the episodic emotion of pride and the character trait bearing the same name. But, the term is also used as a near synonym of arrogance. When the term is used in this way it refers to individuals who are conceited, haughty, arrogant, or vain. These are a plethora of vices that have been collectively labelled as the vices of pride (Roberts & Wood, 2007, p. 77). I refer to them as vices of superiority which I discuss in Chapters 5 and 6. The considerations offered so far should be sufficient to establish that there is another character trait that pertains to proud individuals but is not a vice.

Intellectual pride is related to, but different from, intellectual modesty. Unlike pride, modesty is compatible with lack of ambition. Moreover, modest individuals who do not strive to achieve might always be at risk of falling into self-abasement or fatalism. Pride is a corrective to these dangers. However, pride can be a virtue rather than a mere a prophylactic against vice. Pride involves a desire to improve, to become accomplished. This is the desire to acquire more epistemic goods for oneself, it is also an incentive to persevere in one's endeavours and to increase the level of one's performance. Further, this trait is a consequence of intellectual

---

[21] Hence, contra Hazlett (2017) there is more to intellectual pride than the acknowledgement of one's strengths.

evaluative self-respect understood in part as setting epistemic standards for oneself by which one lives.[22] For all of these reasons pride is best thought as distinct from modesty and as a virtue.

Even though pride as a character trait is distinct from the episodic emotion of pride, some of the psychological research on that emotion helps to deepen our understanding of the trait. Psychologists distinguish between authentic and hubristic pride (Ashton-James & Tracy, 2012; Tracy et al., 2009; Tracy & Robins, 2007). These two emotions do not have distinct phenomenologies; instead, they differ in their consequences and in their intentional objects. Hubristic pride is pride in successes that are experienced as due to inalterable features of the self (e.g., I succeeded because I am smart); authentic pride is pride in successes that are experienced as due to features of the self that are under one's control (e.g., I succeeded because I worked hard). When people are made to feel hubristically proud of something, they become more arrogant and conceited, they feel superior to others; they are more prejudiced because they experience less empathetic concern for other people. However, when individuaals are encouraged to experience authentic pride, they feel more confident, have enhanced sense of self-worth, are more generous and less prejudiced, and feel more humble (Ashton-James & Tracy, 2012; Tracy & Robins, 2007).

It should be apparent from the discussion presented above that hubristic pride is an emotion that is never fitting since it consists in responding, in the manner appropriate for an achievement, to a success for which one cannot take credit. Further, this is not an honest mistake since hubristic pride is self-satisfaction experienced in cases where one construes one's success as the outcome of a feature of the self that is not something over which one has control. Authentic pride is pride in things that one perceives as achievements because one thinks that they are valuable, and that one can take credit for them. Hence, authentic pride can be a fitting emotion.

The distinction between hubristic and authentic pride helps to clarify which emotion of pride proud individuals are disposed to experience. People who suffer from the vices of pride are prone to experience hubristic pride, but those whose pride is a virtue have a tendency to experience authentic pride. That is, they are only proud of those successes that they think are truly a credit to them and only because of what they perceive to be their genuine worth.[23] The distinction between these two emotions also brings to the fore the relation of pride to self-esteem.

There is evidence linking authentic pride to secure high self-esteem. Self-esteem is an evaluative attitude to the self that is high when the attitude is positive.

---

[22] There might be differences between pride as a character trait and self-respect, but in my view they are intimately related. Evaluative self-respect is respect that is proportional to what one takes to be one's admirable features. It is different from recognition self-respect which all individuals deserve merely qua agents. I borrow this distinction, with substantial modifications, from Dillon (2004).

[23] They might on occasion make genuine mistakes on either count.

It is said to be secure, as opposed to defensive or fragile, when positivity is recorded in implicit as well as explicit measures.[24] Individuals whose self-esteem is secure are confident without being defensive. Conversely, defensive high self-esteem is associated with hubristic experiences of pride and with arrogance (Ashton-James & Tracy, 2012). These consideration support the view that proud individuals, when they have occasion to experience the emotion of authentic pride often and about a variety of accomplishments, develop an attitude to the self that is positive but not defensive because their episodic pride is not hubristic.

The discussion above provides evidence that there is a kind of pride that is a virtuous character trait. It also suggests that this pride is based on strong attitudes, serving knowledge and value expressive functions, directed at those among one's cognitive abilities, skills, character traits that are perceived as acquired and at those intellectual successes that are experienced as achievements. These attitudes are combined with a conscious motivation to achieve and succeed. These attitudes and motivations result in the ambitious and assertive behaviour characteristic of proud individuals.

In my view the attitudes characteristic of pride in each individual overlap with those that are the basis of modesty. This claim is counter-intuitive; but its alleged implausibility is a feature of the tendency to think wrongly that proud people are those who often experience pride. However, if pride is properly understood as a desire to have genuine achievements to one's name which, if satisfied, leads to secure and appropriate confidence in one's acquired abilities and achievements, the apparent incompatibility with modesty disappears.

Even though pride and modesty are based on overlapping attitudes, they differ in their typical expressions. We tend to think of pride as the disposition to seek accomplishments for oneself.[25] It is thus a buttress against the risks of excessive modesty or self-abasement. We tend to think of modesty as the disposition to acknowledge one's strengths while caring to get it right, rather than of being right. Modesty, therefore, serves the role of protecting one from the temptation to become arrogant.

In addition, the contents of the attitudes on which pride and modesty are based are likely to be partly different. When attempting to understand their level of ability, human beings tend not to test themselves against objective standards but to compare their level of performance with that achieved by other people (Mussweiler, 2020; Mussweiler & Rüter, 2003). Individuals who are motivated to understand their true abilities tend to compare themselves to others that are relevantly similar to them. Those who want to improve instead measure themselves against those whom they wish to emulate (Corcoran et al., 2011). Since intellectually virtuous individuals are motivated to improve and to know their true

---

[24] See Chapter 3, Section 3.1.4 for a description of explicit and implicit measures.
[25] On intellectual pride as acknowledgment of strengths see Hazlett (2017).

strengths, they are likely to engage in comparisons of both sorts. Nevertheless, since pride is linked to ambition it is likely to be based on comparisons driven by a desire to improve, while modest self-appraisals are derived from interpersonal comparison guided by concerns for accuracy.

It might be thought that feeling proud in discovering that one is better than other people is a sign of arrogance, and is incompatible with authentic pride. One might even claim with Morgan-Knapp (2019) that comparative pride is never fitting, since no achievement becomes more valuable in virtue of its positional character. If sailing solo around the world is a great achievement, its value is not increased by the mere fact that one is the first to complete the task. I agree that being proud that one is better than other people can be a sign of arrogance. However, the discovery that one has outperformed other people might be evidence of one's achievement about which one feels proud. The object of pride is the value of the achievement which is one's own, rather than the fact that one has outperformed others.

That said, there are cases where implicitly comparative pride can be fitting and compatible with modesty. Feeling proud that one has made an important discovery after one has worked hard at it, would seem to be an example of authentic pride. Yet, it is a sort of comparative pride since what makes the discovery such a worthy achievement is that it is a novel addition to scientific knowledge. Part of the epistemic value of this success lies in the fact that one is the first to acquire this piece of knowledge. Examples such as this one suggest that there are successes that are creditable to individuals which acquire part of their worth by their comparative nature. Figuring out the same point at a later date, even if this is arrived at independently of the original discovery, seems less worthy because it makes a lesser contribution to the shared pool of knowledge. Hence, contra to Morgan-Knapp (2019), some comparative pride is fitting. Its experience on the part of those who possess the kind of pride discussed here need not be detrimental to their virtuousness.

4.4 The Virtue of Caring for One's Own Intellectual Reputation

I have argued that an important difference between those who are only modest and those who are also proud lies in how much they care about their own accomplishments. Individuals who are modest without being proud love the truth. Thus, they care that an important discovery was made but, because of the absence of egocentric concerns, they might not put any value on the fact that it was them who made it. Proud individuals also care that the discovery is made by them. However, unless their pride is that of the arrogant, they only value their successes if, and to the extent to which, they are accomplishments that are creditable to them. These considerations show that pride and modesty also partly differ in their proximate motivations since the first but not the second includes a desire to excel. In this section I discuss a virtue, that is distinct from pride, but is together with pride an essential component of secure self-esteem. This is the virtue of caring that others give one the credit that one merits.[26]

Human beings usually care at least to some extent that they have a good reputation. There are prudential reasons why this concern is well-placed. Many aspects of individuals' professional lives are more successful when they enjoy a good reputation. They are more likely to receive promotions, to secure other people's support and collaboration. For those who pursue careers in academia or public life possessing a good intellectual reputation opens many doors. It is instrumental in obtaining research grants, for example. Reputational rankings are pervasive in academia. Information about esteem is collected by universities and governments and is relied upon by students and their families when deciding where to study. There is thus no doubt that it is in individuals' self-interest to be concerned with their reputations.

I think of intellectual reputation as the socially shared property of being esteemed by others for one's intellectual qualities. Esteem is the psychological state of taking a positive or negative stance towards a person because one judges her to possess some good or bad quality. In particular, to esteem someone is to hold her in high regard. Often it also involves judging her to be a model or exemplar worthy of imitation. Thus, individuals who are recipients of esteem are sometimes thought to have good features that others do not have or possess to a lesser degree. Similarly people who are disesteemed are often presented as the target of disapproval because they are thought to have bad features that are either uncommon or are not often possessed to such a high degree. When a person is thought as being particularly disesteemable, she is singled out as a cautionary example.

Individuals are esteemed for their qualities. One may esteem a person for the incisiveness of her questions, without esteeming her for other features. Sometimes we speak of esteeming a person without singling out any qualities for which we hold her in esteem. I assume that in these cases we are indicating that she has many qualities and we esteem her for each of them. Not every feature, however, is something for which a person can be esteemed. Rather we only esteem people for features that we take to be valuable (or disvaluable) in some way and that can be credited to them. In other words, people are esteemed only for those features for which they could be properly proud or ashamed. Pride and shame are emotions directed at the self for some of its features when one presumes that one is

---

[26] My discussion here is indebted to Brennan and Pettit (2004). I have already discussed some of these issues in Tanesini (2018b).

responsible for them and that they are either valuable or disvaluable. Esteem and dis-esteem are their other-directed counterparts.

The psychological state of esteem therefore can be fitting or not. It is fitting when the attitude matches the quality for which the target is esteemed or disesteemed because this quality is genuinely good or bad. But also when the individual who is the target of the attitude is responsible for having the quality in question. The attitude is not fitting when one or both of these conditions are not satisfied.[27] This characterization leaves room for a vast range of qualities as suitable grounds for esteem. It includes categorical properties such as having passed an exam, positional features such as being top of one's class and qualities that belong to continua and attract esteem in proportion to the perceived nature of the accomplishment.

Esteem is closely related to admiration. However, we appear to reserve admiration for those qualities that are thought as defining of a person and deserving high levels of esteem. For example, we might esteem a competent and reliable scientist but we are likely to admire those who have made remarkable contributions to the advance of science. In short, we appear to reserve admiration for excellence of character, while we are prepared to esteem what is good, without being superb, irrespective of whether we take it to be defining of the person (cf. Zagzebski, 2017, pp. 30–40). There is a tendency to use the vocabulary of admiration even with regard to features that are not subject to the person's control. I argue in Chapter 8 that this tendency can be fitting when the features in questions are components of the person's character. That said, the vocabulary of admiration is often used in ways that are not fitting. Hence, we might admire a person for his good looks. In my view this tendency is based on the mistaken assumption that one's looks reflect well or badly on whom one is.

Being the recipient of others' esteem can grow into a reputation when one is held in esteem by many individuals some of whom base their attitude, at least in part, on the testimony of others as expressed through words or other markers of esteem. For instance, a scientist can acquire a reputation for her facility in developing new experimental paradigms. Initially, she might have been esteemed for this quality by the leader of her team, but as her experience grows others also observe at first hand her talent and esteem her for it. As time goes by her team leader emphasizes her exceptional ability in reference letters or mentions it when talking to other scientists. Further, this early career researcher might become the recipient of prizes or awards dedicated to budding leaders. In this way the esteem in which she is held develops into a reputation as other scientists rely at least partly on the team leader's word and on her public successes to form an opinion about

---

[27] Brady (2017, pp. 17–18) claims that people are often esteemed for features for which they are not responsible. I disagree with him, but I suspect our disagreement is purely verbal since he thinks that we can only be responsible for what is within one's control and I do not.

her capacities. This is not surprising since knowing that people whom one esteems hold another in high esteem is defeasible evidence that the target of esteem actually possesses the good quality which would make her worthy of the accolade.[28]

Although esteem is a psychological attitude directed at other people for their qualities, it is manifested through numerous external markers. These outwards expressions of esteem include words and actions. They range from explicit praise of individuals for their qualities, to awards, prizes, and promotions. They also include elections to fellowships, selection for editorial boards and research councils' review colleges. Individuals with a reputation for excellence are called upon to offer their opinion on others' qualities by writing blurbs for books and refereeing submissions to journals. In these, and other ways, the esteem in which some individuals are held by their peers is made public.

Markers of esteem are twice removed from the estimable qualities that they are intended to track. Esteem as a psychological state if well-placed indicates the presence in another person of a good quality that makes them worthy of esteem. The markers of esteem, if the person who produces them is sincere, are meant to track the presence of the psychological attitude. Given the indirect connection between esteem markers and estimable qualities, it is not surprising that these indicators often are not wholly reliable.

Reliance on esteem markers is, therefore, potentially dangerous even though practically necessary. It is necessary because especially in societies in which knowledge is highly specialized, each epistemic agent is largely dependent on others in the pursuit of knowledge. It is completely unfeasible for creatures whose abilities are limited to become experts in every area of one's own discipline, let alone other areas of study. Hence, one must rely on the results obtained by others.

It is not always obvious whether so-called experts can be trusted, knowing about their reputation among fellow scientists often supplies the only available evidence on which to base one's judgment. Nevertheless, reliance on reputation is risky because communities can develop practices of esteem that largely fail to track estimable properties. There are various incentives that might cause this phenomenon.

First, some practices of esteeming are beneficial to both the recipient and the bestower of esteem. Election to a fellowship is an example since being elected is a marker that one is held in esteem, but if one has an excellent reputation, one's election might enhance the value of the fellowship and thus improve the

---

[28] This comment should not be taken to suggest that I endorse a reductionist account of the epistemology of testimony. Rather, testimony about esteem is unusual because esteem is a rivalrous good. Its nature always gives individuals an additional incentive to seek some independent evidence that esteem is well-placed since the esteem in which others are held potentially impacts upon one's reputation. On these points see Tanesini (2018b).

reputation of existing fellows. Reputations built in this mutually advantageous fashion might be especially unreliable indicators.

Second, practices of esteem are influenced by socially shared biases and prejudices. In societies, like ours, where members of some subordinated social groups are unwarrantedly thought to be less intellectually capable and credible simply because of their group membership markers of esteem are likely to be at odd with the estimable properties possessed by these individuals.[29] Widespread prejudicial beliefs affect the esteem in which they are held. The resulting deflation in the esteem that they receive has knock-on effects on those public markers of esteem that are the building blocks of reputations.

Third, and relatedly, the reliability of practices of esteem in an epistemic community also depends on the prevalence within it of individuals who suffer from vices such as intellectual vanity and timidity that have distorting effects on the bestowing of esteem and reputation. Intellectually vain or narcissistic individuals, for instance, seek to acquire others' esteem at all costs. They are thus even prepared to steal other people's credit, and to mislead people so that they form more favourable judgments about them than they merit (cf. Campbell et al., 2000). Notwithstanding these dangers, reliance on reputation is often unavoidable in the course of epistemic activities. That said, one must always be alert to distortions in the practice, and be prepared to compensate for in-built biases.

I have argued that being the recipient of other people's esteem is prudentially valuable for the esteemed person and that the presence of a practice of esteeming is of epistemic value to communities that have it. But, being esteemed by others is also epistemically valuable to the person who is the recipient of these attitudes. Others' esteem is evidence that we can use to understand our qualities. It is often the case that we learn the true significance of any of our intellectual accomplishments thanks to other people's appreciation. Hence, knowing about the esteem in which one is held supplies important information in the aid of self-knowledge.

Being esteemed is also epistemically valuable because of its motivational role. Wanting to be held in high esteem by those people whom one esteems is an incentive to improve one's performance so that one becomes deserving to be credited with a number of achievements and with the possession of a range of intellectually good qualities. Some individuals, especially those who are virtuously proud, might not require the extra incentive of gaining other people's high opinion as a stimulus to raise one's performance. But, as a matter of fact, other people's views of one's abilities are an important driver for many epistemic agents.

---

[29] For arguments that less powerful individuals tend not to receive the credit that they merit see Bruner and O'Connor (2017). This phenomenon is a distributive version of epistemic injustice according to which individuals suffer an injustice when an epistemic good such as intellectual reputation is distributed unfairly (Coady, 2010, 2017).

Most importantly, insofar as the esteem in which others hold one partly guides their behaviour towards one in epistemic exchanges, being held in high regard is essential if we are to be able to engage successfully in a range of social epistemic activities such as debating or offering expert judgments. One's performance in these epistemic activities is, in part, dependent on other people's perception of one's epistemic authoritativeness. Being allocated the amount of authority that is consonant with one's expertise is of great epistemic value to each epistemic agent.

There is, therefore, a close connection between caring that others' esteem one for one's qualities and demanding that others respect us in a manner that is consonant with the level and the extent of our accomplishments. That is, in the same way in which pride is necessary for intellectual self-respect, the desire that others bestow upon one the esteem which one deserves is another pre-requisite of self-respect because demanding that others give one the respect that one is owed is a component of treating oneself with respect. For these reasons, the epistemic value of caring that others allocate to one the esteem which one deserves is intrinsic rather than a mere means to a further epistemic end such as the acquisition of knowledge. It is therefore plausibly thought as a virtue when one's love for honours in recognition of one's intellectual qualities is only in proportion to one's credit and only sought from the right sources (Aristotle, 1985, 1125b 1–25).

One may grant these points and yet claim that the desire that others hold one in high esteem is self-stultifying because it cannot be rationally pursued (Elster, 1983). The person who cares that others esteem her acts in ways designed to seek attention, since it is not possible to be esteemed unless one is noticed. However, if, as it seems plausible, this behaviour is not impressive, then barring dissimulation the attempt to attract others' esteem is bound to result in a lowering of the opinion that others have of us. In response, one may point out that although seeking to be esteemed more than one merits often meets with others' disapproval, in contemporary Western societies at least seeking to attract credit that is proportional to one's merit does not make one the target of negative attitudes. For example, a scientist's attempt to draw attention to her contribution to a collective accomplishment does not necessarily appear unimpressive if she is only attempting to gain the recognition which is due to her.

In my view the attitudes to one's cognitive abilities, skills, and achievements characteristic of those seeking the credit for one's intellectual qualities that is commensurate to one's merits overlap in each individual with those distinct clusters of attitudes that are the bases of pride and acceptance of one's intellectual limitations. This claim is counterintuitive; but part of its alleged implausibility is a feature of the tendency to think wrongly that individuals who care for honours are always vain. The person who only seeks the kind of esteem that is commensurate with her merits must be proud of her achievements but also transparent about her limitations.

The person who wishes to merit the esteem of other people must in ordinary circumstances have a disposition to experience a benign form of envy. Benign envy is a painful experience that one lacks some good feature that is possess by some others (Kristjánsson, 2006; Protasi, 2016). It is the result of social comparisons of one's abilities with others whom one judges to be one's superior in the relevant domain in order to improve. This experience prompts one to emulate others and attempt to acquire the good feature for oneself. It is this kind of envy that motivates a person whose concern for honours is virtuous to improve so as to merit the credit they desire. Such emotional experience is predicated on an acceptance of one's own existing limitations together with a hopeful or optimistic outlook about one's ability to improve.

Even though caring for being esteemed and accepting of one's limitations are based on partially overlapping attitudes with their informational bases, they differ in their typical expressions. We tend to think of caring for others' esteem as the disposition to seek recognition for one's accomplishments. It is thus a buttress against the risks of excessive timidity. We tend to think of acceptance of limitations as the disposition to acknowledge one's weaknesses. Acceptance of limitations, therefore, serves the role of protecting one from the temptation to become vain.

To summarize, modesty and acceptance of limitations are virtues that are based on attitudes of self-evaluation that are driven by the knowledge motivation and the commitment to value truth and other epistemic goods. These two virtues together constitute intellectual humility. Pride in one's intellectual achievements and a concern that these are acknowledged by other people are virtues that are distinct from, but related to, modesty and acceptance of limitations. Pride includes a motivation to have intellectual accomplishments. Thus, it is a the root of the drive to improve that is essential to epistemically virtuous agents. It is complemented by a virtuous concern for others' esteem that comprises a tendency to experience benign envy as a spur to self-improvement. The care for recognition of one's merits includes a motivation to demand that others' acknowledge one's epistemic qualities, one's authority and one's accomplishments. Thus, in addition to being a pre-requisite of intellectual self-respect, seeking recognition for one's contributions is essential when playing one's role in epistemic exchanges. For example, borrowing a theme from Fricker's (2007), unless one is treated as an informant rather than a mere source of evidence, one is unable to fulfil the role of a testifier. If this is right, caring that one is esteemed is a virtue of epistemic agents who stand in relations of epistemic dependence with other epistemic agents.

Each of the four virtues discussed in this chapter are each flanked by two vices—one, seemingly of excess and the other of deficiency. In Chapter 5 I detail the four vices opposed to modesty and pride; in Chapter 6 I turn to those which antagonise acceptance of limitations and care for one's reputation.

5
Superbia, Arrogance, Servility, and Self-Abasement

This chapter is dedicated to those vices that oppose intellectual modesty and pride. These are: haughtiness (*superbia*), intellectual arrogance, servility, and self-abasement.[1] Although ultimately mistaken, Aristotle's conception of virtue as a golden mean which is flanked by vices of excess and deficit is helpful to develop initial broad descriptions of these vices. Arrogance is characteristic of those who lack modesty about their own intellectual strengths, whilst self-abasement typifies individuals who are exceedingly modest since they belittle their own successes. *Superbia* (haughtiness) and servility are related to these qualities. *Superbia* is similar to arrogance and involves excessive pride in one's achievements which leads one to try to diminish other people in order to be their superior. Servility is close to self-abasement and is characterized by lack of pride. However, while those who self-abase tend to think of themselves as worthless, those who are servile retain a sense of self-worth by being accepted as low ranked members of the epistemic community.

Superbia and arrogance are vices of superiority (cf. Bell, 2013). The label is apt for several related reasons. First, these are vices that are in part constituted by unwarranted feelings of superiority. Second, they are traits that include among their manifestations behaviours designed to create or preserve pecking orders in which the subject occupies a high status while other people are diminished to lower ranks. Third, these are vices that are characteristic of people that occupy positions of privilege (Medina, 2013, pp. 30–40).[2] Members of dominant groups are likely to exemplify these vices because, as Dillon (forthcoming) notes, norms of superiority are part of their group identity.

Servility and self-abasement are the corresponding vices of inferiority. These are constituted by unwarranted feelings of inferiority; they are manifested in behaviours indicating the lowly status of their possessors. Individuals who occupy

---

[1] I am aware that readers may come to think that labels such as '*superbia*', 'haughtiness' or 'self-abasement' do not perfectly fit the phenomena I seek to describe. I agree. What matters for my purposes here is that there are clusters of behaviours, emotions, evaluations, and judgments that are plausibly thought as expressions of distinct and distinctive character traits. Whether the labels I have chosen for them have exactly the right connotations in ordinary parlance should not affect the points I want to defend. Thanks to Donald Baxter for raising these issues.

[2] I do not mean to suggest that every privileged individual is necessarily vicious. Rather, my claim is that these people are at higher risk of developing these traits.

subordinated positions in society are especially at risk of developing them (Moody-Adams, 1995).

These vices of inferiority and superiority exemplify ways in which a person may fail to have the true measure of herself. Those who possess these traits are individuals who have faulty estimates of their own personal intellectual worth.[3] These individuals evaluate their cognitive make-up and its components—such as cognitive faculties (e.g., memory, sight), sensibilities (e.g., being observant), intellectual abilities (e.g., facility with numbers), skills (e.g., chess playing), thinking styles and habits (e.g., fact checking), or intellectual commitments (e.g., beliefs and theories)[4]—and treat these as their intellectual strengths or weaknesses. They base their self-confidence and estimate of their own epistemic authority on these evaluations. These clusters of self-evaluations or attitudes toward specific intellectual features of the self, such as one's mathematical abilities, are closely associated with global estimations of the intellectual worth of the self. These global appraisals are forms of self-esteem based on one's agentic qualities which include intellectual abilities, skills, performance, and competence.

The self-evaluations of arrogant, haughty, servile, and self-abasing individuals are faulty because they are not sensitive to the actual epistemic value that pertains to their intellectual features.[5] Instead, their attitudes have been formed and are maintained to serve either the need to defend the self against alleged threats or the need to be accepted as a member of one's affinity groups. If formed to defend the self, as in the case of arrogant and haughty people, these attitudes are associated with the defensive or fragile high self-esteem characteristic of those who have high self-esteem when this is measured explicitly by means of self-reports, but appear low in implicit or indirect measures of self-esteem, such as that provided by an Implicit Association Test (Haddock & Gebauer, 2011).[6] If formed to fit in within one's community, as is characteristic of individuals who are servile or self-abasing, these attitudes are associated with the damaged self-esteem characteristic of those who have low self-esteem according to explicit measures, but whose self-esteem is high when measured implicitly (Schröder-Abé et al., 2007a). Hence, underlying

---

[3] An epistemic agent's personal intellectual worth is relative to the epistemic value that accrues to her beliefs, skills, intellectual habits, and abilities. It is thus possible for one person to be intellectually more worthy than another person. For an account of personal intellectual worth that makes it primarily a function of desire for intellectual values and goods, see Baehr (2011).

[4] In addition, these vices plausibly involve also attitudes about the products of one's intellectual agency such as items which may be said to count as one's intellectual property. Hence, one may think of these vices as evaluations of one's cognitive make-up in an extended sense. For reasons of space, I shall not address this issue here.

[5] Faulty does not in this context mean inaccurate. These estimates are faulty because they are sensitive to the wrong properties such as effectiveness in the protection against threats rather than in the formation of true beliefs. One's estimate could be faulty in this way even though because of luck it happens to result in an accurate evaluation of the intellectual worth of one's abilities, skills, etc.

[6] See Chapter 3, Section 3.1.4 for these kinds of attitude measurements.

these vices are discrepant attitudes towards the personal intellectual worth of the self.

In this regard, the framework of attitudes reveals some important aspects of the opposition of these vices to the virtues of intellectual modesty and pride. First, these virtues are closely associated with a sense of self-esteem or self-worth that is high and secure. The vices of superiority instead are related to high self-esteem that is insecure because defensive. Those of inferiority are related to self-esteem that is damaged. Second, superbia and arrogance are not in reality the vices of excessive pride and deficient modesty. The framework of attitudes reveals that they are the vices of defensive or hubristic pride and evaluation of one's intellectual strengths. Similarly, servility and self-abasement are not best though as lack of pride and excessive modesty. Instead, they are the vices of sacrificing self-esteem for social acceptance.

This chapter consists of four sections each dedicated to one vice. In every case I argue that the vice in question is based on attitudes towards one's own intellectual strengths and weaknesses. In each instance possession of false beliefs that overestimate or underestimate one's own intellectual good qualities is neither sufficient nor necessary for an individual to be vicious.[7] Section 5.1 deals with intellectual haughtiness or *superbia*; Section 5.2 is concerned with arrogance; Section 5.3 with servility or obsequiousness; finally Section 5.4 with self-abasement.

5.1 Intellectual Haughtiness (*Superbia*)

Superbia is a disposition to try to 'do others down' in order to elevate oneself.[8] It includes feelings of superiority, a tendency to arrogate special entitlements for oneself, a propensity to anger quickly and often as well as tendencies to engage in behaviours designed to humiliate and intimidate other people.[9] In this section, I first provide a description of some characteristic manifestations of this intellectual vice. I show that it does not consist in an overestimation of one's good qualities. I explain why *superbia* causes individuals to behave angrily in

---

[7] Nor, more weakly, is absence of a true belief about the same a sign that one is vicious.

[8] These are the people whom in the *Comedy* Dante (1994) describes as *superbi* (Purg., XVII vv 115–17). *Superbia* is usually translated into English as 'pride'. This translation is highly misleading since 'pride' in contemporary English has come to signify something akin to self-love. *Superbia* was conceived in the Middle Ages as the kind of distortion of self-love that involves trying to thwart other people's efforts to excel. Spinoza offers a similar account in his *Ethics* (1985) EIIIDefAffXXVIII.

[9] Roberts and West (2017) identify each of these behaviours as characteristic of a distinct vice of pride. Since 'pride' is often used as a translation of '*superbia*', I presume that we are talking about the same vice which they are slicing more thinly than I do. Nothing hangs on this since one could seek to identify the specific informational bases and individual attitudes in the cluster responsible for each of these behavioural dispositions.

inappropriate ways. Finally I defend the claim that *superbia* is based on a cluster of strong attitudes serving a defensive function.

We are all familiar with the range of behaviours that are typical of haughtiness and which tend to cluster together.[10] These include: bragging and boasting about one's own alleged intellectual achievements; aggressively interrupting or otherwise intimidating other people and looking down on their successes; treating others as one's intellectual inferiors including ostentatiously dismissing their views by shaking one's head, rolling one's eyes, or making a show of expressions of disbelief; behaving as if one thought that one knew it all and that one is always right; conceiving of oneself as naturally talented (Lynch, 2019).[11] The same individuals will often interrupt other people or talk at the same time as them. To my mind, two not uncommon haughty reactions to criticism in debate crystallize what lies at the root of this trait.

The first is typified by the 'I do not understand' objection to a speaker's academic presentation. It is not unusual to hear a prominent member of the audience simply stating in response to a speaker's views that *he* does not understand the speaker. In ordinary circumstances saying that one does not understand is an admittance of a shortcoming on one's part and, perhaps, a request for assistance. But in other contexts, the same words are uttered and interpreted by all present to mean that the speaker's presentation was nonsense. For my purposes here two aspects of this move are particularly relevant. The first is that it can only work in a context in which the questioner can presume that the audience rates him very highly for smartness and does not rate the speaker more highly than the questioner.[12] Thus, the questioner when saying 'I do not understand' to mean 'you are talking nonsense' relies on, and re-enforces, his pre-eminent place in the pecking order. The second aspect of the move is that it is akin to a kind of illocutionary disablement. Instead of addressing the views expressed by the speaker and raise pertinent criticisms, the questioner feigns that no proper question can be asked because the content of what the speaker purported to assert is not discernible. The speaker is thus deprived of any rational comeback since if he explains his views using different words or asks for a clarification of which aspect was not understood, he misses the point of the intervention. One can of

---

[10] My discussions of intellectual vices such as haughtiness are idealized in at least two dimensions. First, individuals can be haughty about some of their features but not others. Here, I focus on people who are haughty tout court because they demonstrate this attitude on most occasions and towards most of their features. Second, haughtiness is a matter of degree. I concentrate on the extreme versions of these vices.

[11] I focus here on verbal behaviours that typify haughtiness, but the latter also finds expression in characteristic bodily postures such as manspreading, pumping up one's chest, or aggressively staring down other people.

[12] The same point has been made by Kieran Healy (2016, April, 28). Such an intervention can also function as a snarky remark made by someone who presumes that he should be rated higher than the speaker, even though he has no reason to believe that his view is shared. Thanks to J. Adam Carter for the observation.

course respond to rudeness with rudeness, but there is no way of advancing the debate. Thus, the questioner has succeeded in strengthening his superior position to the speaker in the smartness ranking.

The second notable expression of haughtiness in criticism is characteristics of speakers. It consists in anger and aggression or at least intense irritation in response to what often seem reasonable criticisms.[13] The speaker in these cases treats a criticism of his views as a personal affront or insult. Such behaviour might appear puzzling until one realizes that at the root of haughtiness lies the conviction that one is entitled to deferential treatment because of one's presumed superior epistemic authority, an entitlement that one does not attribute to other people.[14]

In addition to these typical behaviours, haughtiness also finds its characteristic expression in feelings, emotions, and preoccupations. Individuals who suffer from *superbia* generally feel superior to other people, and are prone to anger.[15] They are also usually preoccupied with rankings by intelligence and with pecking orders of authoritativeness. Many of the most typical haughty behaviour are designed to enforce and establish one's privileged position within these rankings. Since haughty individuals consider themselves to be epistemically authoritative, they naturally take themselves to be entitled to special treatment and react with anger whenever they are addressed in egalitarian ways. Therefore, haughtiness is manifested in a disposition to experience frequently the episodic emotion of hubristic pride. This is the kind of pride that is typical of those who have a 'high opinion' or are 'full' of themselves. It is associated with feeling superior because of fixed and innate putative good qualities and with conceited and prejudicial behaviours (Tracy & Robins, 2007).

It would be a mistake to identify this sense of authoritativeness and entitlement, concern with rank, and 'high opinion' of one's own intellectual worth with possession of a belief in one's intellectual superiority to most other people that one would be prepared to endorse.[16] Such a belief in one's superiority is neither necessary nor sufficient for haughtiness. It is not sufficient for haughtiness because

---

[13] It goes without saying that not every angry response to a criticism is an expression of haughtiness.

[14] Roberts and Wood describe intellectual arrogance as an illicit inference that one is entitled to special epistemic treatment (2007, pp. 243–244). In my view this sense of being entitled is more characteristic of what I label as haughtiness than of arrogance proper. It may be that this dispute is purely semantic.

[15] Anger is not the preserve of the arrogant. It is also plausibly an important emotion to motivate those who are oppressed to resist their oppression. Anger can thus be an important weapon in the arsenal of the activist. For insightful discussions of the positive role of anger in promoting progressive change and of the personal costs it exacts, see Tessman (2005, pp. 116–125).

[16] To some extent whether belief in one's superiority is necessary for arrogance depends on the nature of belief. Those who are arrogant consistently behave in superior ways. This fact alone can be taken as sufficient evidence that they possess a dispositional belief that they are superior. This might be so. What I am highlighting is the fact that these people could deny that they think of themselves as superior; and these denials could be sincere. Thanks to Quassim Cassam for raising this point.

it is possible to have formed this judgment without thereby treating other people with contempt.[17] Some people are better than others at a number of intellectual endeavours: they may know more, understand some things better, have superior mathematical abilities, see answers to puzzles more quickly, or be more creative. One may be fully aware of one's talents, skills and achievements, believe that they are more significant than those of others around one, without feeling superior to them or wishing to put them in their place. It is even possible to hold a belief about one's intellectual superiority, be mistaken about it, and not be haughty. The person who is in error about his intellectual strengths may be making an honest mistake without thereby exhibiting haughty behaviour. For example, one may overestimate the significance of one's discovery which, in hindsight, may turn out not to have been the breakthrough one thought it was. The individual who makes such an error need not be haughty about his own successes.

A belief in one's intellectual superiority is also not necessary for haughtiness at least insofar as one could sincerely deny believing this and yet be haughty. One may feel superior without endorsing the thought that one is intellectually superior to most others. One may, for instance, studiously avoid considering whether one's feeling of superiority is warranted.[18] One may refrain from explicitly comparing oneself to some accomplished individuals; thus, failing to form any belief about one's ranking in relation to them. At the same time, a person who is haughty may instead compare himself for differences to other agents that are clearly less capable than he is. In sum, a person may have a 'high opinion' of himself and behave in superior ways without endorsing the view that he is superior to most other people. On the contrary, he may put effort in remaining ignorant of how he may be different from accomplished individuals.

I have noted that individuals who suffer from *superbia* are prone to anger.[19] This claim might be surprising since anger has often been associated with narcissism rather than with vices akin to arrogance (cf., Nussbaum, 2016; Stocker & Hegeman, 1996). This association is partly due to pervasive conflations between arrogance and narcissism in both the philosophical and psychological literature.[20] In order to see why this is a mistake it is useful to begin by noting that anger is a negative emotion directed towards a person for something that he has done which is perceived to be intentional and to have slighted oneself or someone whom one

---

[17] Roberts and Wood make the same point using as an example the case of an individual who is actually intellectually superior to other members of his epistemic community (2007, pp. 243–245).

[18] Possibly in order to avoid feeling guilty, it is not uncommon for those who are privileged to develop sensibilities that promote ignorance. I discussed this sensibility in Chapter 2 and I return to these issues in Chapter 7. The connection between privilege, arrogance, and active ignorance is also explored by Medina (2013, pp. 30–40).

[19] For a more extensive discussion of these points see Tanesini (2018a).

[20] In psychology, for example, defensive high self-esteem has been often associated with arrogant behaviours but also with narcissism (McGregor et al., 2005). There are reasons to doubt this association since evidence of defensiveness among the narcissists is inconclusive (Campbell & Foster, 2007).

holds dear. In addition, anger might also include a desire for retaliation.[21] It should not be surprising that individuals who are preoccupied with being able to feel superior to other people often feel slighted. Anytime they are treated in egalitarian ways, they are bound to experience this conduct as an affront since it denies them the special entitlements and status they arrogate for themselves. Hence, haughty individuals are prone to experience perfectly legitimate behaviour as insulting. In response they attempt to assert their superiority by trying to get even and diminish those whom they perceive as disrespectful. In short, haughty individuals are disposed to anger.

Narcissism is different from haughtiness because of its close connection with vanity. Haughty individuals wish to be superior to others. They are not particularly concerned with the regard in which they are held by them. Vain individuals, instead, want to be admired by other people. They are therefore less likely to try angrily to put people in their place since this behaviour is unlikely to attract the love and admiration craved by those who are vain. If, as I argue in Chapter 6, it is a deepening of vanity into a form of self-infatuation, narcissism is unlikely to manifest itself through anger.[22] On the contrary, one would expect those who are vain or narcissistic to experience spiteful envy for other people's successes. That said, it is possible that some people might be both haughty and vain. They might have a propensity to anger, but if what I have said so far is correct, this emotional reaction is an expression of their haughtiness rather than of their vanity.

The connection of haughtiness with anger is evidence of the defensive character of this vice. Aristotle notes that anger is an implicit acknowledgement of vulnerability to threats (*Rhetoric* 1379a 49–1379b 2, Aristotle, 2007, p. 119). In his view, anybody who responds angrily to behaviours that are dismissive of his qualities must be insecure as to whether these are genuinely excellent. Those whose self-esteem is secure are not thrown into doubt about their own worth by other people's insults. Hence, they can safely ignore offensive behaviour with magnanimity. Whilst I am doubtful of the view that anger is always an expression of insecurity, there are examples when anger is defensive precisely in these ways. In particular, in the absence of obvious and continuous hostility on the part of others, a tendency to be always on the verge of anger indicates defensive attitudes.

---

[21] Aristotle in the *Rhetoric* defines anger as a 'desire, accompanied by [mental and physical] distress, for apparent retaliation because of an apparent slight that was directed, without justification, against oneself or those near to one' (1378a 30–33, Aristotle, 2007, p. 116). Contra Aristotle, not all anger is vengeful. Sometimes the angry person might be seeking a simple apology. However, arrogant anger often seems vengeful.

[22] That said, narcissists might react in anger when all their attempts to be admired are frustrated. My point here is that anger is not their first and most frequent reaction to being challenged. This claim is controversial since some have claimed to have shown that narcissism is linked to aggressive behaviour in response to criticism (Bushman & Baumeister, 1998). In Chapter 6 I discuss the possibility that these results are a consequence of conflating narcissism and defensive or hubristic pride. The latter is what I call *superbia* and is the topic of this section.

These observations get to the core of the psychology of *superbia* and of the angry disposition that accompanies it. Anger in this instance is a defensive mechanism to protect one's own self-esteem from alleged threats. The haughty person is hyper-vigilant. She will perceive innocent behaviours as threatening because her self-esteem depends on sustaining the illusion of her superiority over other people. Being prone to anger is therefore a background disposition, an existential feeling (Ratcliffe, 2008), that colours every aspect of life.[23]

These considerations support the hypothesis that *superbia* is based on attitudes towards the self and components of one's cognitive make-up that are defensive. In particular they support the suggestion that the manifestations of *superbia* are expressions of attitudes to the self that are characteristic of defensive high self-esteem (Haddock & Gebauer, 2011).

This form of self-esteem is characteristic of individuals who have high explicit and low implicit self-esteem. In other words, they appear to have a high opinion of themselves as elicited from self-reports and responses to questionnaires, but their self-esteem is low as measured in tests of another sort: e.g., when asking participants how much they like their own names (cf. Chapter 3, Section 3.1.4).[24] These individuals display a tendency to possess attitudes about all kinds of objects and topics, such as the arrangement of furniture in one's office or climate change, which are strong in the sense of being easily accessible and that serve an ego-defensive function (Haddock & Gebauer, 2011, p. 1283).[25] In addition, there is evidence that they are particularly disposed to respond arrogantly to threats (McGregor et al., 2005); to boasting (Olson et al., 2007); to self-enhancing (Bosson et al., 2003); and to anger (Schröder-Abé et al., 2007a). They are more prejudiced towards members of other ethnic groups than people whose self-esteem is not discrepant (Jordan et al., 2005). They are hypervigilant to threats and have a propensity to perceive events as threatening. Thus, their defensiveness is always heightened (Haddock & Gebauer, 2011, p. 1280). These agents suffer from a fear of failure, as evinced by their low implicit self-esteem, to which they respond defensively through aggression and self-aggrandizement to boost their explicit self-esteem.

These are all features that are plausibly typified as characteristic expressions of arrogance and haughtiness. Intellectual arrogance, and haughtiness, are thus plausibly caused by defensive self-esteem and its associated clusters of highly

---

[23] This emotional dimension is missing in those who might superficially appear arrogant but who in reality behave arrogantly to give themselves courage or to suppress feelings of shame.

[24] There are different implicit measures of self-esteem and these are poorly correlated (Bosson et al., 2000). It should not be assumed that explicit and implicit measures measure different constructs, instead, the discrepancies may be due to reporting tendencies. Some individuals with low self-esteem may wish to present themselves as self-confident, thus measuring high in self-esteem as measured explicitly (cf. Olson et al., 2007).

[25] This conclusion is somewhat controversial as others have claimed that attitude accessibility is a moderator of implicit and explicit self-esteem correspondence (LeBel, 2010). That is to say, attitudes towards the worth of the self which show little discrepancy between implicit or explicit measures would be more accessible.

accessible (that is, strong) positive explicitly measured attitudes directed towards aspects of one's own cognitive make-up such as one's skills, habits, faculties, and views. In short, these are attitudes towards the self and its components, evaluating them for their intellectual worth. These positive explicitly measured attitudes of favouring, and feeling good about, aspects of oneself have been formed and maintained because they satisfy the need to protect the self against perceived threats. The person who possesses this range of attitudes will, therefore, like those aspects of his cognitive make-up which are efficient at repulsing threats and inflating his self-esteem. Intellectual arrogance is, in other words, a sort of fight response to perceived threats.[26]

A positive explicitly measured attitude towards the self (high explicit self-esteem) would be only one component of a larger cluster of strong attitudes, together with their informational bases, that take as their objects aspects of one's cognitive make-up. Intellectual arrogance and haughtiness are best understood as being based on the whole cluster rather than solely on attitudes towards the self, since it is entirely possible for an individual to be arrogant about some of their abilities without being arrogant about others. It is also possible, however, that attitudes towards the self play a crucial role in the formation and maintenance of the cluster. For instance, low implicitly measured self-esteem could be the initial root of the development of strong defensive attitudes about various objects and ultimately lead to the formation of positive explicitly measured attitudes directed at the self and the components of one's cognitive make-up.

Low implicit self-esteem would give rise to mostly negative behavioural reactions in a range of ordinary situations in which one's intellectual worth is salient. These avoidant behaviours are uncomfortable and thus the subject attempts to avoid their occurrence by adopting a range of strategies designed to make them less frequent.[27] One avoidance strategy is aggressive defence. The subject may be hostile to what he perceives to be the sources of threats and may seek to neutralize the alleged threat by way of attack or dismissal. The subject may also develop a strong preference for what makes him feel good about himself and thus counteracts the negative reaction.[28]

The account of *superbia* as based on a cluster of highly accessible defensive attitudes, and their informational bases, directed to the self and towards components of one's cognitive make-up can explain why the behavioural and affective manifestations of this vice cluster together. They are all expressions of a fight

---

[26] It should be noted that according to self-affirmation theory the threats need not be perceived as threats to one's intellectual worth. There is robust evidence that defence responses that boost self-esteem are effective even when they compensate for the threat by boosting an unrelated aspect of one's self-concept (Watt et al., 2008, p. 204).

[27] This kind of discomfort need not be accessible to consciousness or it may be experienced as a vague sense of uneasiness.

[28] These are very tentative speculations as attitudes towards the self are still not very well understood.

response initiated by hypersensitivity to threats that is caused by a fragile sense of self-worth or esteem.

Another advantage of the account is its ability to explain the close connections of haughtiness or *superbia* to closed-mindedness, dogmatism, and active ignorance. Individuals who have high defensive self-esteem tend to overestimate the degree to which others agree with them (McGregor et al., 2005). They thus are unlikely to notice the availability of points of view alternative to their own. Further, these individuals are high in attitude certainty (McGregor & Marigold, 2003). They are certain about the correctness of their views, and are confident that they know what they think. Those who are certain of their attitudes are more likely to pay attention only to evidence that supports their pre-existing views (Brannon et al., 2007). They, thus are likely to be closed-minded. There are also suggestive results that discrepant self-esteem might be predictive of a high dispositional need for cognitive closure (Jost et al., 2003). If this is right, this motivational disposition, combined with the high confidence in one's abilities to achieve closure that one would expect of people that display high defensive self-esteem, should result in the dogmatic resistance to new counterevidence associated with the freezing tendencies characteristic of this thinking style (Kruglanski et al., 1993). In addition, there is also evidence that defensive attitudes in general are fairly resistant to rational persuasion since defensiveness biases one's processing of information (Sherman & Cohen, 2002). Finally, individuals whose high self-esteem is defensive are prone to compensatory or hardened and extreme convictions because they form certainties in order to banish unwanted realizations (McGregor & Marigold, 2003). In short, they have an uncanny ability not to notice inconvenient truths, thanks to their wilfully ignorant sensibility.

These characteristic ways of thinking are what we would expect if these individuals form evaluations, including self-evaluations, that are shaped by the motivation to defend the ego against threats. This motivation induces them implicitly to formulate directed questions that they use to select the information that they take to be pertinent to the evaluation of target objects. In addition, because of the higher risks associated by mistaking a threat for something unthreatening, these individuals are disposed to appraise negatively positions opposed to their own. One would also expect them to form positive opinions of their own abilities since the hardening of one's own views into certainties also promotes self-certainties (Clarkson et al., 2009).

To summarize, there is a growing body of empirical literature on defensive attitudes and defensive self-esteem that shows these psychological states to be predictive of those behaviours and emotions that I have independently characterized as being typical of *superbia*. Identifying attitudes as the causal bases of these manifestations of haughtiness provides insights into the ways in which this trait promotes the development of epistemically harmful dispositions to dogmatism, closed-mindedness, and studied ignorance. It also throws light on the links between *superbia* and its emotional manifestations that include anger, hubristic pride, and epistemic feelings of certainty and self-certainty.

5.2 Intellectual Arrogance

There is a version of arrogance whose signature overlaps with superbia but also partly differs from it. This kind of arrogance manifests itself as an extreme form of self-reliance which is best described as hyper-autonomy (Roberts & Wood, 2007, p. 236). It is the kind of arrogance that is characteristic of those who behave as if they are totally epistemically self-reliant and as if they have no intellectually debts towards anybody else. Those who are arrogant in this way display the coolness and fearlessness typical of individuals who think of themselves as being so powerful to be invulnerable to threats. This is the kind of arrogance that was exhibited by those bankers who, prior to the financial crisis of 2008, gambled with, and lost, other people's money. Arrogant individuals might be less likely to boast shamelessly than people who suffer from *superbia* since they consider themselves to be so far removed from the common folk that they would find such behaviour to be undignified. They are also less prone to anger, and are more disposed to experience contempt and thus to withdraw from those one judges to be below oneself (Bell, 2013, p. 44). Some aspects of the character of Mr Darcy in Austen's *Pride and Prejudice* exemplify this sort of arrogance.

I think of arrogance as a deepening or exacerbation of tendencies that are already found in *superbia*. The person who is haughty feels that he is superior to other people, but the arrogant person feels that he is the standard by which worth is measured. That is, those who are haughty feel that they are better than other people because they possess independently valuable features. Those who are arrogant measure the value of people's qualities by reference to whether it is a property they share. There is a sense in which the arrogant thinks of himself as the measure of all things. A similar phenomenon has been described by Spelman (1990) and Lugones (2003) as 'boomerang vision' and consists in taking oneself as the standard by which others' worth is to be measured. It is sadly taught from a young age. Hence, white children are told that black people are okay because they are just like them. However, these white children never hear it said that they must be okay, because they are just like black people.

Supremely arrogant people take this attitude one step further and behave as if they think that things must be as they say simply because of their saying so. In other words, arrogant individuals behave as if the world must adjust to their views, rather than the other way around.[29] Of course, I am not suggesting that they

---

[29] Frye (1983) characterizes the vision of the arrogant eye in similar terms. I have argued elsewhere that the arrogant when purporting to be making an assertion does not take himself to be committed to

literally believe this since to do so would be pathological. Nevertheless, arrogant people think of their opinions as not being open to question. It is this denial of answerability to the facts that I want to convey when I say that arrogant individuals take themselves to be the measure of all things.

So understood two features crystallize intellectual arrogance: an attitude of complete self-reliance which leads one to distrust other epistemic agents;[30] and an implicit conviction that one is the measure of epistemic value so that the mere fact that they belong to one would confer additional epistemic value to one's beliefs and cognitive faculties. Thus, instead of measuring his personal intellectual worth in accordance with the epistemic value that accrues to components of his cognitive make up, the arrogant person concludes that a skill, an ability, or belief must be valuable because he exhibits it. Hence, as Lynch notes, the epistemically arrogant person thinks that his views cannot be improved upon (Lynch, 2018).

Arrogance and haughtiness are thus distinct although in practice they may often be found together. It seems plausible to think of haughtiness as a route to full blown arrogance so that the second is a deepening or an exacerbation of some of the features of the first. The person who is haughty tries to safeguard his high self-esteem by ignoring or dismissing others whom he perceives as an actual or potential threat. The person who is arrogant has become even more insulated from possible criticisms because he has developed a stance of total self-reliance. Since he thinks and feels that he does not owe any intellectual debt to anybody, and since he strives to secure that others' views make no impact on his opinions and emotions, the arrogant individual has found a more extreme way of neutralizing any possible threats to his self-esteem. Because nothing others may say can count as evidence which provides rational pressure to update his own high opinion of himself, his positive stance towards his own cognitive make-up, in so far as he succeeds in being arrogant, becomes totally invulnerable to any considerations based on the beliefs of other agents that would force a downward revision.[31] In his aloofness the arrogant person, unlike the haughty one, is no longer concerned with how he may compare with other epistemic agents.[32]

Like haughtiness, arrogance is not to be identified with beliefs in one's superior or excellent intellectual qualities since humble individuals may possess these beliefs (see Chapter 4). The arrogant person, and the haughty individual, take delight in their achievements but this fact alone does not define them. What is distinctive about these people is the character of their self-evaluations. They take

---

having the required epistemic standing vis-à-vis the asserted proposition. Rather he presumes that his preparedness to assert secures that he has such epistemic standing (Tanesini, 2016a).

[30] Zagzebski (2012, pp. 58–60; 2015, pp. 217–219) describes this tendency as egoism in the realm of the intellect.

[31] This failure to encounter any resistance is a serious obstacle to the acquisition of knowledge (cf., Medina, 2013, p. 32).

[32] I owe the idea that there are two kinds of arrogance to Dillon (2004, 2007).

pleasure in their intellectual strengths because they make them feel good about themselves and thus increase their self-confidence. Thus, they are not delighted because of the epistemic worth of their strengths and achievements; rather what delights them is that these epistemically valuable qualities belong to them. In particular, haughty and arrogant individuals have positive evaluations of those aspects of their intellectual characters that boost their self-esteem and which protect it from any perceived threats. Thus, these individuals use their self-confidence as a defence shield to protect their self-esteem. This appears to be true in the case of arrogance also, since aloofness and contemptuous withdrawal are defensive strategies.

The self-protective character of aloofness and of acting entitled is best illustrated by self-sabotage. This is a strategy used to preserve self-confidence in one's abilities in the face of a potential failure showing that one is less talented than one thinks. In these circumstances individuals with a high sense of entitlement engage in behaviour that undermines their chances of success. For them, not appearing to practice or put any effort seems to be as important as achieving their goal. In truth, this seemingly bizarre tactic is an excellent way of preserving self-esteem since success is evidence of ability, whilst failure can be explained away by lack of application rather than inability or poor skill. There is evidence that individuals who have high defensive self-esteem engage in this type of behaviour (Lupien et al., 2010). This result strengthens the plausibility of my view that intellectual arrogance, like *superbia*, should be identified with high defensive self-esteem. Arrogance would differ from *superbia* in feigning invulnerability as a defence tactic by adopting strategies such as self-sabotaging that insulate one from evidence about one's true qualities.

Intellectual arrogance would thus be based on clusters of defensive attitudes which overlap with those that are responsible for haughtiness. These attitudes, however, would not be exactly the same. The beliefs, dispositions, and affects that figure in the informational contents on which attitudes are based are likely to be somewhat different. These contents as well as informing the attitude are among the causes of behaviour so that two individuals, even though they share the same attitude with the same function, may act differently in the same situation when the contents of their attitudes are different (Maio & Olson, 2000a). It is plausible that in the case of haughty individuals, social comparison judgments play a more important role in attitude preservation than they do for arrogant people. In practice, this claim is hard to substantiate fully since most people who are arrogant are likely to also display haughty tendencies.

As I mentioned in Chapter 4 when people form evaluative beliefs about their abilities, including intellectual abilities, they tend not to judge these by reference to objective standards. Instead, they gauge them by comparing themselves with others (Mussweiler, 2020). These comparisons can be motivated by the desire to have an accurate assessment of one's capacities; by the desire to improve, or finally by the need to enhance self-esteem (Corcoran et al., 2011).[33] Those whose comparisons are driven by self-enhancement tend to compare themselves downward for differences and upward for assimilation. Thus, when they compare themselves to accomplished individuals, they seek to confirm the hypothesis that they are similar to them. However, they mostly compare themselves downward to confirm the proposition that they are better than the people in question (Vohs & Heatherton, 2001).[34] Either way individuals who base their evaluations of their own abilities on social comparisons driven by the self-enhancement motive end up with a distorted estimate of their abilities that promotes an unwarranted high opinion of oneself. This dynamic captures what I discussed in Section 5.1 when I explained the feelings of superiority of haughty individuals.

In addition to the empirical evidence that these downward comparisons are characteristic of those with high defensive self-esteem (Vohs & Heatherton, 2001, 2004), there are results showing that individuals whose self-esteem is defensive engage in malicious (aggressive) envy, wishing the fall and failure of other individuals whom one judges to be better than oneself (Smallets et al., 2016).[35] These findings provide further support for the claim defended here that *superbia* as a feeling of superiority and entitlement combined with a propensity to do other people down is best understood as an expression of attitudes of defensive self-esteem based on social comparison judgments. There is also evidence in favour of social comparison as a route from haughtiness to arrogance as hyper-autonomy. Individuals possessing high self-esteem and responding to threat situations by making downward social comparisons, rate—after the comparison—themselves more highly in independence and become especially alert and sensitive to their own successes, abilities, and traits (Vohs & Heatherton, 2004).

Intellectual arrogance shares many of the epistemically harmful features of *superbia* since it brings dogmatism, ignorance, and closed-mindedness in its trail. But it is likely to promote additional vices. These include intellectual laziness born of the opinion that one's position needs no improvement (Medina, 2013, p. 32). Importantly, several of these vices concern the treatment of other epistemic agents in the community. Those who are intellectual arrogant are not team players. Because they think that they owe nothing to others, they are unlikely to be generous about other people's contributions to shared successes. In short,

---

[33] In Chapter 4 I have noted that humble and proud individuals engage in social comparisons motivated by the needs for accuracy and self-improvement.
[34] The motivation to defend the self against threats to its self-worth would explain these patterns. But see Wheeler and Suls (2020, pp. 14–16) for scepticism about downward comparisons as a response to threats.
[35] In Chapter 6 I argue that spiteful envy is characteristic of vanity. Both spiteful and aggressive envy are malicious. Aggressive envy that is a manifestation of arrogance and especially of *superbia* seeks to deprive others of the envied good, spiteful envy that is characteristic of vanity and narcissism seeks to spoil the envied good when one judges it to be unattainable (Protasi, 2016).

intellectual arrogant individuals are likely to inflict significant and pervasive epistemic harms on others (see Chapter 7).

Recently, Dillon (forthcoming) has argued that in conditions of oppression arrogance is a virtue because it contributes to asserting self-respect. Dillon acknowledges that women and members of others subordinate groups are labelled 'arrogant' or 'uppity' for behaviours that are merely assertive and self-respecting. These same behaviours are admired in members of dominant groups. However, she also claims that there are cases when subordinated individuals have an arrogant sense of entitlement. She defines this kind of arrogance as 'unwarranted claims arrogance' that she characterizes as a disposition to arrogate things of worth for oneself in the service of self-enhancement (Dillon, forthcoming, p. 8). Dillon illustrates virtuous arrogance with examples of subordinated individuals who defy the legitimacy of authority. In particular, Dillon mentions Antigone's violation of Creon's edict by burying the body of her brother and Sethe's (the protagonist of Toni Morrison's *Beloved*) murder of her baby daughter to spare her from the ordeal of slavery. Dillon thinks that these actions are expressive of hubris, and are therefore arrogant. Nevertheless, she also think that they are manifestations of self-respect. She concludes that in these instances arrogance is virtuous.

Dillon's characterization of these behaviours as manifestations of hubris is, in my view, mistaken. It is true that such conduct is often interpreted in this way by dominant society. But, as Dillon also notes, subordinated individuals are often misdescribed as arrogant when they resist subordination by 'usurping' the roles traditionally assigned to members of dominant groups. Thus, the verdicts of majorities does not by themselves determine whether Sethe and Antigone suffer from hubris or instantiate the virtue of pride. Further, the motives that move Sethe and Antigone to act as they do are not related to self-esteem or self-enhancement, which Dillon originally identified as essential to unwarranted claims arrogance. If this is right, these are not examples of virtuous arrogance. Instead, one might think of these as instances of proud behaviour.

5.3 Intellectual Servility or Obsequiousness

In this section I offer an account of the first of the vices of inferiority that I discuss in this book. Intellectual servility or obsequiousness is best thought of as manifested in persistent feelings of inferiority accompanied by a desire to ingratiate oneself to powerful individuals.[36]

The individual who behaves in an intellectually servile manner is exceedingly deferential to, and unduly influenced by, the views expressed by others. He adopts

---

[36] I have also addressed these issues in Tanesini (2018e). A few paragraphs in this section are borrowed with light revisions from this article.

this position either because he feels intellectually inferior or because he consciously thinks that adopting an obsequious stance is an effective strategy to obtain what he wants given his circumstances. If the former is true, the person who is servile shows thereby a lack of pride. For this reason, servility could be thought as the vice of inferiority that opposes haughtiness or *superbia* as the vice of hubristic pride. If the latter, we may say that the person acts in a servile way out of expediency without being servile.[37]

Intellectually servile individuals tend to belittle their own abilities. They attribute any success, achievement, or strength of theirs either to a stroke of good luck or to the easiness of the task at hand. They consider any failure or weakness to be a consequence of their limitations, and lack of skill. This tendency to attribute failures to unchangeable features of the self, and success to external circumstances is referred by psychologists as depressive attributional style and its close association to low self-esteem is well-established (Schröder-Abé et al., 2007a).

These negative evaluations of one's own talents and abilities are partly the result of frequent experiences of episodic shame because of one's alleged inadequacy. One of the most telling features of intellectual servility is the development of a persistent sense of shame for who one is. Whilst shame is an episodic emotion, shame-proneness is a trait. It is this latter that is characteristic of servility, the emotion is instead also a feature of the affective life of those who possess the intellectual virtue of pride.

Episodic shame is a negative global emotion of self-assessment. It is negative because it is painful. It is global because it is focused on who one is, rather than what one has done. It conveys an assessment of the self as having failed to meet some standards, where that failure reflects poorly on the worth of the self (Deonna et al., 2011; Dolezal, 2015; Galligan, 2016). Whether the standards that the shamed subject fails to meet are set by the individual herself or by her society is a matter of some controversy (cf. Galligan, 2016). Those who are impressed by the power of shame to motivate moral correction focus on the connection between shame and the desire to live up to one's principles (Taylor, 1985). Others see shame as derivative of a more primitive emotion promoting submissive behaviour in a social hierarchy (Maibom, 2010).

Two considerations provide some evidence that shame can be experienced as a response to a failure to meet standards set by others. First, publicity worsen feelings of shame which in turn motivate behaviours to avoid it. Hence, when ashamed, people wish to hide, run away or cover themselves up. Second, it is possible to feel ashamed for not meeting standards that one does not endorse. Thus, a man who sees nothing wrong with crying in public, might nonetheless be

---

[37] For example, domestic servants often feigned stupidity and servility as an effective strategy of resistance. Employers would speak freely in their presence presuming that the servants would be unable or unwilling to exploit those words to their advantage (cf. Collins, 1991, pp. 55–58; 91–93).

ashamed of appearing emotional. These observations do not establish that the standards whose failure to meet trigger shame are always set by one's group. It seems possible to be ashamed in private for having failed to meet standards that one has set, even though they are not endorsed by one's group. These contradicting considerations can be reconciled if we distinguish circumstances in which shame is fitting from circumstances when it is not.[38] It would seem that the kind of shame that is an occasion to recommit to one's ideals can be both fitting and a warranted response. Shame in these circumstances is a salutary emotion that is compatible with virtuous pride.[39] Episodes of shame in response to behaviours who are designed to shame the individual are, on the other hand, often not fitting.

Shame-proneness is not fitting since this is the disposition to feel acutely ashamed in circumstances that only warrant slight shame (Deonna et al., 2011, pp. 165–168).[40] It is also a chronic disposition to be hypervigilant to possible occasions for shame in one's environment. Further, when the environment is often hostile, the shame-prone individual frequently experiences shame. Irrespective of whether these episodes of shame are fitting, there are reasons to think that feeling this way is to be resisted because of its damaging effects on people's wellbeing.

Feminist philosophers and race theorists have often pointed out that the chronic sense of shame that is characteristic of intellectual servility results from being the target of repeated episodes of shaming and humiliating treatment (Card, 1996; Césaire, 1972; Fanon, 1986; Tessman, 2005).[41] The effects of these experiences are recorded by W. E. B. Du Bois as inducing a 'sense of always looking at one's self through the eyes of others' (1990, p. 8). Du Bois notes that this experience generates something akin to a double-consciousness. On the one hand one sees oneself through one's own eyes measuring oneself by standards one endorses. On the other hand, one sees oneself through 'the revelation of the other world'. One thus finds in oneself 'two warring ideals in one dark body' (Du Bois, 1990, pp. 8–9).

Ingratiation as a family of tactics designed to gain the approval of those who hold power over a person is a common response to being shamed or humiliated by others who hold one in low regard. Even though one might respond in anger to the perceived insult, servile individuals often react to degrading treatment by enhancing those who treat them badly.[42] It is the response of the so-called

---

[38] Shame is fitting when the circumstances are actually shameful.
[39] See Deonna et al. (2011) and Kristjánsson (2014) on this positive face of shame.
[40] Intellectually servile individuals therefore experience a kind of shame which is frequently not fitting. It is thus a wholly negative emotion. The negativity of shame-proneness is acknowledged even by those who think that shame can be an incentive to self-improvement (cf. Deonna et al., 2011, pp. 165–168). See Dolezal (2015) on the distinction between chronic and acute shame.
[41] I return to these themes in Chapter 7.
[42] In social psychology ingratiation is thought as a form of impression management through benign and obsequious behaviour designed to gain social acceptance. Individuals, especially those suffering

'Uncle Tom'. The person who is intellectually servile is the individual who responds to those who hold him in low esteem with behaviours seeking their acceptance. He defers to their views and accepts for himself the negative estimate that they possess of his intellectual skills and abilities in the hope that, because of his compliance, they will come to like him. He might at the same time feel as if he could explode with anger.[43]

The shame proneness and ingratiating tendencies that are coping strategies in response to shaming and degrading treatment are deeply connected with feelings of inferiority, low self-esteem, and negative evaluations of one's intellectual abilities that are characteristic of those who are intellectually servile. These features also explain some of the other manifestations of servility such as the conformist tendency to parrot the views of the majority, or to agree with the opinions of whoever holds power on a given occasion. The habituated tendency to respond to shaming with shame also explains why those who are intellectually servile come to submit or even accept disrespectful behaviour as if it befitted their lack of merit.

It would be a mistake to identify intellectual servility with belief in one's intellectual inferiority.[44] This belief is neither sufficient nor necessary for servility, although it is commonly associated with it. Servility is a matter of feeling inferior and having a deprecating or negative estimation of one's own personal intellectual worth. This estimate however is an affective, rather than an exclusively doxastic, stance. Thinking of oneself as intellectually inferior to others is not sufficient for servility because one may have these thoughts about oneself without thereby humiliating oneself in front of them or seeking to be in their good books. Instead, one may have developed an honest assessment of the qualities of one's own intellectual character.[45] It is also not necessary since it seem possible for a person to be aware that one is intellectually equal to many other intellectual agents and yet be unable to shake off the sense that one is inadequate. In the same way in

---

from low self-esteem, often respond to insults or rejection not with overt anger and aggression but with behaviour that seeks the approval of those who have rejected them. For the connections between ingratiation, social acceptance, and self-esteem see, Wu et al. (2011) and Romero-Canyas et al. (2010).

[43] The overt expression of anger might therefore be instrumental in the fight against discrimination because it sustains a motivation to resist. Thus, anger might be a virtue in circumstances of oppression. It is however a virtue that is burdensome since it damages the well-being of those that are prone to it. On this kind of anger see Tessman (2005, pp. 116–125).

[44] I thus disagree with Whitcomb et al.'s (2017) identification of servility with the underestimation of one's intellectual abilities. Spinoza's accounts of humility and abjection as sad passions also bears a close similarity to my views on servility and self-abasement but differs from them in this regard. See *Ethics* (1985), EIIIP55S; EIIIDefAffXXIX; EIIIDefAffXXIXExp.

[45] This may sound counterintuitive because we tend to believe that no person is worse than everybody else at absolutely everything. Instead, we think that everyone is better than someone else at something. But the point stands, a person could have limited intellectual abilities, be aware of the fact, without becoming obsequious. The same person could also accept these features of his intellectual character without belittling himself in self-abasement.

which one may feel superior without judging oneself to be such, one may feel inferior even when one knows that one is not.[46] It might simply prove impossible to shake off the anxious thought that one might be less able, skilful, or talented than other epistemic agents.[47]

The behavioural, affective, and doxastic manifestations of servility are what one would predict if these were the consequence of negative self-evaluations, based on social comparisons, motivated by the need for social acceptance. For those for whom preserving social bonds is an extremely important aim, inclusion as a low status group member is preferable to social exclusion. The motive of social acceptance biases how these individuals evaluate themselves. Thus, these people assess their personal qualities for their effectiveness in fostering social bonds, rather than—for instance—in gaining knowledge of the social environment.[48] One way of promoting good social relations is to enhance the self-esteem of prominent members of one's elective social group by communicating one's favourable opinion of their abilities. A particularly effective way of doing this is by making other people feel superior to oneself (Vohs & Heatherton, 2004); another is to underperform so that they can excel in comparison (White et al., 2002). Thus, portraying oneself as inferior to others is an effective strategy of gaining their social acceptance. One would expect this strategy to be particularly effective when social groups include individuals who display the trademarks of *superbia*.

It is likely that initially such ingratiating behaviour does not reflect one's beliefs. It might be a strategy that a child picks up from the behaviour of the adults belonging to the same stigmatized group as himself. Alternatively, it might be something a person hits upon by chance or trial and error, but that becomes ingrained because of its effectiveness in gaining a modicum of social acceptance. However, as the research on cognitive dissonance illustrates, over time one's attitudes often tend to become consistent with one's behaviour. Thus, the person who initially only behaved in inferior ways may eventually evaluate himself as inferior and thus form negative attitudes towards his intellectual qualities.[49]

In short, individuals, who are likely to suffer from discrimination, if they want to belong to the social group that rejects them, respond to the risk of exclusion by engaging in ingratiating behaviour. Over time, partly because of cognitive dissonance, these individuals develop some negative evaluations of their abilities.[50] In

---

[46] And the same issues related to the nature of belief are pertinent here. See note 172.

[47] Bartky (1990, p. 93) observes a similar phenomenon among some of her female students.

[48] The motive of social acceptance shapes both the selection of the evidence relevant to the evaluation and the asymmetric thresholds of evidence required to reach a conclusion.

[49] For a review of the literature on cognitive dissonance see Cooper (2008). In the cases under consideration agents try to avoid having to think of themselves as liars and deceivers. It is this threat to the concept of oneself as honest that over time produces the conformity of attitudes to behaviour (cf. Wood, 2000, p. 546). My thanks to Jonathan Webber for pressing this point.

[50] Another factor promoting low self-evaluation is the conformism of the ingratiator. Since those who ingratiate also come to share the views of those whose favour they seek, they develop a low estimation of their abilities if that is the opinion of those they are trying to ingratiate.

addition, they compare themselves negatively with other people and thus suffer from feelings of inferiority. Hence, one would expect members of stigmatized groups to be at risk of developing low self-esteem (negative attitudes towards oneself) as a result of trying to satisfy their need for social acceptance.[51] Unfortunately, these negative attitudes serving a social-adjustive function generate a vicious circle of further negative comparisons with others' abilities and a consequent lowering of self-esteem.

Du Bois' observations about a divided consciousness including two warring factions that threaten to tear one apart suggest that servile individuals might be those whose self-esteem is said to be damaged (Schröder-Abé et al., 2007a). These persons typically exhibit a discrepancy between measures of self-esteem in the opposite direction of that recorded in individuals whose high self-opinion is defensive. Individuals whose self-esteem is damaged possess high self-esteem as measured implicitly but are low in explicit self-esteem. Several of the features characteristic of this group are those one would expect in servile individuals. They have a depressive attributional style (Schröder-Abé et al., 2007a, p. 330; Vater et al., 2010); they exhibit heightened nervousness or anxiety (Schröder-Abé et al., 2007a, p. 331); they report the highest levels of suppressed anger (Schröder-Abé et al., 2007a, p. 327); and lack self-confidence as expressed in controlled behaviour (Rudolph et al., 2010).[52]

Haughtiness and servility are based on attitudes informed by social comparison judgments. However, when under threat people with high explicit self-esteem engage, as I mentioned above, in downward comparison, whilst those with low explicit self-esteem engage in upward ones. Thus they judge people to be better than they are (Vohs & Heatherton, 2004, p. 178). This response would be maladaptive if it served the need to defend the ego, since it fails to enhance self-esteem. This strategy, which is essentially an other-enhancing ingratiation strategy, makes sense if it serves the need to secure social bonds (Vohs & Heatherton, 2004, p. 171). Low explicit self-esteem individuals who ingratiate also tend to express higher levels of conformity with the views of the group whose acceptance they seek (Romero-Canyas et al., 2010, p. 803). Individuals who often check that their attitudes match social expectations are usually labelled high self-monitors (Snyder, 1974). These people tend to form attitudes fulfilling the need to foster social bonds (Watt et al., 2008). Their attitudes fit their social contexts and thus display high levels of conformism. In addition, these individuals

---

[51] Some of the literature on this topic treats ingratiation as a response to a threat directed at the self and thus as a way of defending the ego. I presume that they conceive of it in this way because social exclusion is thought to be a threat to the self. Nevertheless, it would seem that whatever their ultimate motive may be, the actions of these people are guided by a proximate motive of seeking social acceptance.

[52] These behaviours are treated in this literature as expressive of modesty, leading psychologists to conclude that modesty is not a wholly positive feature (Schröder-Abé et al., 2007a, p. 322). In my view this is a mistake. These behaviours are the manifestation of servility.

conceive of themselves as more interdependent after they ingratiate; they also show deeper appreciation of others' successes and are more liked by other people in return (Vohs & Heatherton, 2004). These observations further confirm the hypothesis that such individuals have attitudes towards the self serving social-adjustive needs. The motivation of social adjustment explains why some people develop servility in response to being held in low regard whilst others reject society's judgment.

These individuals pay a price for their tendency to compare themselves negatively to others when their self-esteem is under threat. The threats that instigate downward comparisons impact negatively on explicit self-esteem, while the comparisons fail to restore it to pre-threat levels.[53] Therefore, these people may be caught in a downward spiral when facing repeated threats since every threat compromises their explicit self-esteem and their responses fail to provoke a rebound (Vohs & Heatherton, 2004). These individuals are therefore subject to increasing self-doubt and engage in behaviours that are confidence sapping and anxiety inducing. These studies all lend support to the conclusion that the manifestations of intellectual servility (low self-esteem, feelings of inferiority, intellectual conformism, ingratiating behaviours) are based on negative attitudes to the self (low self-esteem) which serve the need to foster social bonds.

5.4 Self-Abasement or Self-Humiliation

Obsequiousness can also develop into the deeper vice of self-abasement.[54] When this happens a person turns onto oneself the humiliating viewpoint that the servile attempts to deflect through ingratiation. I refer to such an individual as self-abasing. He is the person who has come to belittle himself, and thinks that he has no intellectual strengths. So understood self-abasement is an exacerbation of servility since the person who humiliates himself has learnt to find comfort in thinking of himself as intellectually worthless.

Self-abasement is also a kind of heteronomy of the intellect. For this reason, it is the opposite of arrogance understood as hyper-autonomy and excessive self-reliance. The individual who belittles his own ability is not intellectually autonomous. He does not give sufficient weight to his own views; he is likely to accept without questioning what others believe. He has a heteronomous intellect because

---

[53] Paul Bloomfield has raised the question of impacts on self-esteem as measured implicitly. It seems not affected by these comparisons. I am not aware of psychological research that specifically answers this question.

[54] I borrow the term from Wollstonecraft who uses it in the *Vindication of the Rights of Woman* (1792) to refer to self-humiliation and debasement (Wollstonecraft, 1992, p. 231). Thanks to Paul Bloomfield for alerting me to the existence of this passage.

his deliberations often consist in trying to find out what others think and uncritically to second it.[55]

Obsequiousness and self-abasement are similar in their manifestations. Both are characterized by attitudes of deference and tendencies to ingratiate others by boosting the ego of those who hold positions of power. In both cases, individuals live with a perpetual sense of shame. This propensity to shame is not to be understood as mere persistence of episodic emotions of shame. Rather, shame is a kind of affective sensibility. It is a disposition to scan one's environment for shame related risks. These individuals are extremely sensitive to shaming opportunities in a way that is related to the hypervigilance to ego threats of those who are haughty.

There might, however, also be differences in the manifestations of servility and self-abasement. I take it that ritual self-humiliation is the trademark of the self-abasing individual. Bartky describes that self-abasing behaviours were common among women in a course she taught. The students were experienced teachers taking a professional development class. Yet when submitting assignments each declared aloud that she was ashamed of her piece of work (Bartky, 1990, p. 89). A similar approach is adopted by those who preface their interventions in discussions with self-undermining qualifications suggesting that their questions might be naïve or stupid or betraying a misunderstanding of these issues. These are strategies to diminish the self; they appear to be adopted to inspire pity and thus to pre-empt the humiliation that one fully expect to be otherwise forthcoming.

In this regard self-abasement is the opposite of narcissism. Both the narcissist and the self-abased make their self-esteem wholly dependent on imagining others' attitudes towards the self. Narcissists are charming because they wish to be admired. They expect to be the target of approving looks because they believe that they are special. Individuals who are self-abasing think of others as disapproving of the self. They think of themselves as deserving of this alleged negative evaluation that consequently they turn onto themselves.

I have described the intellectually servile individual as possessing a kind of double consciousness. He holds himself in low regard but he has hidden reserves of strength as revealed by his high, implicitly measured, self-esteem. These resources offer the possibility for a revaluation of the self in a more positive direction. They offer opportunities for learning to become proud of one's successes.[56] Self-abasement is the character vice that pertains to those who do not have such hidden resources. If this is right, self-abasement like servility is based on negative

---

[55] See Zagzebski (2012, pp. 24–25) for a discussion of heteronomy in belief formation.
[56] For this reason damaged self-esteem has also been described as being more responsive to both positive and negative feedback and thus to being less stable than congruent low self-esteem (Jordan et al., 2013).

attitudes towards the self and towards aspects of one's cognitive character serving social-adjustive functions. However, whilst the high self-esteem that is recorded by implicit measures offers, in the case of obsequiousness, a glimmer of hope for developing a more positive assessment of the self. This might be missing in individuals whose low self-esteem is congruent. These individuals lack the internal conflict that is characteristic of those whose self-esteem is damaged and thus might report higher levels of well-being (Jordan et al., 2013). These considerations suggest that effective interventions to bolster self-confidence in those who are self-abasing might be harder to design. Hence, this vice is deeper than servility also because it might prove more difficult to dislodge.

In this chapter I offered accounts of the four vices that are opposed to intellectual modesty and to intellectual pride. Two are vices of superiority characterized by an unwarranted sense of entitlement, feelings of superiority, hubristic pride, anger, defensiveness, and hyper-autonomy. Haughty and arrogant individuals assess their personal qualities not for their intellectual worth, but for their role in protecting the ego against real or imagined threats. Hence, their self-evaluations are not based on the motivation to know one's strengths and weaknesses. Instead, they assess their properties purely as means to boosting self-esteem. Servility and self-abasement are vices of inferiority typified by unwarranted deference, feelings of inadequacy, shame-proneness, ingratiation, and heteronomy. People who are servile or self-abasing appraise their features not for their intellectual worth, but for their effectiveness in securing social acceptance and deflecting threats of social exclusion. Like their domineering counterparts, these individuals are not motivated to understand themselves; they are instead prepared to compromise their self-esteem in order to get along with others.

6
Vanity, Narcissism, Timidity, and Fatalism

This chapter is dedicated to those vices that oppose acceptance of one's own limitations and proper concern for being esteemed by other members of the epistemic community. These are: intellectual vanity, narcissism, intellectual timidity, and fatalism about one's alleged intellectual limitations. Vanity is characteristic of those who show an excessive concern for being held in high esteem by other people, especially by those who occupy high-ranking positions within the epistemic community. Timidity is instead exemplified by those whose fear to be exposed as intellectually inadequate is so extreme that they shun being noticed by other epistemic agents. Consequently, they exhibit insufficient concern for being held in esteem by their epistemic community. Narcissism is related to intellectual vanity. It involves a failure to accept one's intellectual limitations due to an infatuation with one's own intellectual abilities. Fatalism is a strengthening of timidity that consists in a disposition to resign oneself to the alleged intractability of one's own intellectual limitations.[1]

Vanity and narcissism are vices of superiority, while timidity and fatalism are vices of inferiority. I use these labels to indicate three features that these pairs of vices share with superbia, arrogance, servility, and self-abasement (see Chapter 5). First, the vices of superiority involve feelings of superiority, while those of inferiority include feelings that one is inferior and inadequate. Second, these vices contribute via their manifestation to creating and entrenching pecking orders. Vain individuals, for example, often show off in the attempt to establish for themselves a high-ranking position in the epistemic community. Third, individuals from privileged backgrounds are at higher risk than people with subordinated social identities to develop the vices of superiority. The converse holds for the vices of inferiority.

These vices of superiority and inferiority are the outcome of deeply flawed evaluations of the self for its worth in the intellectual domain. Individuals who suffer from these vices appraise their cognitive make-up and its components—such as cognitive capacities (e.g., perception and memory), sensibilities (e.g., being observant), intellectual abilities (e.g., spatial orientation) skills (e.g., reading

---

[1] As I mentioned before these considerations should not be read to indicate that these vices are best classified in terms of excess and deficiency in accordance with the Aristotelian doctrine of the golden mean. In my view the descriptions in terms of these extremities are at best superficial, a better understanding of the nature of these vices is provided by analysing their motivational structures.

medieval manuscripts), thinking styles and habits (e.g., playing devil's advocate), or intellectual commitments (e.g., beliefs and theories)—and treat these as their intellectual strengths or weaknesses. Their self-appraisals, however, are skewed since motives such as seeking social acceptance or fearing social exclusion contribute to determining the informational bases of these evaluations and to setting the evidential thresholds for reaching a conclusion. These clusters of assessments of intellectual features of the self are closely associated with estimations of the intellectual worth of the self as a whole. The latter are forms of self-esteem with regard to one's agentic epistemic qualities.

The self-evaluations of those who are vain, narcissistic or timid and fatalistic are, like those of their arrogant or self-abasing cousins, faulty because they are not responsive to the epistemic worth of the personal qualities that these evaluations assess.[2] These self-appraisals are formed and sustained to address the needs either to be accepted by one's elective social group or to defend the self against alleged threats. Individuals who are vain or narcissistic appraise their qualities for their capacity to attract others' admiration irrespective of these qualities' actual epistemic worth. Those who are timid or fatalistic evaluate their intellectual features for their tendency to make the self vulnerable to threats.

This chapter consists of four sections each dedicated to one vice. In every case I argue that the vice in question is based on attitudes, together with their informational bases, towards one's own intellectual strengths and weaknesses. In each instance possession of false beliefs that overestimate or underestimate one's own intellectual good qualities is neither sufficient nor necessary for an individual to be vicious.[3] Section 6.1 deals with intellectual vanity; Section 6.2 is concerned with narcissism, Section 6.3 with intellectual timidity, and finally Section 6.4 with fatalism.

6.1 Intellectual Vanity

Intellectual vanity is a disposition to behave in ways designed to attract the admiration and esteem of other people and especially of those who are themselves held in high esteem by the epistemic community.[4] Intellectually vain individuals have no intrinsic concern for being worthy of the admiration they seek, although they might pursue epistemic self-improvement as a means to gain others' approval.[5] Intellectual vanity is also characterized by a broadly positive appraisal

---

[2] As I mentioned before, faulty does not in this context entail that they are necessarily inaccurate.
[3] Nor, more weakly, is absence of a true belief about the same a sign that one is vicious.
[4] Some of the ideas discussed in this section extend points I already made in Tanesini (2018b).
[5] For this reason Matthew Kieran (2017) has argued following David Hume that vanity is a vice close to virtue since one can foster in vain individuals the desire to be worthy of esteem by relying on their pre-existing desire to be esteemed.

of one's own intellectual abilities and talents together with an unwillingness to accept any intellectual limitations.[6] In this section, I first provide a description of some characteristic manifestations of this intellectual vice. I explain why vanity causes individuals to become predisposed to malicious and especially to spiteful envy. Finally I defend the claim that vanity is based on a cluster of attitudes with their bases that serve the need to gain social acceptance.

Vanity manifests itself in the intellectual domain through a range of characteristic behaviours and emotional responses. Intellectually vain individuals are deeply concerned with their reputations. It matters to them that they are noticed and admired because of the pleasure they gain from being the object of these attitudes.[7] Hence, they might repeatedly google their own name to see what others are saying about them. If they are writers or academics upon coming across a book or an article in their area of expertise, they might first of all browse the references to check whether their own work is cited. They might also check their h-index by using Publish or Perish or other similar software.[8] In addition to seeking evidence of their own good reputation, intellectually vain individuals also especially care to be seen to be part of the in-crowd. Hence, researchers who are intellectually vain tend to circle around big stars at conferences in the hope that they might be included among the selected few invited for a drink or a meal. These behaviours are not always indicative of full-blown intellectual vanity. Some people might indulge in these activities because they have a tendency to vain behaviour; but as their dispositions are not consistent across situations or stable, it would be inaccurate to attribute to them vanity as a character trait. In addition, there are contexts in which one might behave in these ways without being in the least vain. One may wish to network with powerful people at conferences because of the potential benefits for one's career of establishing such contacts. One might want to know whether others are engaging with one's work, in order to find out whether they are formulating pertinent criticisms of one's views. Knowing these facts is important in order to refine one's position and to engage in dialogue.

I have claimed that vain individuals desire to be admired and thus seek the spotlight, since one must first be noticed to be esteemed. When those who are vain succeed in gaining others' admiration, they often become self-important and conceited. It is not that uncommon to see vain individuals sing their own praises. Partly, they behave in this way in order to attract admiration. But since vanity is not regarded as an admirable quality, such behaviour risks attracting others'

---

[6] Such unwillingness to accept one's shortcomings is compatible with being preoccupied to hide from view any limitations that one fears one may have. I say more on this point below. As I explained in Chapter 4, acceptance of limitations requires that one openly acknowledges their existence and is prepared to reveal these limitations to other people. Vain individuals do not accept their limitations even when they know about their existence, because they wish to cover them up.
[7] See also Nuyen (1999) for the idea that vanity is a desire to receive others' praise and admiration for the sole purpose of personal gratification.
[8] This index measures the productivity and influence of academics.

disapproval. Vain individuals often engage in it because they have developed an inflated self-conception without fully appreciating that their self-regard might come across as overbearing.

In addition, people who are vain, seem to believe the praise that is bestowed upon them even when it is blatantly disingenuous. Hence, researchers who have achieved positions of power within institutions are often surrounded by yes-men who tell them that they are clever, witty, that their research track-record is unsurpassed, and their visions for the institution or research team clearheaded and strategic. It is surprising how often the individuals upon whom such praise is heaped believe what they are told. They behave like peacocks parading their alleged successes, while it is obvious to all outside their coterie that, like the proverbial emperor, they have nothing to show off about. In this manner individuals who are vain often become incapable of noticing their weak points or failures.

If vain individuals become impervious to their weaknesses when they are powerful, the same vain individuals can obsess over alleged limitations if others' praise is denied to, or withdrawn from, them. When this happens, vain individuals' concern is not to address their weaknesses but to hide them from others' scrutiny. For example, the vain academic who has received a pertinent criticism of her views that she could not address satisfactorily, might in subsequent days worry more about the impression that her inability to defend her view might have made on the audience than about the substance of the criticism or whether it can be fully answered. In short, vain people when powerful and admired do not notice their weaknesses; when they are not powerful or admired, vain individuals obsess about their shortcomings, but their efforts are directed to covering them up rather than dealing with them. In these ways those who are intellectually vain seem unable to accept their limitations.

This behaviour is what we would expect if, as I claimed above, vain individuals crave the admiration of others but are not intrinsically concerned to be worthy of that praise. In the eyes of a person who suffers from vanity if a personal shortcoming is not noticed by other people, and thus does not influence the esteem in which one is held, than that feature is not really a limitation since it is not an obstacle to gaining what one wants: that is, the pleasant feeling of being thought highly by other people.

To summarize, there are three main components to intellectual vanity. First, it involves a high sense of self-regard or self-importance that is fuelled by a desire to be accepted as an admired member of the community. Second, it includes an inability to accept one's shortcomings which is manifested either in a tendency not to notice them, or in a propensity to hide them from others' views. Third, it comprises a desire to receive others' approval and admiration for the pleasure one gets from being regarded in these ways and irrespective of merit. It is this third component of intellectual vanity that is fundamental to this trait and explains the other two features that characterize it.

I have argued in Chapter 5 that the emotional lives of people who suffer from *superbia* are suffused with anger at perceived slights caused by behaviour that fails to acknowledge the entitlements that they arrogate for themselves. The lives of those who are servile, I have also claimed, are coloured by shame engendered by others' disapproval and the need to avoid experiencing it. In the lives of people who are vain envy plays an equally encompassing role.

Envy is a negative emotion that is directed at others because they possess a feature or occupy a social role that makes them superior to oneself in some regard that is of concern to the envious individual. Thus, envy can be thought as the unpleasant emotion that we feel when we compare ourselves to others finding ourselves wanting in some regard, whilst desiring to occupy instead the position of the superior individual (cf. Protasi, 2016). It is commonplace in philosophy and psychology to distinguish at least two kinds of envy. Benign envy is the painful experience that one lacks some good feature or status prompted by comparing oneself to another who possesses it, and is, thus, judged to be superior to oneself in that regard. The pain engendered by one's perceived shortcoming supplies a motive to emulate the other and acquire the good feature for oneself. Benign envy is thus a driver to self-improvement.[9]

Malicious envy is the painful experience that others have some good feature prompted by comparing oneself to these people and thus judging them to be superior to one in that regard.[10] Malicious envy is aggressive when it involves a desire to bring others down to one's level so that they are no longer one's superiors. So, whilst benign envy would involve an effort to level things up, malicious envy when aggressive would lead to attempting to level them down by depriving others of the good features that one covets (Kristjánsson, 2006).[11] This species of envy, which comprises a desire to level down one's perceived superiors, leads the envious to engage in hostile behaviour designed to take other people down a peg. As I argued in Chapter 5 this kind of aggressive levelling down is characteristic of *superbia*; this vice is associated with malicious envy that is aggressive.

There is, however, a different species of malicious envy that is better described as spiteful. Spiteful individuals try to spoil the good that is the object of their envy. For example, an academic who has never succeeded in having a paper published in a specific high-ranking journal might let it be known that she thinks that the journal is going downhill or that their peer-refereeing procedures are not up to scratch. This sour grape phenomenon is a common manifestation of envy when one feels unable to gain the envied good for oneself. It is an attempt to make the

---

[9] This characterization can be found in Aristotle's Rhetoric (2007, 1388a 30–36). It is also discussed by Zagzebski (2015).
[10] For the distinction between malicious and benign envy in psychology see, van de Ven et al. (2009).
[11] I mentioned benign envy in Chapter 4 as a characteristic emotion of virtuous concern with being esteemed.

quality one envies seem to be not worth having. This reaction, therefore, is not an attempt directly to diminish the person one envies. Rather, it tries to change views about what is worthy of pursuit and admiration. Hence, levelling down does not capture what the spiteful person seeks to achieve.

Another reason to be suspicious of the account of spiteful envy in terms of levelling down is that it makes spite wholly irrational. As Gabriele Taylor (2006, p. 46) notes, it would be inane of someone who envies another's beauty simply to desire that they become ugly, since the satisfaction of such desire would not seem to give one what one wants. One might experience schadenfreude as a result of this other person's misfortune, but the need whose frustration generated the spiteful envy remains unfulfilled as a result. Fulfilment may instead be gained by convincing others that beauty is only skin deep. Relatedly, the spiteful person does not necessarily want to have the envied feature. Taylor notes that a person might envy an individual for the position she holds—such as being prime minister for example—without wishing to occupy the burdensome role oneself (Taylor, 2006, p. 47).

I have suggested that individuals who are vain are prone to spiteful envy because they want to get the credit that comes with admiration irrespective of whether they merit it. I have described vanity as being characterized by a sense of self-importance that is primarily dependent on the conviction that one is the object of the admiration and esteem of one's community. If this is right, those who are vain are liable to be envious of others who seem to them to attract more admiration than they do. Perversely, they are also keen to be the target of others' envy. The reason for the desire to be envied is twofold. First, to be envied is to be the target of someone's attention, and those who are vain crave attention. Second, to be envied is to be taken to have qualities that one thinks attract the admiration of the community; admiration is also something sought by the vain.

These considerations about the association of vanity to spiteful envy highlight the relations of this vice to servility and to *superbia*. Vanity is closely related to *superbia*. Here and in Chapter 5 I have highlighted the differences between these two vices which are often confused or conflated with each other.[12] It seems plausible, however, that these vices will be often embodied by the same individuals. Individuals who suffer from either vice have an inflated sense of their own self-importance; they are both likely to feel superior to other people, and have big egos. Nevertheless, one can imagine the case of a vain but rather insecure individual who fluctuates between feeling on top of the world after having received praise for some success, and feeling low because she obsesses about what others might think of her. Such a person would not seem to fit the description of someone who suffers from *superbia*. The relation between servility and vanity is

---

[12] Tiberius and Walker (1998) for instance assimilate vanity to arrogance.

one of complementarity. Those who are vain like to be surrounded by individuals who display servile features since the latter are disposed to show the deference and bestow the praise craved by the vain. Of course, these subordinates cannot be total outsiders since vain individuals only seek the admiration of those whose admiration enhances the social reputation of the vain person.

Intellectual vanity so conceived is likely to be based on a cluster of attitudes to the self, and their informational bases, that are positive but prone to cross-situational inconsistency. These attitudes are formed and sustained to satisfy the need to be socially accepted. I am not aware of empirical research that directly supports this hypothesis, there are however results that can be taken to offer some indirect evidence for my view. The description of vanity provided so far strongly suggests that vain individuals must be highly concerned with impression management. That is to say, since they are pre-occupied that others hold them in high-regard, they spend a lot of effort trying to make a good impression on others. In particular, they must engage in self-presentation activities dedicated to the strategic control of the information about the self that they are willing to reveal to other people.[13] Intriguingly, there is good evidence that individuals that are very preoccupied with self-presentation engage in high levels of self-monitoring of their attitudes to ensure that these match what they think is required (by others) in that given context. These individuals are described as high self-monitors whose attitudes match what they take to be socially appropriate in context (Snyder, 1974). Unsurprisingly, these individuals have also been characterized as 'chameleon-like'.

People who are primarily concerned with getting along in the way that is characteristic of obsequious individuals also engage in impression management and self-presentation. They too exhibit high-self monitoring. Their behaviour is a strategy for getting along given that they care about social acceptance and occupy a position that makes the achievement of a high social rank extremely unlikely. But not all people who are preoccupied with making a good impression also occupy a lowly social position. Some do not. In my view, vanity is the expression of the preoccupation with impression management and self-presentation in individuals for whom achieving high social status in some domain is perceived as a realistic possibility. If this is right, intellectual vanity is based on attitudes to the self and to aspects of one's cognitive make-up which are responsive to the need to make a good impression for the purpose of gaining social acceptance. Vain individuals evaluate positively, and treat as their intellectual strengths, those features of themselves that are instrumental in gaining the approval of society. Since different features might garner social approval in varied contexts and social

---

[13] For a review of some empirical literature on impression management (including ingratiation) and on self-presentation see Schlenker and Pontari (2000).

groups one would expected these attitudes to change accordingly. This prediction is supported by empirical evidence that indicates that high self-monitors have attitudes serving a social adjustive function that are susceptible to contextual variation (Watt et al., 2008, p. 197).

These considerations offer some empirical support for the view defended here that intellectual vanity is based on attitudes designed to facilitate the making of a good impression that lack stability across situations. If this is right, we should expect intellectually vain individuals to change their views frequently to match their social environments and to have an inflated self-esteem which is unstable and prone to ups and downs. This characterization matches folk-psychological descriptions of the character of vain individuals.

6.2 Narcissism

Narcissism is a deepening of intellectual vanity into a kind of self-infatuation. Whilst intellectually vain individuals are keen to obtain the admiration of other people, narcissists are less needy of others' approval since they bestow upon themselves all the praise and admiration that they crave for. Narcissists are also less likely to think of others as people whose opinion matters, and this might be why they do not always seek to be likeable. In short, intellectually vain individuals are motivated by the desire that others think well of them; narcissists instead want primarily to think well of themselves, others' opinion is of import only in so far as it promotes the satisfaction of the desire for high self-regard. If vanity is the love of honours, narcissism is a morbid form of self-love (Nuyen, 1999, p. 621).

In this section I describe some of the manifestations of narcissism that differentiate it from intellectual vanity, although the two vices are closely related. I also briefly review some relevant empirical literature on narcissism. Psychological theories of narcissism are not well supported. Whilst a scale to measure narcissistic tendencies has been developed, it has led to contradictory results.[14] I diagnose a confusion of narcissism with arrogance at the root of the conflicting results psychologists have obtained. I also cautiously endorse recent proposals that see narcissism to be a manifestation of attitudes to the self that are high in the agentic domain but low with regard to the pro-social or communal traits of generosity, empathy or benevolence. Thus, conceived narcissists have a high opinion of their own intellectual abilities and competence but do not think that they are liked by other people or that they are particularly good at personal relations.

---

[14] Narcissism is measured by means of the Narcissistic Personality Inventory (Raskin & Terry, 1988).

Perhaps the most significant difference between narcissism and mere vanity is a sense of one's own specialness.[15] Narcissists like the sound of their own voices. They turn any discussion into a lecture, since they presume that what anybody should be interested in is what the narcissist thinks about the topic rather than the topic itself.[16] Given that people intensely dislike being lectured at, narcissists appear to have a tin ear to the fact that their self-centred behaviour is perceived by others as boorish, vainglorious, and unadmirable. In this regard, those who are narcissistic lack the awareness for others' perceptions that is possessed by some individuals who suffer from vanity.[17]

Narcissists might also be less likely to experience episodic pangs of spiteful envy than individuals who are vain. Since narcissists have a keen sense of their own specialness, they might take their personal features as defining of the admirable. That is, they might think of any quality that it must be admirable if they possess it, and that it can't be admirable if they do not have it. Individuals with this mindset do not often experience pangs of envy because they have convinced themselves that the qualities they do not have are not worth having.[18] That said, narcissists might have fewer experiences of episodic spiteful envy than vain individuals simply because they have more successfully spoiled those goods that they do not have, thus reducing the need for future spiteful behaviour.

To summarize, narcissism can be thought as a version of vanity because it is characterized by an inflated sense of one's own self-worth and self-importance. This inflated ego is even more extreme in the case of narcissists who tend to have grandiose thoughts about their own specialness and uniqueness. Vain individuals desire to be admired by the social group to which they wish to belong and thus are motivated by a desire to be esteemed. Because they strive to be admired, they are unable to accept their limitations. Narcissists also want to be admired, but the only opinion they value is their own. Thus, they desire to be admirable in their own eyes; they crave for the esteem that they bestow upon themselves. Because of this urge to seem admirable in their own eyes, narcissists are also unable to accept that they have any limitations.

The psychological literature on narcissism is complex and contradictory. In what follows I ignore the clinical literature on narcissism as a personality disorder. Instead, I review some of the psychology of narcissism as an individual difference

---

[15] This need for uniqueness or specialness has been associated with a predilection for conspiracy theories (Imhoff & Lamberty, 2017).

[16] Aikin and Clanton (2010, p. 415) describe this behaviour as characteristic of the deliberative vice of egotistical filibuster. I agree that the behaviour is a manifestation of egotism, but I would not characterize as filibustering since it does not involve intentional time-wasting.

[17] These matters are not clear-cut since there is no neat separation between people who are vain and those who are narcissistic. I suspect that in many cases people who suffer from one of these vices also possess the other to some degree.

[18] Self-abasement is therefore the opposite of narcissism. This is borne out in some empirical results (e.g., Emmons, 1984).

in personality (that is, a personality variable).[19] So understood narcissistic tendencies are measured using the Narcissistic Personality Inventory (NPI) or some of its simplified variants. The inventory in its most popular form consists in a forced-choice questionnaire involving forty paired statements. For each pair, participants need to select the statement that most closely reflects their feelings. Pairs include claims such as: A. I am no better or worse than most people. B. I think I am a special person; and A. I have a natural talent for influencing people. B. I am not good at influencing people (Raskin & Terry, 1988). The pairs included in the inventory point to different factors of narcissism, but there is no agreement about these (Campbell & Foster, 2007, p. 117). Ackerman et al. (2011), for example, have suggested a three factor analysis in terms of Leadership/Authority, Grandiose Exhibitionism, and Entitlement/Exploitativeness. Other factor analyses have yielded a larger number of components such as: exhibitionism (a preference for showing off); vanity (a focus on appearance); authority (thinking one is a leader); entitlement (thinking one deserves the best); exploitativeness (thinking that one is good at manipulating others); superiority (thinking one is better than other people); and self-sufficiency (valuing independence).

This uncertainty over the dimensions of narcissism probably plays a role in explaining some of the contradictory results obtained in empirical studies. For example, narcissism has been seen by some to be linked to defensive high self-esteem (McGregor et al., 2005; Schröder-Abé et al., 2007a). Others have voiced deep reservations about this connection (Campbell et al., 2007; Gregg & Sedikides, 2010; Haddock & Gebauer, 2011). A plausible explanation of these contradictory results is that the NPI tracks some features of narcissism and other features that are more characteristic of arrogance.[20] For example, exhibitionism, and vanity are closely related to narcissistic tendencies. However, superiority, exploitativeness, and authority are features that narcissism shares with arrogance, whilst self-sufficiency and entitlement stand arguably in a closer connection to arrogance than narcissism. If this is right, the NPI measures both arrogance and narcissism.

This confusion would explain why the relationship of narcissism to self-esteem is so messy. Those who measure highly in narcissistic tendencies as revealed by the NPI are likely to be individuals who are both arrogant and narcissistic. Thus, even though there is a positive relation between narcissism and defensive high self-esteem, it does not follow that this kind of discrepant self-esteem is the basis of narcissism. Intriguingly, recent research has cast further doubts into the identification of narcissism and defensive self-esteem. Campbell et al. (2007) have argued that narcissists only measure low in implicit measures of self-esteem when these focus on associations of the self to communal traits (such as love and generosity). When association to agentic qualities (such as assertiveness or enthusiasm) are

---

[19] For a review see Campbell and Foster (2007).
[20] Some factor analyses of narcissism even list arrogance as one of its factors (Emmons, 1984).

measured, narcissism is positively related to high implicit self-esteem. This result has prompted the speculation that narcissists rate highly (both explicitly and indirectly) their competence, but do not have the same view of their likeability. This conclusion coheres with the account of narcissism offered above. Narcissists desire to admire themselves, but they have some awareness that this is not generally regarded as an admirable feature. This recognition is what is recorded in their low self-assessment of pro-social qualities, such as helpfulness or likeability, as implicitly measured.

One might conclude from these considerations that attitudes towards the self serving the need to be socially accepted cannot be the causal bases of narcissism, since narcissism involves behaviours that do not foster that goal. Further, narcissists exhibit some awareness of the fact since they negatively associate the self to socially likeable features. If this is right, narcissism must be radically different from vanity. I do not have a full answer to this objection. However, narcissism is, like vanity, positively correlated with high self-monitoring (Emmons, 1984). This result strongly suggests that narcissists monitor their attitudes to make them fit their situation. Therefore, at least some of their attitudes must serve the need for social acceptance.

Contrary to first impressions, this conclusion is plausible, if we consider that the narcissists' self-admiration is indirectly reliant on others' esteem, even though narcissists would deny this fact. Narcissists want to think of themselves as immensely talented, and tend to discount those who do not share their high opinion of themselves. Nevertheless, being admired by others is for narcissists evidence of their admirability. Thus, narcissists will tend to surround themselves with people whose friendship reflects well on them. To this extent, then it is likely that narcissists are, like vain individuals, preoccupied with the strategic presentations to others of information about the self. If this is correct, some of the attitudes that are the bases of narcissism are formed to serve the need to attract the right kind of response from other people. Narcissism, like vanity is a craving for esteem, and this is why it is based on some attitudes serving social-adjustive functions.

6.3 Intellectual Timidity

Intellectual timidity is a disposition to self-silence because of an overriding fear to be exposed as lacking in intelligence, talent or ability. It is also characterized by a lack of motivation to persevere, take intellectual risks or attempt to improve.[21] Those who are timid prefer not to be noticed and thus do not demand that others acknowledge their merits. Intellectually timid individuals, therefore, show

---

[21] Some aspects of this section are based on points I made in Tanesini (2018e).

insufficient regard for being esteemed in their community. In what follows I first describe the characteristic behavioural, affective, and doxastic manifestations of timidity. Second, I argue that the emotional lives of those who are timid are dominated by fear and anxiety that are corrosive of self-confidence and self-trust. Third, I illustrate how the framework of attitudes can explain the psychology of intellectually timidity. Finally, I compare timidity to intellectual servility in order to highlight the similarities and differences between these two vices.

I think of intellectual timidity as the vice that is characteristic of those who are extremely risk averse in intellectual inquiry. Timidity, and the related vice of fatalism, are therefore opposed to intellectual arrogance since excessive risk-taking is a characteristic feature of the latter. Those who are intellectually timid suffer from something close to intellectual cowardice because they are afraid of being exposed as fools or stupid. This fear of social exclusion dominates their behaviour and explains their tendencies to self-silence and avoid notice. Those who are timid adopt the motto attributed to Denis Thatcher: 'It is better to keep your mouth shut and be thought a fool than open it and remove all doubt.'[22] Hence, those who are intellectually timid adopt a policy of self-silencing.

The fear of exposure is closely associated to feelings of inadequacy. Intellectually timid people often feel intellectually inferior to other people. They might be aware that they have no solid evidence supporting a belief in their inferiority. They might even acknowledge that they are likely to be as capable as most other people. However, they cannot shake off feelings of doubts in their ability. These epistemic feelings undermine self-trust, self-certainty and self-confidence, even for those people who sincerely would not endorse the claim that they are intellectually inferior to other epistemic agents. For this reason those who are intellectually timid are riven by self-doubts and hold themselves in low regard.

Perhaps because of their low self-esteem, intellectually timid individuals do not respond to their feelings of inferiority by trying to improve or to challenge their fears. Instead, they adopt a fixed mindset (Dweck, 2006). They seem to assume that their limitations are fixed and cannot be addressed. In addition, fear itself blunts their responsiveness to quality differences in evidence (Baron, 2000, p. 244). These factors impede their performance and undercut any motivation to improve.

I have claimed that intellectual timidity is a vice opposed to intellectual humility. This claim might strike one as odd. First, timidity is more naturally opposed to courage. Second, since timidity encourages meekness, it might seem to be a component of humility rather than opposed to it. In response I wish to point out that one vice might be opposed to more than one virtue. Being fearful to have

---

[22] This quote is attributed to Margaret Thatcher's husband by the BBC on its news website http://news.bbc.co.uk/1/hi/uk_politics/2669923.stm (accessed: 17 December 2018).

one's alleged incompetence exposed is opposed to humility since the latter includes acceptance of one's perceived limitations and a willingness to reveal them to others. It is also opposed to intellectual courage because hiding one's alleged limitations displays a lack of courage.

Fear is the characteristic emotion of intellectual timidity. This is a fear that corrodes one's intellectual self-trust. Repeated self-silencing, I suspect, might cause one to come to believe that one is incompetent and has nothing to say. Imagine a student who never raises her hand in class even when she thinks she knows the answer. This student might be anxious because she has been mocked in the past or because the teacher has previously ignored her contributions. Her reticence might also have temperamental origins. Be that as it may, she routinely bites her tongue out of fear of being humiliated. Initially this habit would be at odds with her beliefs about her knowledge. We should expect her to experience cognitive dissonance since she is aware that she 'freely' engages in behaviour that is inconsistent with the standards of honesty and courage she has set for herself (cf. Wood, 2000, p. 546). Hence, I suspect that individuals might reduce the cognitive dissonance between their actions and their self-knowledge by conforming what they believe about themselves to their actions.[23] Thus, the individual who initially bites her tongue ends up honestly believing that she has nothing to say. In this manner, her emotions, actions, and beliefs interact in a vicious circle of ever lowering self-esteem.

The clustering of behaviours (self-silencing, shying away from the limelight), affects (fear of being found out associated with so-called rejection sensitivity,[24] feelings of inferiority), and beliefs about one's alleged shortcomings typical of intellectual timidity is intelligible if this vice is based on mostly negative attitudes to the self and to elements of one's cognitive make-up that are motivated by the need to defend the ego against the threat of social exclusion. Intellectually timid individuals form negative attitudes, and treat as their bad qualities or limitations, those features of the self that may threaten their already low self-esteem. These attitudes are characteristic of those who adopt the flight response to threats. They protect themselves by avoiding being noticed. These individuals will assess negatively those among their features that might attract attention.[25] Thus, they are averse to displaying ability or to speaking up. Having negative evaluations of the self and of its qualities rationalizes adopting behaviours that help to escape notice.

---

[23] See Cooper (2008) for an introduction to theories about cognitive dissonance.
[24] This term used by psychologists is intended to refer to an unusually high sensitivity to the possibility of rejection. The literature on this topic tends to pay insufficient attention to the unjust environmental circumstances that lead people to become especially fearful of being dismissed or ignored.
[25] Their self-appraisal are skewed because the motive of defending the ego biases the selection of the evidence used in the self-evaluations and sets a lower threshold for concluding that something is a threat to self-esteem compared to the evidence required to judge that something is not a threat.

Hence, these attitudes serve an ego-defensive function since they contribute to satisfying the need to avoid the threat of being exposed.

There is some empirical evidence in support of this analysis. There is work on self-silencing of women in academic settings that indicates that they stop themselves from intervening out of fear of negative judgments about them and of the risk of being socially ostracized. This fear extends to failing to take up opportunities for self-improvement if these also carry a risk of exposure (London et al., 2012). There is also independent evidence that individuals who are extremely sensitive to the possibility of rejection suffer from low self-esteem (Wu et al., 2011). These considerations when combined suggest that some individuals who hold themselves in low regard, self-silence because of fear of being attacked. It is therefore plausible to think that intellectual timidity is based on defensive negative attitudes towards the self and to elements of one's cognitive make-up.

The hypothesis that timidity is to be understood in terms of attitudes helps to explain the complex relationship between this vice of inferiority and intellectual servility. These two vices, which are usually characteristic of people who occupy subordinate positions, overlap but are distinct. It is possible for a person to be intellectual obsequious without being timid. A person can be excessively deferential without fearing the limelight. On the contrary, such a person might try to attract attention so that the people whom she is trying to ingratiate notice her. It is also possible to be intellectually timid without being servile, since a person might self-silence without trying to please those who are more powerful than she is. Nevertheless, many individuals who suffer from one of these vices also possess to some extent the other. They might ingratiate themselves to the powerful in some circumstances whilst biting their tongue in others.

These similarities and differences between these two vices can be made intelligible in terms of the differing needs served by attitudes. Servility and timidity are both mostly negative forms of self-assessment. The first is developed to foster social acceptance, the second to defend the self against the threat of social exclusion or disapproval. It is perfectly possible for someone's attitudes to have been formed and sustained in the service of both needs. How these attitudes are manifested might depend on the details of the occasion. If a person who is both timid and servile finds herself in a situation where, in her opinion, she cannot shift the negative views that she thinks others have of her, she is likely to believe that ingratiation would be futile. In such a circumstance she might choose to be silent. If however she thinks that by praising others, she might get them to like her, the same person might engage in deferential behaviour designed to secure acceptance. In short, timidity and servility are distinct vices that flow from low self-esteem. Even though, the vices are different, they might be based on overlapping attitudes because attitudes can have multiple motivations.

6.4 Intellectual Fatalism

Intellectual fatalism is a deepening of timidity into a state of hopelessness. Fatalism thus conceived is an exacerbation of the resignation that is characteristic of intellectual timidity. In this section I identify fatalism with unresponsive low self-esteem. I argue that this kind of low self-regard that is motivated by fear of exposure leads to hopelessness and despair out of a sense of the futility of attempts at self-improvement.[26]

Timidity and fatalism are closely related but they differ because the intellectual life of those who are timid is suffused by fear and anxiety, whilst the dominant emotion of fatalism is loss of hope, despair, and profound disappointment with oneself. Fatalism is thus characterized both by a sense that many desired outcomes are simply not achievable and by an utter lack of motivation. The fatalist feels hopeless and despairs because she cannot see how she could succeed in her epistemic activities. She feels that her abilities are both inadequate and immutable. Her lack of motivation and of perseverance is partly the consequence of a fixed mindset that conceives of intelligence and other intellectual qualities as unchangeable (Dweck, 2006). This conception makes any attempt to improve and succeed seem futile and thus causes motivation to falter. This sense of hopelessness can be chronic without being a form of clinical depression.[27] It manifests itself in an attitude of disappointment in oneself, because one feels that the standards one has set for oneself are not achievable. In this manner, fatalism is wholly undermining of intellectual self-trust since if one is hopeless about one's ability to succeed one does not trust one's own intellectual abilities or one's capacity to improve upon them.

Hopefulness plays an important role in epistemic activities. Nancy Snow (2013) has argued that hope can be an intellectual virtue when it consists in a perception of some outcomes as epistemically good, a belief that those outcomes can be achieved but are not certain, and a desire to achieve them. This is a standard (or 'bare bones' view) of hope. These beliefs and desires might be necessary for hope but they are not sufficient because hope includes an emotional stance which supplies distinctive reasons for action (Martin, 2014). For example, the perception of a discovery as good, combined with a belief that it is possible, and a desire to achieve it, are not by themselves always sufficient to justify activity directed at the pursuit of the activity. One might desire something which one perceive as both good and possible without seeking to attain it because of the existence of

---

[26] I characterize this orientation as one of resigned hopelessness which combines hopelessness and despair. Cobb would describe it as one of despair because it includes a commitment to the impossibility of obtaining what one wants (2019, p. 66).

[27] In psychology hopelessness theory seeks to study a clinical condition closely related to depression and suicidal tendencies (Abramson et al., 1989). I am interested in non-clinical varieties of hopelessness as a response to the extreme stress caused by fear of exposure.

countervailing reasons against taking the required course of action. In this case one merely wishes for the outcome rather than hopes for it. What hope supplies in addition to belief, perception, and desire is a determination to act, since to treat an outcome as hoped for is to treat it as something which one has sufficient reasons to try to bring about (Martin, 2014, p. 62). Snow does not mention the reason-giving role played by the emotion of hope, but it is this feature of hope that makes it a key component of epistemic agency. Successful inquirers set themselves epistemic goals and plan how to achieve them. Unless investigators have a hopeful attitude they are not likely to be open to take reasonable chances, and thus set challenging but achievable goals for themselves. In this way hopefulness has a direct influence on the skills, sensibilities, and thinking styles of epistemic agents.

Snow argues that hope promotes a motivation to seek the truth for its own sake, makes one resilient but also flexible in one's epistemic endeavours, and generates a new methodological approach of openness to the opportunities that present themselves to one (Snow, 2013, pp. 162–164). Hence, hope goes hand in hand with a realistic optimism about one's chances of success that is necessary if one is to be motivated to take on difficult challenges. Once hope is conceived in this manner, it becomes apparent how its diminution manifests itself in a lack of motivation and of intellectual courage and, thus, a deepening of timidity. It also becomes clear how hope can be thought of as opposed to arrogance in so far as the latter includes a kind of self-satisfied certainty in one's ability to succeed that seems to obviate the need for hopefulness.

These considerations also throw light on the connections between hope and the acceptance of one's own intellectual limitations that is a component of intellectual humility (see Chapter 4). It is only if we accept that we do have limitations that some desired outcomes can be perceived by us as uncertain but possible. But acceptance does not merely consist in knowing that one has limitations, it also requires realistic optimism about one's ability to improve. Without hope, as the discussion in this section has illustrated, intellectual humility degenerates into a resigned attitude of disappointment with oneself. This attitude fosters a belief that all effort is futile; and this belief is an obstacle to any epistemic activity. In this regard, hope appears to be an important component of human agency in all its manifestations, including epistemic activities (cf. McGeer, 2004).

The framework of attitudes offers a powerful explanation of the clustering of affects (e.g., feelings of hopelessness and disappointment), behaviours (e.g., failure to attempt difficult tasks), and beliefs in one's own constitutional inadequacy. According to the account, fatalism is based on negative attitudes to the self that are caused by fear of exposure.[28] This fear—which is labelled 'rejection-sensitivity' by

---

[28] I should say that it is certainly possible to be fatalist about outcomes that are genuinely out of one's control without fearing exposure. My interest here is on fatalism about intellectual failure that has become a character trait.

psychologists—motivates individuals to adopt risk-averse tactics in impression management. Thus, instead of trying to boost their self-esteem, they cut their losses and adopt self-protective strategies (Wood et al., 1994). These results offer some support to the view that both timidity and fatalism are the expression of low self-esteem understood as a cluster of negative attitudes directed to the self and to the elements of one's cognitive make-up.[29] These attitudes serve the need to protect the self from further losses by shielding one from the risk of exposure. Hence, those who are timid and fatalistic are hyper-vigilant against possible threats to the ego.[30] This is a tendency that they share with individuals who suffer from *superbia* and arrogance. The latter however respond to threats by trying to self-enhance, the former by attempting to self-protect (Wood et al., 1994).[31]

Thinking of timidity and fatalism as a defensive low self-esteem accounts for the feelings of inadequacy and disappointment that characterize these vices. The fact that these low self-assessments serve a defensive role explains the tendency to hide, to avoid even trying to succeed. All of these behaviours can be seen as consequences of adopting a strategy of self-protection based on the attempt to insulate the self from any risks of rejection. When low self-esteem is accompanied by the conviction that one's shortcomings are fixed as is typical of a fixed mindset, the manifestations that are typical of fatalism ensue. For example, in a study of undergraduates from lower socioeconomic backgrounds, Rheinschmidt and Mendoza-Denton (2014) found that those who were hypervigilant about social exclusion because of their class origins, and who thought that intelligence is a fixed quantity that cannot be modified through effort, experienced more feelings of hopelessness and of personal failure than students from a similar social background that thought that intelligence and academic achievement can be improved through effort. I suspect that these negative feelings stand in a mutually reinforcing connection with low self-esteem.

Timidity and fatalism are therefore, like servility and self-abasement, vices of low self-esteem. These four vices are all distinct from each other but not unrelated. One of the explanatory advantages of the framework of attitudes over other approaches is its ability to explain the connections and differences between

---

[29] This identification also receives some support from the sociometer theory of self-esteem (Leary & Baumeister, 2000). According to this position self-esteem is an attitude to the self that serves the need to monitor social acceptance and exclusion. Low self-esteem registers that one perceives oneself not to be valued by others; high self-esteem records one's impression that one is socially accepted. I do not think that self-esteem exclusively functions in this way, but I agree that one's sense of self-regard is powerfully shaped by the perception that one is accepted or rejected by other members of one's affiliative group. See also Cobb (2019) for some remarks on how other people can facilitate the development of either agentic or resigned emotional orientations.

[30] See Mendoza-Denton et al. (2002) for evidence that people who experience discrimination for features (such as group identity) that are not malleable can become especially vigilant about social exclusion.

[31] See Wheeler and Suls (2020) for scepticism about these claims.

these vices. What timidity and fatalism have in common with servility and self-abasement is a root in low self-esteem understood as a cluster of negative attitudes to the self and its components. They differ in the needs served by these attitudes. Those who are timid or fatalistic adopt a low opinion of the self out of a fear of social exclusion. Those who are servile and self-abased, instead, adopt a low self-regard wishing to gain social acceptance.

For this reason, some have described the damaged self-esteem that I have claimed in Chapter 5 is characteristic of servility as a kind of responsive self-esteem. Individuals who possess this form of self-esteem are able at least temporarily to increase their opinion of themselves following positive feedback (Jordan et al., 2013). It is plausible to attribute this responsiveness to their high self-esteem as implicitly measured. This positive attitude furnishes them a 'glimmer of hope' that manifests itself in an enhanced self-regard after experiences of social acceptance. I speculate that fatalism is a manifestation of a low self-esteem that is less responsive to positive feedback because it is congruent across explicit and implicit measures. Admittedly, however, this is speculation since to my knowledge there is no conclusive evidence in its support. Nevertheless, results showing that those whose low self-esteem is congruent do not feel less depressed after receiving positive feedback are suggestive of the identification of fatalism with a kind of self-esteem that is not responsive to episodes of social acceptance (cf. Jordan et al., 2013).

To summarize, this chapter has provided an account of four intellectual vices opposed to acceptance of one's own limitations and to proper concern for being esteemed. These are two vices of superiority—vanity and narcissism—based on positive attitudes, serving the need to be socially accepted, directed to the self and its cognitive features, and two vices of inferiority—timidity and fatalism—based on negative attitudes, serving the need to defend the ego from threats, directed to the self and its cognitive features. Each of these vices is characterized by distinctive emotions that function as powerful motives for some of the behaviours characteristic of these vices. Those who are vain are especially prone to spiteful envy; narcissism is rooted in morbid self-love. Timid individuals are riven by fear and those who fatalistic are the victims of hopelessness.

This discussion concludes my investigation of the psychology of those vices of superiority and inferiority that are opposed to intellectual humility. Having thus examined the structure of these vices, I am now in a position to explore in the next two chapters the influence of these vices on effective and responsible inquiry. In Chapter 7 I focus on the epistemic harms and moral wrongs to self and others that flow from the vices of superiority and inferiority. I show how *superbia*, arrogance, vanity, and narcissism generate unwarranted intellectual self-trust which in turn fosters vicious sensibilities and thinking styles. Servility, self-abasement, timidity, and fatalism diminish self-trust with equally deleterious consequences for an agent's effectiveness in inquiry. These intellectual vices are also harmful to the epistemic community as a whole since arrogance, for example, inhibits the free exchange of ideas, whilst vanity fosters the production of bullshit and other epistemic pollutants. Finally, these vices damage other epistemic agents. Individuals who are servile, for instance, deprive speakers of vital criticisms that could assist them in the refinement of their views. In Chapter 8 I discuss responsibility for these vices.

PART III
EPISTEMIC HARMS AND MORAL WRONGS

7
Harms and Wrongs

The vices of superiority and of inferiority comprise evaluations of one's own intellectual abilities, competencies, and skills for their intellectual worth that track the effectiveness of these qualities in defending the ego or gain social acceptance rather than appraising them for their epistemic value. There is, therefore, something inherently self-deceptive about these vices. What makes them vicious is that the motivations of ego-defence and social-acceptance give rise to further motives to turn away from epistemic goods. Hence, the arrogant and the vain, for instance, are motivated to avoid learning inconvenient truths about the intellectual worth of their abilities and skills. The individuals who possess the vices of superiority and inferiority are likely to be in denial about their motives, and deluded about their intellectual qualities.

Even though these intellectual vices are characterized primarily by their motives rather than their consequences, there is no doubt that in ordinary circumstances, numerous epistemic harms flow from them. For example, these vices are obstacles to the acquisition of self-knowledge; they promote the development of unwarranted self-confidence in haughty, arrogant, vain, and narcissistic individuals, and a corrosive lack of intellectual self-trust in those who suffer from the vices of inferiority. They facilitate the transmission of false information; they inhibit free, constructive but critical debate. Finally, they breed the development of other vices such as dogmatism, closed-mindedness, cowardice as well as promoting vicious thinking styles such as wishful thinking and sensibilities like wilful ignorance.

This chapter is concerned with the epistemic harms caused by the vices of inferiority and superiority. That is, it provides an analysis of some of the ways in which these vices effectively function as obstacles to inquiry that is conducted responsibly and effectively—that is to say, in the manner that is responsive to reasons and promotes the acquisition of knowledge and other epistemic goods (Cassam, 2016, 2019). I characterize these consequences of intellectual vices as epistemic harms because they constitute setbacks to the interest we all have in the acquisition of goods such as truth, knowledge, epistemic authority, and trust. The chapter consists of three sections. The first considers the negative influence of the vices of superiority and inferiority on inquiry. It focuses on their role in promoting motivated cognition and impeding self-regulation and self-control. The second section discusses the role of the vices of superiority and inferiority in distorting intellectual self-trust, obstructing self-knowledge and promoting self-deception.

The Mismeasure of the Self: A Study in Vice Epistemology. Alessandra Tanesini, Oxford University Press (2021).
© Alessandra Tanesini. DOI: 10.1093/oso/9780198858836.003.0007

The third section focuses on the epistemic harms that these vices cause to other agents and to the epistemic community as a whole.

7.1 Epistemic Harms to Epistemic Performance

I have already described some of the negative epistemic consequences of the vices of superiority and inferiority. For example in Chapter 5 I have mentioned that individuals who possess defensive high self-esteem are more prejudiced than other people and tend to overestimate the extent to which others agree with them. I have used these empirical findings to defend my position that intellectual *superbia* and arrogance are based on defensive attitudes and to illustrate the explanatory power of the attitude framework. In this section I take that discussion further by exploring the potential mechanisms responsible for these phenomena and by examining a broader range of epistemic harms that flow from the epistemic vices discussed in Chapters 5 and 6.

Social psychological research on the influence of attitudes on information processing and on responses to persuasive messages identifies attitude function as an important variable. Attitudes shape what novel information we attend to, how we process and interpret it, which messages we find persuasive and what we remember. In particular, the motives informing the development and maintenance of attitudes are crucial. People tend to prefer information that agrees with their pre-existing attitudes but what they consider, ignore, or reflect upon is also determined by the needs those attitudes have been formed to satisfy. For instance, people whose attitudes serve the function of ego-defence pay particular attention to information that is relevant to this motive. In short, the functions served by attitudes bias cognition. Since these functions are the result of motives that shape attitudes, cognition that is biased by attitude function is motivated cognition.

Supporters of the notion that cognition is motivated argue that cognitive processes are not purely cognitive (Kunda, 1990). Instead, motives are important drivers of cognition. These motives include the desire to be accurate, to be socially accepted and to enhance one's self-esteem. Motives shape cognition in two complementary ways. First, they determine which information should be considered. Second, they influence how that information is evaluated (Scott-Kakures, 2000). These influences are at work also in the cognitive processes leading to attitude formation. These processes are themselves primary examples of motivated cognition.

When faced with new objects, people are likely to try to figure out what they think and how they feel about them. The evaluation of the object is based on the information subjects have. However, not every bit of information is relevant. For example, when considering a potentially dangerous animal, it might be unimportant to consider that they have a shiny green skin. Which information is relevant depends on what we are trying to figure out. Thus, depending on whether we are attempting to make sense of the object or ascertaining whether it is a danger, we will select different information as the basis for the attitude. In this way, motives determine what is included in the attitude content. Second, motives also shape the evaluation process because they induce asymmetries in the costs associated with making errors. If the attitude to an object is shaped by the need to defend the self, less evidence is required to conclude that the object is dangerous than to be confident that it innocuous. This is because prudentially speaking false positives are less costly than false negatives. In this way, motives determine how the attitude itself is reached.

The ways in which motives shape attitude formation are examples of motivated cognition. The phenomenon, however, is meant to be pervasive and to shape cognitive processes of all kinds.[1] In what follows I interpret results that indicate that pre-existing attitudes bias information processing as examples of motivated cognition. It is plausible that attitude content and function (that is, the motive to fulfil a specific need) influence attitude-relevant information processing in addition to the attitude itself. If this is right, as robust function-matching effects in persuasion overwhelmingly indicate, the motives that sustain an attitude also subsequently shape the processing of information that is potentially relevant to that attitude. In other words, individuals pay more attention to information that is relevant to the motives that have guided the formation of their attitudes and that sustain their retention. That is, there is a match between the function(s) served by attitudes and the effort spent on processing information that is relevant to it (Watt et al., 2008). But this deep processing of information is biased by the relevant motive (Chen et al., 1999), and thus generally result in belief formation that is not sensitive to the evidence.[2]

Attitudes shape what information people access, how they process and interpret it, and what they remember. In general, people prefer to look at, and spend more time on, information that agrees with their pre-existing views and attitudes. This phenomenon is known as selective exposure effect (Maio & Haddock, 2015, pp. 58–60).[3] People also interpret information in ways that are biased in favour of their pre-existing attitudes (Maio & Haddock, 2015, pp. 61–62). Finally, individuals tend to remember better what they agree with. This is a congeniality effect that is generally believed to be small (Maio & Haddock, 2015, pp. 63–66).[4]

---

[1] The view that motives play a fundamental role in biasing cognition is not uncontroversial. Several psychologists have argued that numerous phenomena that have been taken as evidence of the role of motivation in cognition should be explained differently. For instance Hahn and Harris (2014) have pointed to methodological errors in the motivated cognition literature.

[2] See also Chapter 3, Section 3.1.2.

[3] See Fischer (2011) for a review that proposes a non-motivational account of the selective exposure effect.

[4] It is also not consistently present since there is evidence that people have good memory for arguments with which they are in disagreement (Eagly et al., 2001).

In sum, if unconstrained, on the whole people attend to, consider and remember better, information that supports their views rather than information that goes against them. There are, however, numerous variables that amplify, qualify, or inhibit these effects. These moderators include attitude functions such as defensiveness or meta-cognitive features such as certainty. I argue below that several properties of the attitudes that are the bases of the vices of inferiority and superiority are known to exacerbate these biasing effects. These results offer some empirical support for the view that these vices have especially pernicious epistemically negative consequences.

In addition to biasing the interpretation of new information, pre-existing attitudes also influence the manner in which we process this information. More specifically, the contents and functions of current attitudes contribute to determining whether we scrutinize some information or skim it superficially primarily by relying on some of its features as cues. The dominant models of attitude change following exposure to novel information are the Elaboration Likelihood Model (ELM) (Petty & Cacioppo, 1986) and the Heuristics Systematic Model (HSM) (Chen et al., 1999). Both models postulate the existence of a dual way of processing information. In some cases, subjects examine the content of the persuasive message and assess its probative strength. When this approach is adopted, people engage in cognitive processes that are slow, deliberative, and conscious. On other occasions, subjects to do not pay much heed to the content of the message, but rely on possibly irrelevant features of its source (e.g., whether the person is famous), to decide whether it is persuasive. These models agree that people scrutinize messages whenever they are able and motivated to do so; they rely on heuristics only when they are unable or are not motivated to consider the content of the message.

Whilst mention of two routes to persuasion by way of exposure to messages is reminiscent of dual processes theories of cognition (Evans, 2008), it would be more accurate to think of these models as postulating multiple routes to persuasion lying on a spectrum from wholly deliberative to fully heuristics (Petty et al., 2000). Hence, these frameworks are committed to the existence of numerous different kinds of cognitive processes rather than postulating the existence of two systems one of which would be conscious, slow, and deliberative (system 2) whilst the other would be unconscious, fast, and automatic (system 1) (Kahneman, 2012).

ELM and HSM also predict that messages that match the function or content of existing attitudes are more likely to persuade. These effects are well-established (Maio & Haddock, 2015, pp. 114–122). Subjects tend to process more deeply messages that speak to the content of the attitude and to the function it serves; they rely more on heuristics otherwise. If as I have proposed in Chapter 3, we understand attitude function in motivational terms, these effects are best understood as instances of motivated cognition. The motivations that have shaped and sustained the attitudes are also operative in the processing of messages that concern the objects of the attitudes. Subjects scrutinize more closely messages that are relevant to their motivations. Close scrutiny is not, however, the same thing as unbiased scrutiny. On the contrary, subjects often engage in processing that is both systematic and biased in favour of their pre-existing attitudes.[5]

Psychologists have found that people, who scrutinize a message, are more likely to find it persuasive than individuals who have not paid much attention to it. However, the phenomenon obtains only if the argument contained in the message is of good quality. This is because individuals when they subject arguments to close scrutiny become more sensitive to how well the premises support their conclusions (Lavine & Snyder, 1996; Petty et al., 2000, p. 140). It might seem that this claim flatly contradicts the claim that deep processing can be biased. Indeed, the psychological literature appears to support this objection since it often vacillates between claiming that systematic processing can be biased and asserting that it is also responsive to the evidence (e.g., Petty et al., 2000, comparing p. 140 and p. 145).

This objection can be answered if systematic processing is an instance of the kind of motivated cognition that I described above. A message that speaks to the motive sustaining the attitude will be selected as relevant to answering the directional question (e.g., questions such as: 'Is this thing a threat to how I see myself?') with which motivated cognizers address novel information. This is why this message is subjected to systematic processing.[6] In addition, motivation contributes to setting different evidential thresholds. More specifically, for example, cognizers motivated by the need to defend the self are prepared to run the risk of false positives to avoid false negatives. Hence, defensive individuals require less evidence to be persuaded that something is dangerous for their self-esteem than that it is not. This is why their systemic processing is biased. Nevertheless, this kind of bias is compatible with being sensitive to the differences in strength between different arguments that something is a threat (or indeed between arguments that it is not). If this is right, we would expect people whose attitudes to an object are defensive to find arguments about the dangers associated with the object to be more persuasive than arguments addressing other aspects of the object. This should occur because the threshold for judging the evidence to be sufficient to justify thinking of the object as a threat is set unusually low. There are several empirical results establishing what these conceptual considerations predict (Lavine & Snyder, 1996).

---

[5] Motives also influence the processing of information when one is denied the opportunity to scrutinize the message. In these cases messages that address a need that matches the attitude function are rated more positively than other messages. This occurs because the addressed need is treated as a cue (DeBono, 1987).

[6] Alternatively one can argue that the high importance of the issue raises the sufficiency threshold for certainty higher than it is set for uninteresting questions and thus induces more effort being spent on thinking about the issue (Maheswaran & Chaiken, 1991).

I have claimed that people who suffer from the vices of superiority and inferiority possess characteristic motivations. That is to say, their attitudes toward vast ranges of objects serve the same functions. Hence, arrogant but also timid people are in general defensive. Servile and also vain individuals have attitudes that serve a social-adjustive function. I am therefore committed to the view that there are individual differences in the kind of attitudes that people have (Snyder & DeBono, 1989). This approach predicts that different individuals will be systematically prone to some biases rather than others because of the kind of attitudes they possess. Defensive people, for instance, assess arguments that speak to their defensiveness as being more persuasive than other people judge them to be. These considerations support the conclusion that people whose attitudes serve functions other than knowledge are likely to display characteristic biases when attending to some new information, when processing and interpreting it, and subsequently when attempting to remember it.

The argument so far indicates that the vices of superiority and inferiority are obstacles to inquiry because they include characteristic motivations that systematically bias cognition when forming attitudes, considering new information, assessing arguments, and evaluating whether the evidence warrants changing one's view. These vices are especially pernicious because individuals who suffer from them adopt attitudes serving characteristic functions even with regard to objects for which the corresponding need seems irrelevant. For example, it is prudentially rational to have one's attitude to a bully being shaped by the motive to defend oneself. But, the adoption of a defensive attitude towards all sort of objects including one's own cognitive abilities is misplaced. Individuals who possess the vices of superiority and inferiority possess distinctive motivational profiles that puts them in an epistemically worse position compared to those occupied by other cognizers whose motivations are more mixed.

Features directly or indirectly pertaining to the affective components of the attitudes underlying the vices of superiority and inferiority also aggravate the situation. My focus here is on three such variables, and their biasing effects on cognition. They are: aspects of attitude strength including certainty, extremity and accessibility; low self-esteem; directed emotions. In what follows I discuss how these variables moderate the effects of motives on cognition.

Attitude certainty amplifies some biases (Clarkson et al., 2008). More precisely, when information is perceived as familiar, certainty about one's attitude exacerbates the tendency to prefer information that confirms one's pre-existing views (selective exposure effects) (Knobloch-Westerwick & Meng, 2009; Sawicki et al., 2011).[7]

---

[7] I suspect that if as I argue throughout those who suffer from arrogance are overconfident, they are extremely likely to judge that they have already considered the arguments presented by other people. Thus, I presume that these individuals tend to default in judging information presented by others as familiar.

Attitude certainty also biases judgment in favour of the existing attitude, provided that it is not ambivalent (Clarkson et al., 2008, 2011; Tormala, 2016; Tormala & Rucker, 2007). These results should not be surprising. It is rational to resist persuasion if one is quite certain of the correctness of one's current view. Such approach seems especially pertinent if the counterevidence is familiar (and thus presumably previously evaluated), and if one's attitude is not ambivalent because one's evidence is unequivocally in its support. These considerations are predicated on the assumption that the certainty with which the attitude is held in the first place is warranted. However, if such certainty is misplaced, its presence amplifies the probability of errors.

This is precisely the predicament of individuals who suffer from *superbia* and from arrogance. They are especially prone to form firm convictions to compensate for uncertainties they are motivated to suppress (McGregor, 2003; McGregor & Marigold, 2003; McGregor et al., 2005). That is, they have a tendency to be certain even when the evidence would not warrant this judgment. Existing certainties subsequently amplify the biased selection of information and its biased processing and evaluation. In short, they aggravate motivated cognition. In addition a tendency to be certain of one's attitudes also promotes self-certainty, where the latter is understood as confidence in one's abilities and general competence (Clarkson et al., 2009). Once again, this conclusion would be rational if the initial certainties were warranted. When they are not the connection between attitude certainty and self-certainty appears to promote a vicious circle of ever inflated confidence in one's views and oneself that is ill-placed.

I argued in Chapter 6 that narcissism (and vanity from which it is not distinguished in the psychological literature) is often conflated with arrogance because it is understood as being based on defensive high self-esteem (Gregg & Sedikides, 2010). I cannot exclude that this conflation explains results indicating that narcissist and vain individuals are also especially prone to be certain of their views (McGregor & Marigold, 2003; McGregor et al., 2005). Nevertheless there is evidence linking narcissism to overestimation of one's abilities (John & Robins, 1994).[8] If this is correct, the effects of certainty on biased thinking outlined here might well on the whole also apply to narcissism.

Although attitude certainty is a measure of people's judgments about their confidence that their attitudes are correct, it is generally presumed that subjects base these judgments on their epistemic feelings of confidence (Petty et al., 2007, pp. 256–257; 260–266). Given the role of epistemic feelings of confidence in the regulation of inquiry, we can explain the effects of attitude certainty on information processing in these terms. Feeling that one is certain about one's current position makes one more resistant to being persuaded to change one's mind. If

---

[8] See Moore and Schatz (2017) for a word of caution.

one is motivated to preserve the feeling, as is the case when the feeling of conviction is compensatory for an underlying lack of certainty, one is led to select and consider only information that is confirmatory of one's existing views (Petty et al., 2007, p. 261). Feelings of confidence should also play a role in determining how much effort one dedicates to examining a persuasive argument. If one is already certain of one's views one is unlikely to dedicate much time to considering counter-arguments. In addition, feelings of certainty should indicate the asymmetric levels of evidence required to reach a conclusion in motivated reasoning. The defensive person settles more quickly on identifying objects and people as threats rather than as unthreatening because less evidence of threat is necessary to inspire a feeling of certainty than it would be required to conclude with confidence that the object is not a danger to the self. These tendencies to experience premature feelings of certainty contribute to explaining why arrogant people are especially prone to overestimating the extent to which others agree with their views (McGregor et al., 2005), to holding prejudicial beliefs about members of stigmatized social groups (Ashton-James & Tracy, 2012; Jordan et al., 2005), and to be unrealistically optimistic (Bosson et al., 2003).

Attitude certainty positively correlates with attitude extremity. That is, people who are very confident of their views also tend to have extreme views (Petty et al., 2007, p. 261). It is therefore no surprise that individuals whose high self-esteem is defensive tend to hold extreme views (Haddock & Gebauer, 2011). Extremity is predictive of increased bias in some judgments. For instance, those who hold extreme views also tend to attribute to others views that are equally extreme. Hence, they perceive debates to be polarized (Van Boven et al., 2012).

Whilst attitude certainty exacerbates bias in some circumstances, lack of certainty is deleterious in others. When information is perceived as unfamiliar, uncertainty aggravates selective exposure (Sawicki et al., 2011; Sawicki et al., 2013). Uncertainty can also lead to more systematic processing of information (Maheswaran & Chaiken, 1991; Tormala, 2016); whilst certainty is associated with dedicating less effort to information processing (Tormala & Rucker, 2007, p. 474). Increased elaboration of the content of persuasive messages does not indicate that such processing is less biased, although there is evidence that people who are made to feel uncertain are more sensitive to differences in argument strength than those who are certain of their views (Tiedens & Linton, 2001). This result is hardly surprising since it indicates that when people pay attention to arguments they are more sensitive to differences in quality among them. It is also compatible with enhanced bias if these individuals tend to agree with whatever argument is presented to them.

In addition, the enhancement of selective exposure when faced with unfamiliar information, would suggest that in these circumstances people who lack confidence in their own views suffer from an increased liability to biased thinking. I hasten to add that it is rational to consider more deeply information that is relevant to one's views when one is uncertain about their correctness. Issues arise only when one is chronically uncertain, as is the case for individuals who are depressed or who suffer from the vices of inferiority. These individuals lack in self-confidence and thus might experience persuasive messages as relatively unfamiliar (since they might not be confident that they have already addressed them) and thus as requiring extensive evaluation.

If my accounts of the vices of inferiority are correct, the empirical literature on the effects of attitude uncertainty on information processing might fail to distinguish the characteristic profiles of those who are timid and of those who are servile. In my view, individuals who are timid or fatalistic are chronically prone to experience fear as well as self-doubt, whilst those who are servile experience uncertainty and are prone to shame. To the best of my knowledge, those results that indicate an association between attitude uncertainty, increased message elaboration or scrutiny, and increased sensitivity to argument strength have focused on inducing emotions such as sadness that are only moderately associated with uncertainty (Tiedens & Linton, 2001).

There is, instead, evidence associating fear with increased selective exposure (Mathews & MacLeod, 1994) and also with increased reliance on heuristic processing and decreased sensitivity to argument quality (Baron, 2000; Gleicher & Petty, 1992; Wood, 2000). This set of seemingly contradictory results can be explained if the influence of attitude uncertainty on information processing is moderated by other factors. If the moderator is fear, as is the case for individuals who are timid and fatalistic, then attitude uncertainty increases bias in favour of one's current opinion because it encourages superficial engagement with arguments and a preference for information that is congruent with one's existing views. If the moderator is shame or sadness, as with individuals who are servile and self-abasing, then attitude uncertainty might lead to increased effort in the processing of information when one is unfamiliar with the arguments under consideration.[9] Presumably such increased elaboration is in the aid of understanding the attitudes endorsed by others in order to get along with them.[10]

The discussion of the biasing effects of attitude certainty and uncertainty highlights similarities to the consequences of dispositional need for closure (Kruglanski, 2004). As I explained in Chapter 2 this motivational feature of cognition is responsible for a tendency to freeze one's current opinions when one thinks one is already well-informed and is confident in one's ability to achieve closure. This is precisely the kind of closed-mindedness that is a consequence of

---

[9] The association between fear and uncertainty is much stronger than that between shame and uncertainty (Smith & Ellsworth, 1985, p. 827).

[10] Chen et al. (1996) indicate that individuals who are motivated to get along are biased in favour of agreeing with those with whom they are in discussion.

the certainty in one's views and self-confidence that is characteristic of arrogance and narcissism. For this reason, these vices of superiority are capital vices (Kidd, 2017a). Their presence promotes the development of other vices. More specifically, the vices of superiority foster the acquisition and strengthening of closed-mindedness, dogmatism, and prejudicial ways of thinking.

The other tendency that is characteristic of the dispositional need for closure is seizing on novel information (Kruglanski, 2004). It is manifested in situations in which one feels uninformed or unable to achieve closure. This tendency bears a similarity to the effects of attitude uncertainty on information processing. Those lacking in confidence in their views seize on the information that is presented to them either because fear inhibits cognitive effort or because the desire to get along leads one to share the opinions of one's conversational partners. For this reason, the vices of inferiority are also best thought of as capital vices. Timidity fosters closed-mindedness whist servility also promotes unthinking conformism (Romero-Canyas et al., 2010).[11]

Low self-esteem has also been found to have significant effects on the processing of information. It amplifies selective exposure with regard to value-relevant information (Wiersema et al., 2012). This phenomenon has been described as a defensive attempt to avoid facing unpleasant truths (Maio & Haddock, 2015, p. 60). This description is suggestive of the tendency of those who are timid and who out of fear prefer not to think about challenging issues. In addition, low self-esteem also aggravates a congeniality effect so that one tends to remember better information that is congruent with one's opinions (Wiersema et al., 2010). This phenomenon too seem to involve some form of defensive strategy.

Finally, the characteristic emotions of the vices of inferiority and superiority also contribute to extensive biasing of information selection, processing and recall. I have already mentioned how fear inhibits careful scrutiny of information. But the effects of anger, envy, and shame are also detrimental. Anger promotes certainty and its attendant biases (Tiedens & Linton, 2001).[12] Malicious envy amplifies selective exposure (Crusius & Lange, 2014) and biases memory (Hill et al., 2011). Finally shame promotes attitude uncertainty and its resultant effects (Smith & Ellsworth, 1985).

The negative consequences of the vices of inferiority and superiority on epistemic conduct are not limited to the biasing effects of their motivational and affective components on the selection, processing and recall of information. In

---

[11] Interestingly, some have found that attitude accessibility, which is a feature of those attitudes that are the causal bases of humility, reduces selective exposure effects (Roskos-Ewoldsen & Fazio, 1992). However, since much of the work on this topic aggregates measures of attitude accessibility and certainty, it is hard to have any confidence in some of these findings.

[12] Pettigrove (2012) also discusses a number of experiments showing that anger can impact negatively the quality of judgments about outgroups, threats, and risks.

addition, these vices impede inquiry by promoting failures of self-control or self-regulation. Self-regulation is understood as the ability to make and keep commitments that are appropriate given one's abilities and goals.[13] Individuals with defensive high self-esteem show poor self-regulation of behaviour, and might become aggressive especially when they feel threatened (Baumeister et al., 1996; Lambird & Mann, 2006). Further, because they are unrealistically optimistic about their abilities, unwarrantedly certain of their opinions, and overestimate consensus with their views, they are unlikely to set for themselves goals that are conducive to success in their epistemic activities. These same people have a tendency to self-handicap (Lupien et al., 2010); that is to say, they do not put in the preparation required to succeed in a task. This is a defensive strategy since it allows to attribute failure to lack of effort rather than to inability.[14]

In addition, the propensity to anger that is characteristic of arrogant people also facilitates losing self-control. Similarly, spiteful envy, which is a characteristic emotion of vanity and narcissism, contributes to losing control because it depletes the resources available to engage in cognitive tasks (Hill et al., 2011). In general, it would seem that narcissists suffer from self-regulatory failures akin to those that are characteristic of arrogant individuals (Ashton-James & Tracy, 2012).

The vices of inferiority are also implicated in loss of control because of failures in monitoring and regulation. Individuals, whose self-esteem is said to be damaged because it is low when measured explicitly even though it is high in implicit measures, are prone to ruminating (that is, mulling over and over the same thoughts) (Phillips & Hine, 2016). In addition, feelings of ambivalence and self-doubt can lead to procrastination (van Harreveld et al., 2009). These tendencies predictably result in failures of self-regulation since rumination depletes cognitive resources that cannot therefore be allocated to carrying out other cognitive tasks. These same individuals have high levels of maladaptive perfectionism (Zeigler-Hill & Terry, 2007). This propensity is an obstacle to efficiency in inquiry. Further, the experience of being rejected that is associated with servility is known to generate a sense of loss of control as well as the directed emotion of shame (Gerber & Wheeler, 2009). Finally, fear might cause lapses of self-regulation (Baumeister & Heatherton, 1996).

This large body of literature provides abundant evidence in favour of the conclusion that the attitudes I have identified as the causal bases of the vices of superiority and inferiority are causally responsible for epistemic activities such as thinking, assessing arguments, collecting new information that are less than successful because they are marked by motivational biases and by a lack of self-regulation. These considerations support the view that possession of these attitudes is an obstacle to effective and responsible inquiry (Cassam, 2016, 2019).

---

[13] See Baumeister and Heatherton (1996) for an overview of failures of self-regulation.
[14] For added complexity see Leary and Baumeister (2000, p. 30).

Relatedly, the evidence reviewed in this section also supports the claim that the intellectual character vices of superiority and inferiority foster the development of vicious thinking styles and sensibilities. Since the vices of inferiority and superiority alike promote selective exposure, they are associated with the development of wilfully ignorant sensibilities because of a predilection for attending to information that is congruent with what one already believes. I have already indicated that arrogance, narcissism but also self-abasement might be associated with different tendencies that are characteristic of the dispositional need for closure. There is also work connecting a propensity to adopt conspiratorial explanations (conspiracy mentality) with narcissism (Cichocka et al., 2016), the need for cognitive closure (Marchlewska et al., 2018), and the need to feel special (Imhoff & Lamberty, 2017). In addition, if narcissism predicts overestimation of one's abilities as I indicated above, it is likely to involve a tendency to engage in wishful thinking.[15] These results indicate that the vices of inferiority and superiority have pervasive negative consequences for epistemic conduct in every context ranging from observation, to argument evaluation, to the ability to set and commit appropriate epistemic goals.

7.2 Intellectual Self-Trust, Self-Knowledge, and Self-Deception

In this section I argue that the vices of inferiority and superiority are at the root of unwarranted forms of self-trust and distrust. I also show how these vices are responsible for persistent and extensive self-deception. These claims are not surprising given the pervasive negative effects of these character traits on epistemic conduct as a whole.[16]

I think of intellectual self-trust as a three-place relation between an agent, her intellectual faculties and abilities, and some domain or context.[17] In my view there are at least three components to intra-personal trust, each of which is necessary for a person to trust herself. The first is a tendency to rely on one's faculties and abilities; the second is a propensity to be confident in one's willpower; the third is a disposition to experience at least occasionally positive epistemic feelings of certainty and confidence.[18]

These three components of intellectual self-trust play distinctive roles in inquiry. Reliance on one's faculties and abilities is required to carry out any epistemic activity. Confidence in one's willpower is necessary to be able to commit to one's epistemic goals and plans. Finally, epistemic feelings have an essential role

---

[15] See Moore and Schatz (2017) for a word of caution.
[16] I have offered an account of self-trust and discussed how arrogance and servility lead to forms of self-trust and distrust that are unwarranted in Tanesini (2020).
[17] The idea that trust is a three-place relation can be traced to Baier (1994).
[18] These elements are necessary but they might not be sufficient for intellectual self-trust.

in guiding and monitoring epistemic activities. Feeling doubtful prompts agents to investigate or to double-check the outcome of previous epistemic activities; feeling certain alerts them that they can at least provisionally endorse their current results.

Every facet of epistemic conduct is dependent on reliance on one's faculties and abilities. Without implicitly taking these aspects of the self to be reliable, epistemic activity would simply be impossible. Unless we are at least prepared defeasibly to accept the vast majority of the deliverances of our senses, of memory and of reasoning, we would be condemned to deep seated and crippling scepticism. Genuine sceptical doubt is not a live option for humans. If we are to live and flourish, we need to have beliefs, and thus we must place some trust in our intellectual capacities.[19] Implicit reliance on our faculties does not presuppose that we believe that they are reliable. Very young children possess this kind of intellectual self-trust before they are able to acquire metacognitive beliefs about the reliability of their own faculties. That said, I would expect most adults to rely on their capacities but also to believe that they are at least somewhat reliable.

Reliance on one's faculties presupposes taking them to be up to the task of acquiring and evaluating information. However, in order to trust oneself to carry out epistemic activities successfully, one must also be confident that one has the self-control required to regulate and monitor cognitive processing. Without the exercise of epistemic agency, even though one's faculties might in principle be up to a specific cognitive task, the person might not be up to carrying it out successfully because he is too distracted or unmotivated or lacking in resilience. Therefore, trusting oneself presupposes taking one's will to possess the kind of control required to execute cognitive tasks.[20]

Finally, intellectual self-trust requires that one is not in the grip of crippling epistemic anxiety. I take epistemic anxiety to be persistent feelings of doubt about some of one's beliefs. Epistemic anxiety can temper someone's tendency to excessive certainty about one's views, but if it is ever present or concerns beliefs that are central to the agent's world view, it can become crippling. Jones' example of a person who obsessively checks on her way to airport whether she has packed her passport is an apt example of anxiety (2012). It also demonstrates that an affective element is essential to self-trust.

The person who is in the grip of doubts about the whereabouts of her passport might sincerely believe that it is in her bag, because she remembers putting it

---

[19] See Zagzebski (2012) for some arguments that a degree of self-trust is rational as well as inescapable.
[20] These two aspects of self-trust can come apart since one may trust one's self-control without trusting one's intellectual prowess. Conversely, one might trust one's abilities without trusting the strength of one's will. In my opinion these two aspects of self-trust also exemplify different kinds of reliance. Agents rely on their faculties in the sense that they predict that they will be reliable, agents also expect their will to deliver. This expectation is not however a mere prediction. It is also a commitment. Hence, trust in one's will is not a matter of mere reliance.

there. Nevertheless, this belief is insufficient to quell anxiety and put an end to searching behaviour. This person has, for whatever reason, set the evidential threshold for resting assured that the passport is in her bag unnecessarily high, so high in fact that it can never be met (cf. Nagel, 2010). It might be objected that one might be able to explain the behaviour of the epistemically anxious by attributing to them inconsistent beliefs about the location of the passport. I have no objection to this view if it is predicated on the thought that to entertain a proposition is, in some sense, to already believe it (Mandelbaum, 2014). My point is rather that this phenomenon has a distinctive affective component. It is this component that plays a motivational role in initiating and halting epistemic activities.

The vices of inferiority and superiority are at the root of decalibrated forms of intellectual self-trust. The vices of superiority are responsible for inflated self-trust, whilst those of inferiority are implicated in the unwarranted deflation of self-trust. There are three ways in which these vices distort the dispositions that constitute self-trust. First, they influence the extent to which one is disposed to rely on one's faculties in each context. That is, they contribute to determining whether one relies on one's abilities in a given situation, even though, for instance, one is tired or ill-qualified. They also partly determine levels of confidence in the deliverances of one's faculties causing over or under confidence. Second, they set the default level of epistemic anxiety in ways that are at variance with what would be epistemically appropriate. Third, they weaken regulatory self-control so that confidence in one's will power (if present) would be unwarranted.

Superbia and intellectual arrogance are characterized by a tendency to experience anger and contempt (cf. Chapter 5). These emotions are indicative of defensiveness and promote compensatory certainty in one's convictions (McGregor, 2003; McGregor & Marigold, 2003). Certainty, in turn, promotes self-certainty (Clarkson et al., 2009). These vices by facilitating unwarranted self-certainty, that is to say confidence in one's ability to form correct opinions, foster a tendency to rely on one's faculties even when such reliance is unwarranted or should be tempered with caution. In short, these vices promote overconfidence in one's abilities. In addition, because these vices are characterized by defensive emotions, they contribute to making potential threats to the ego seem especially salient. This salience sets the evidential threshold for identifying something as threatening as especially low, so that inquiry is terminated prematurely. One might classify these people as being, epistemically speaking, insufficiently anxious. Finally, anger contributes to loss of control and thus further impedes effective inquiry. Because loss of control is not accompanied by a loss of confidence in one's abilities, this element of these two vices of superiority also contributes to the decalibration of self-trust. In conclusion, those who are arrogant or suffer from *superbia* put a lot of trust in their intellectual capacities. Their self-trust is, however, inflated and therefore ill-placed.

Intellectual vanity and narcissism are characterized by dispositions to experience malicious or spiteful envy and morbid self-love (see Chapter 6). These emotions are in my view indicative of a desire to be loved and admired by other people. Narcissism also promotes unwarranted certainty in one's own abilities because it fosters self-serving assessments of their strength (Campbell & Foster, 2007; Campbell et al., 2000). Hence, vanity and narcissism like arrogance and *superbia* promote inflated self-confidence that manifests itself through unwarranted reliance on one's own abilities. In addition, spiteful envy and morbid self-love contribute to making others' opinions seem especially salient. Cognitive effort is thus directed to features of the self and of other people that might influence how one is viewed. This might be reflected in setting the evidential threshold required to satisfy oneself that others hold one in high opinion unusually high, so that individuals who are vain and narcissistic might show heightened epistemic anxiety in this domain since they desire above all to think highly of themselves and to be held in esteem by others (Baumeister & Vohs, 2001).[21] Hence, these individuals have inflated self-trust but also heightened anxiety about others' trust in their abilities (cf. Campbell et al., 2007). The role of envy in inhibiting self-control because it depletes cognitive resources further contributes to causing the inflated and yet anxious self-trust of those who are vain and narcissistic to be at variance with the facts.

Intellectual servility and self-abasement are characterised by a propensity to experience shame (see, chapter five). Since shame is an experience of having failed to meet standards it generates beliefs and feelings about one's lack of ability. These beliefs and feelings are in the case of servile and self-abasing individuals often unwarranted. Therefore, they foster a tendency not to rely sufficiently on one's own capacities. In other words, these vices deflate intellectual self-trust. In addition, shame tends to make aspects of the self that attract public disapproval especially salient. Hence, heightened cognitive effort is directed at monitoring one's own performance. This is why these individuals are high self-monitors that tend to adjust their views, including their opinion of themselves, to the prevailing consensus (Snyder, 1974). I suspect that these concerns will make such individuals exceedingly anxious about their own capacities. They might thus set the evidential threshold to adjudicate which features of their own character are strengths to be inappropriately high. As a result they might show heightened anxiety about their performance combined with a deflated kind of self-trust. This combination of features would explain their tendency to belittle their own abilities but also their perfectionism. Finally, shame has the power in the long term to weaken self-control by depleting cognitive resources (Baumeister et al., 2006; Gerber & Wheeler, 2009;

---

[21] In this regard one should bear in mind that narcissists have a high opinion of their abilities but tend to think that they are not likeable. See Chapter 6.

Vohs et al., 2005).[22] Perversely, this feature of the vice actually lowers the reliability of one's faculties. It thus validates one's tendency not to trust oneself. Nevertheless, it contributes to the decalibration of self-trust because these low assessments of abilities actually lower the reliability of one's faculties rather than record the extent to which one can rely on them.

Intellectual timidity and fatalism are characterized by a disposition to experience fear, hopelessness, and despair (see Chapter 6). People who suffer from these vices have low self-esteem and lack confidence in their abilities and feel especially vulnerable to threats.[23] As a result these individuals lack confidence in their abilities and suffer from deflated self-trust. In addition, they are likely to exhibit high levels of epistemic anxiety. In turn, such anxiety has the perverse effect of damaging regulatory self-control and thus impact negatively on the reliability of the faculties of the chronically anxious person (Mathews & MacLeod, 1994). As in the case of servile and self-abased individuals low self-esteem functions as a self-fulfilling prophecy since it diminishes ability which in turn lowers the level of esteem fitting for one's capacities.

These considerations make it apparent that those who suffer from these vices do not have their own measure. People who are arrogant or servile, vain or timid, harbour motivated false beliefs about themselves or their abilities. For instance, narcissists are known to offer grandiose reports of their performance even when it is in fact objectively poor (Campbell & Foster, 2007). Arrogant people are unwarrantedly certain about their abilities (McGregor & Marigold, 2003). They compare themselves to others in ways that are disproportionately self-enhancing (Vohs & Heatherton, 2004). Conversely those who are servile or timid are prone to underestimate their abilities because they attribute failures to their shortcomings but successes to situational factors (that is, they possess a depressive attributional style) (Schröder-Abé et al., 2007a). They also compare themselves unfavourably to others whom they judge to possess good qualities (Vohs & Heatherton, 2004). In short, possession of these vices constitutes a significant obstacle to self-knowledge.

I have claimed that individuals who suffer from these vices have a significant number of false beliefs resulting from their attitudes about their intellectual abilities or about the epistemic status of their beliefs. Some people might also harbour illusions that they know and understand topics over which their grasp is somewhat tenuous. Others might underestimate their level of expertise. These wide-ranging misconceptions are not mere errors. They are examples of self-deception in the sense of belief or attitude that is formed and preserved, despite abundant counter-evidence, because of some directional motivation, and could

---

[22] However, in the short term anticipating future shame also supplies some incentive to resist impulsive behaviour (Patrick et al., 2009).
[23] On the effects of a chronic sense of vulnerability on intellectual self-trust see Jones (2004).

not be acknowledged without creating a deep conflict between the subject's attitudes and doxastic states. The beliefs about their intellectual abilities harboured by the arrogant are motivated by their need to self-enhance, those of the servile by their need to be socially accepted. The self-assessment of those who are timid are guided by the need to avoid rejection, and those of the vain to be thought of highly. Thus each of these vices results in beliefs about the self that are not sensitive to the evidence because of the biasing influence of motives that are unrelated to accuracy. The self-deceptive nature of these beliefs about the self, and of the attitudes that sustain them, explains why the vices of self-evaluation are stealthy and resistant to change via rational update (Cassam, 2015, 2019).[24]

What makes these beliefs and attitudes self-deceptive is that they are beliefs and attitudes about the self that are false and whose falsity is motivated rather than accidental. In addition, the processes by which these attitudes are acquired and maintained are necessarily opaque to the subjects that have the attitudes since awareness of one's motives would rationally undermine one's attitudes. Finally, in some cases these beliefs are inferred from attitudes that are discrepant. This discrepancy is likely experienced by the subject as a tension or an anxiety about the accuracy of one's views. But even if the discrepancy does not raise to consciousness, it is nevertheless a conflict or dissonance in the cognitive economy of the individuals that moves them to try to solve it. These features of vicious self-assessments show them not to be mere mistakes but examples of self-deception, provided that it is agreed that one might be self-deceived without consciously intending to deceive oneself (cf. Mele, 2001).

The account of arrogance I have offered in Chapter 5 can be used to illustrate these points. The person who is arrogant has an inflated opinion of his ability. His false beliefs are based on attitudes that serve the function to defend the ego by making him feel good about himself. This motivation biases what he considers relevant to assessing his own abilities and how he evaluates the relevant evidence. These evaluations include comparing oneself for similarities to capable individuals so as to gain evidence of one's own competence. The motive to puff up the ego in self-defence is responsible for the tenacity of the false beliefs about the self in the teeth of available counter-evidence. The motivated process of attitude and belief formation results in underestimating the significance of this evidence, or explaining it away or even disregarding it. This is why arrogant self-beliefs are motivated beliefs.

In addition both the nature of the motivations responsible for these beliefs and attitudes and the processes leading to the formation of these cognitive states are opaque to the subject because if one became aware of them, one's beliefs and

---

[24] They are stealthy because possession of the vice inhibits the ability to know that one has that vice; they are resistant to change because possession of the vice inhibits the self-control and motivation required to dislodge the vice.

attitudes would be rationally undermined. With regard to arrogance, if the arrogant individual became aware that he has a high opinion of himself only because having it makes him feel good about himself, he could not sustain his high self-estimate. If one discovers that one's belief in one's intelligence has nothing to do with one's intelligence and everything to do with one's need to feel good about oneself, one would no longer believe in one's intelligence or feel good about oneself. The motive of self-enhancement props up the false belief but the genealogy of the belief cannot be avowed by the subject without undermining self-belief. In short, a true psychological explanation of why the subject harbours some beliefs and attitudes would make some of the psychological states appear rationally untenable in his own eyes (Cassam, 2015). This is why these false motivated beliefs and attitude are self-deceptive. The person who has them must necessarily lack some self-knowledge. Hence, the vice or arrogance is stealthy since those who suffer from it are ill-equipped to notice that they have the vice.

In this regard, these attitudes are different from other motivated cognitive states. A person could be wilfully ignorant of some counter-evidence with regard to some belief of hers. She might be aware that her thinking is motivated but endorses her bias or simply does not care about it. Arguably this person is not self-deceived because she understands herself well (Holton, 2001). The arrogant individual's motivated beliefs and attitudes are sustained only thanks to ignorance about his motives and how they support these cognitive states. Since such a person is necessarily ignorant about the pedigree of his views about himself, it is plausible to think of this as a case of self-deception.[25]

Finally arrogance is based on discrepant attitudes to the self. The arrogant person has positive views of the self as measured explicitly but also possess negative attitudes to self in implicit measures. It is this discrepancy that has led some psychologists to hypothesize that the positive opinions about the self that these individuals express in response to questionnaires whilst sincerely held are a defensive cover for deep seated doubts about the self (McGregor & Marigold, 2003). This discrepancy would thus be evidence of an internal psychological conflict that might or might not be consciously experienced. Either way, the subject struggles to resolve this tension but, as the deep seated doubts are not extinguished, the defensive mechanism remain operative. Hence, arrogant beliefs and attitudes about the self display the kind of inner conflict or tension that is another hallmark of self-deception.[26] This tension or conflict might not be present in every vice of self-assessment. For instance, I have not argued that timidity or fatalism are based on some kind of discrepant self-esteem. However, if the accounts I presented in

---

[25] See Medina (2013, p. 143) on the links between self-ignorance and complicity with oppressive conditions that contribute to spreading ignorance.

[26] The presence of this tension might be a difference between self-deception and self-delusion given that the latter is also an example of motivated belief whose genesis must be opaque to the self.

Chapters 5 and 6 are correct, the remaining six vices of self-evaluations are based on attitudes that are prone to generate cognitive dissonance.

To summarize, the first two sections of this chapter detail the numerous epistemic harms that the vices of superiority and inferiority inflict on their possessors. They damage their ability to engage in effective and responsible inquiry because they dispose them to engage in motivated cognition and they impact negatively their self-regulatory abilities. These same vices harm subjects' ability to acquire and retain a form of self-trust that is calibrated or warranted; they are obstacles to the acquisition of self-knowledge and instead promote delusions and self-deception.

7.3 Epistemic Harms to Others

The vices of superiority and inferiority are not only epistemically damaging to their possessors but they are also causally responsible for behaviours and attitudes that harm the epistemic community as a whole as well as its members. In what follows I first highlight how these vices cause setbacks to other people's epistemic interests before discussing the damage done to epistemic communities. The vices of inferiority and superiority do not merely harm other people; they also wrong them by denying them the full expression of their epistemic agency. The discussion of these harms and wrongs here is not intended to be exhaustive. Instead, I highlight a few examples to convey the gravity and extensiveness of the damage done to people's epistemic interests by the presence of behaviours and attitudes associated with these vices. I shall address questions concerning responsibility for epistemic harms and moral wrongs in Chapter 8.

Individuals who possess some vices of superiority, but also people who suffer from those of inferiority cause setbacks to others' epistemic interests by depriving them of knowledge and thus facilitating their ignorance. A few examples should illustrate the phenomenon. Arrogant individuals overestimate consensus over their views about which they also are excessively confident. The certainty with which they hold their opinions is bound to mislead other people into accepting what arrogant individuals say even though objectively speaking the evidence they possess for their claims might not be strong. Both models of persuasion (ELM and HSM) discussed above predict that messages from sources that are perceived to be more credible are more persuasive than messages of equal quality from sources felt to be less credible both in conditions of low levels of cognitive elaboration (Petty & Cacioppo, 1986) and when cognitive elaboration is high (Petty & Wegener, 1998; Pornpitakpan, 2004).[27] Further, since attitude certainty is likely to enhance the

---

[27] In some cases especially when the message concerns matters of subjective preference certainty about one's own views has the opposite effect (Karmarkar & Tormala, 2010). This is unsurprising since it is foolish to express certainty about one's objective correctness in what is a matter of mere taste.

appearance of credibility, those who are certain of their views are more likely to persuade others to agree with them compared with other people who are less certain of their opinions. This is so irrespective of whether such self-certainty is warranted. In addition, those who are certain of the correctness of their views have a propensity to advocacy (Cheatham & Tormala, 2015). The combined effect of a tendency to proselytize and the unwarranted ability to persuade suggests that arrogant individuals might be especially effective at spreading their views. However, since as I argued above, these are arrived at in highly biased ways, arrogant individuals are likely to transmit more false and misleading information than other people. Given that we all have an interest in receiving truthful information, by spreading false, misleading, or unwarranted beliefs arrogant individuals harm other epistemic agents.

Vanity and narcissism are also detrimental to other people's knowledge acquisition and preservation. Vain and narcissistic individuals do not care about the truth and are likely to say whatever is expedient to obtain the power and admiration they crave. Their disregard for the truth is at the root of their tendency to bullshit. That is to say to put forward claims irrespective of their epistemic value. Since narcissists often also exude an air of self-certainty, their bullshit can be convincing, thus unduly persuading other people. In this manner, vain and narcissists promote other people's acquisition of unwarranted beliefs.

Individuals who suffer from the vice of inferiority are also prone to causing epistemic harm to other agents. For instance, people who are intellectually servile are likely to parrot the views of the powerful and to change their opinion depending on the viewpoint of those whom they are trying to ingratiate. Hence, servile individuals are likely to amplify and transmit the false and misleading beliefs of the powerful. This is harmful whenever further epistemic agents accept these opinions and take them to be true. Similarly timid individuals are likely to be quiet even when they possess information that would be helpful to other people. Hence, timid people can cause epistemic harms to others by depriving them of knowledge which they are in a position to transmit.

So far I have highlighted some the harms, defined following Feinberg (1984, ch. 1) as a setback to interests, that individuals suffering from the vices of inferiority and superiority are likely to cause to other people. Harms so understood are different from wrongs. First, some harms are not wrongs. These include harms that result from natural causes but also harms that result from others' legitimate activities. For instance, if you do not lend me something that you have and I need, you set back my interests but do not wrong me if I have no right to the loan. Conversely, some wrongs might not be overall harmful. People who paternalistically interfere to stop someone acting against his own interests, wrong this person because they violate his autonomy. However, they might overall further his interests rather than set them back. Further some wrongs might not be at all harmful. Imagine a person who has a reputation for breaking her promises, so that no one expects her to keep her word. If she makes and breaks a promise to an individual who does not expect her to do as promised, she has wronged that person but might not have harmed the promissee who had not counted on the promise.

The vices of inferiority and superiority also find their expression in behaviours that wrong other epistemic agents. Here I briefly describe three kinds of wrong. First, arrogant individuals wrong other people by intimidating and humiliating them. This behaviour is morally wrong but it is also causally responsible for a distinctive epistemic wrong. Those who are subjected to these kinds of behaviour often lose confidence in the accuracy of their views and in their intellectual abilities. Such erosion of self-trust is a distinctively epistemic (as well as moral) wrong because it impedes the future full exercise of individuals' epistemic agency. Those who come to believe that they lack intellectual abilities often stop trying to improve. Hence, loss of confidence and self-trust turn into self-fulfilling prophecies.

Narcissists and vain individuals also have a tendency to wrong other people. Because they are spitefully envious of other people's successes, they are likely to downplay the worth of others' achievements by attempting to spoil them and devalue them (Protasi, 2016). These behaviours are disrespectful but they might also contribute to loss of confidence and self-trust in other people if they begin to doubt the value of their achievements.

It might be thought that those who suffer from vices of inferiority are also disposed to wrong others because they engage in behaviours such as excessive deference that could cause others to wrongly inflate self-confidence and self-trust. If a person is surrounded by people who agree with everything she says, she may come to the conclusion that she is exceptionally smart and that her views are irrefutably correct. The development of excessive self-confidence is likely to be harmful to the individual. Thus, insofar as servile individuals are instrumental to this situation, they are causally responsible for harm. This conduct taken singly, however, does not seem wrongful in the requisite epistemic sense. That said, as Fricker also notes, its cumulative effect might be wronging the person who is thereby made to develop a vicious character (2007, pp. 20–21).[28]

Failures to give others the epistemic credit they deserve are the second kind of wrong caused by those who possess the vices of superiority. Arrogant individuals are prone to dismiss or even ridicule other people's views when they disagree with their own. Narcissists are known for stealing for themselves credit that is due to other people (Campbell & Foster, 2007; Campbell et al., 2000). These behaviours

---

[28] The examples of individuals who feign deference and servility as a survival strategy in conditions of oppression or as a deliberate plan to deceive in the pursuit of self-interest are different. These are cases of deceit and thus are by themselves wrongful, even though the wrong might in some circumstances be excusable.

are wrongful because they are failures to recognize other agents as deserving of respect for their epistemic capacities. Arrogant individuals deflate other people's credibility, whilst narcissists reduce the esteem in which other individuals should be held. Whenever these wrongful behaviours that are tantamount to a lack of respect occur systematically, and especially when they target individuals subordinated and stigmatized because of their social identities, they can be rightfully categorized as instances of epistemic injustice, since they are wrongs done to individuals in their capacity as knowers (Fricker, 2007, p. 20).

Finally, the vices of superiority but also the vices of inferiority are, in Kidd's terminology, capital vices (Kidd, 2017a). These are vices that corrupt because they facilitate the development of further off-spring vices. I have already argued that arrogance fosters dogmatism and closed-mindedness, for instance. But these vices are also capital in the sense of promoting the development of vices in other epistemic agents. This phenomenon is a distinctive third kind of wrong that is caused by behaviours expressive of the vices of inferiority and superiority.

Arrogant individuals are prone to behaviours that intimidate and humiliate other people. These would include: shouting down other people, repeatedly interrupting them when they speak, mocking their contributions to debates. Aggressive behaviours are intimidating whilst mockery is designed to humiliate. When individuals are repeatedly intimidated and humiliated, they might fight back in anger. However, different responses are also likely. The person who is frequently at the receiving end of intimidating behaviour might choose to self-silence to avoid future attacks. Such a person will find herself biting her tongue time and time again. Whilst it is possible that she might retain a sense that her contributions would be useful, if she were allowed to make them without fear of reprisal, it is also likely that she rationalizes her silence not as explained by a desire to avoid unpleasant attacks but as resulting from the fact that she has nothing to say.

This phenomenon is known as cognitive dissonance (see Chapter 5). The behaviour of the self-silencing individual is initially at odds with her beliefs. She thinks she has a contribution to make, but she keeps quiet. This discrepancy is explained by her fear of being the target of attack. It might also be partly explained by the belief that speaking up is pointless because others are not interested in the contribution that people like her could make. Either explanation is hard to bear because it entails either acknowledging that one lacks the courage to stand up to bullies or that one is not likely to ever be taken seriously. Sometimes it might be easier instead to believe that one is silent because one has nothing of significance to say (cf. Cooper, 2008, pp. 150–152). Be that as it may, the person who self-silences in the face of repeated intimidation will over time develop the epistemic vice of timidity. Similar dynamics might cause individuals to become intellectual servile. Whenever a person is persistently humiliated by being mocked and dismissed, she might choose silence and become timid. But she might also choose to ingratiate the bully (Romero-Canyas et al., 2010; Wu et al., 2011). When this happens humiliating behaviours promote the development of intellectual servility in others.

Narcissists and vain people need admirers since above all else they crave other people's esteem. It is for this reason that narcissists can be very charming toward some whom they do not experience as immediate rivals (Baumeister & Vohs, 2001). Such behaviour induces low status individuals who are already craving social acceptance to flatter those who are vain and narcissistic. Given that people who ingratiate others are liked better and thought to be more credible by those whom they ingratiate (Vonk, 2002), individuals who seek others' approval have an incentive to flatter and be deferential. Since narcissists and vain individuals promote these behaviours in others, they foster the vice of intellectual servility in other people. Conversely, individuals who are predisposed to ingratiate those who are more powerful than them induce vanity and narcissism in those whom they flatter (Campbell & Foster, 2007). In short, servile, and vain individuals are locked in a dynamic of ingratiation in which their epistemically vicious dispositions are mutually exacerbated.

It should be noted however that these arguments in favour of the conclusion that intellectually vicious individuals engage in behaviours that wrong other people do not by themselves settle questions of responsibility. This is a point to which I return in Chapter 8; for now I wish to note that in some cases a person can wrong another but have an excuse for her behaviour. For instance, individuals who are intellectually timid are unlikely to object when they observe someone make highly prejudicial and bigoted assertions. If these claims are directed at a third party in order to intimidate or humiliate, the timid bystander might have a duty to object. Her failure to do so out of fear is a kind of negligence that wrongs (as well as harms) the target of the attack.[29] Nevertheless, the timid bystander might be excused for her silence especially if she is vulnerable and her fear of reprisal is warranted.

If, as I have argued, intellectual vices include characteristic patterns of motivation, it might, because motivation is hard to establish, prove somewhat difficult to estimate the prevalence of each vice within epistemic communities. That said, some of the harms and wrongs detailed above can be inflicted by individuals who display vicious tendencies without exemplifying the full-blown intellectual vices. For instance, if it is true that, as I argue in Chapter 5, arrogance is based on positive strong defensive attitudes directed toward the self and its features, it is possible for individuals to be disposed to behave arrogantly about some topics and in some situations without being arrogant. For example, those who have positive defensive strong attitudes about some of their features but not others, behave

---

[29] For a different account of this kind of case see Lackey (2018).

arrogantly when they perceive those features to be under attack.[30] They might be less defensive and thus less arrogant about other issues. In addition, some individuals might have positive defensive attitudes that are not strong. These attitudes are not triggered in every circumstance. Instead, situational factors partly determine when such individuals behave in arrogant ways. Hence, even if intellectual vice might be rare, vicious behaviour could be relatively widespread. It is also easier to recognize.

So far I have considered the harms and wrongs that the intellectual vices of superiority and inferiority can inflict on individuals. These same harms and wrongs can also occur when people only have dispositions to behave viciously in some situations and about some limited topics. I now wish to consider the effects of these behaviours on the epistemic community as a whole. In particular I wish to address two related questions. First, does widespread intellectually vicious conduct resulting in the prevalence of mis- and disinformation within an epistemic community make a difference to what should be regarded as intellectual character virtues within that community? Second, could the presence of intellectual character vice in a community be epistemically beneficial to the community as a whole?

In her recent work on closed-mindedness Heather Battaly (2018a) argues that unwillingness or inability to engage with relevant options can in some contexts be an intellectual effect-virtue.[31] In her view some epistemic environments can be defined as hostile because they include widely held falsehoods about a range of topics including beliefs that discredit members of some groups. In these contexts, the disposition to close one's mind by being unwilling to engage with false or misleading but relevant options can have a preponderance of epistemically beneficial effects. If this is right, in these contexts the disposition to be closed-minded would be a virtue, if virtues are dispositions that facilitate the acquisition, retention, and transmission of epistemic goods. Battaly supports this conclusion by arguing that the person who ignores relevant, but false, information in these contexts is epistemically better off than the person who open-mindedly engages with it. Examples of this kind circumvent Cassam's arguments that dogmatism is never a virtue because ignoring false information always causes a loss of justification (and thus of knowledge) even when it is instrumental in retaining a true belief (Cassam, 2019, p. 116). Battaly's examples concern individuals that either have already been robbed of knowledge so that the best they can hope for is to preserve their true beliefs, or for whom losing knowledge but at least preserving their true beliefs is the least bad option. This is in her view the epistemically good effect of

---

[30] That said, any kind of alleged threat makes defensive people become defensive also about unrelated aspects of the self.
[31] What makes a trait an effect virtue is exclusively its nature as a disposition that reliably produces good effects.

closed-mindedness in these instances. That is why in Battaly's view it can be a virtue.

I find Battaly's arguments unpersuasive but first I should note that they do not affect the motivational account of intellectual vice I have defended here. The individuals who ignore false but relevant options when faced with epistemically hostile environments might not according to the motivational account possess the vice of being closed-minded. Whether they do depends on their motivations and on the extent to which they suffer from a high dispositional need for cognitive closure (see, Chapter 2). If this is right, then the examples Battaly considers do not show that closed-mindedness can be a virtue because they might not concern instances of closed-mindedness.

Be that as it may, one may still wonder whether these are cases where ignoring relevant alternatives is for an agent the best epistemic course of action as measured by its epistemic consequences. I think not. Battaly compares the benefits of not engaging with misinformation with the costs of taking it seriously. The person who ignores relevant but false information retains her true beliefs at the cost of possibly losing her justification for them. Were she to engage with misinformation she runs the risk of abandoning her true beliefs and acquiring false ones instead. Hence, if our aim is the maximization of true belief, non-engagement with misleading information might seem the best course of action. But this evaluation of the situation ignores that open-minded (that is, critical rather than gullible) engagement even with false information carries epistemic benefits. Even in a hostile environment there is something to be gained by evaluating misleading information. By engaging with these beliefs one might come to understand both that they are false and why they are widely held. It is thus at best moot whether the aim of truth maximization requires avoiding engaging with misleading information. Further, especially in cases of hostile environments understanding the dominant false ideology is crucial if one is to be able effectively to attempt to dismantle it. Hence, when one takes into account the epistemic value of unmasking the kind of ideological beliefs that make an epistemic environment hostile, there is little in support of the epistemic policy recommended by Battaly.[32]

I do not deny that one can envisage a highly artificial environment in which by cosmic coincidence or demonic intervention the adoption of irresponsible doxastic policies maximises true belief and/or minimises false ones. My point is rather that in ordinary circumstances, even those including communities that are under the yoke of false ideologies, this is unlikely to be the case since critical scrutiny is part of the best strategy for the collective improvement of the epistemic environment.

---

[32] A similar case can be made against Fantl's (2018) view that we should not engage open-mindedly with counter-arguments that one knows to be misleading. He also ignores the epistemic value of understanding beliefs one knows to be false with a view to provide further arguments against them.

These arguments leave open the possibility that individual intellectual vice might be beneficial to the collective epistemic good. For instance, Hookway notices that a research team is likely to benefit from having 'some members who are dogmatic, and unwilling to take on board new possibilities, while others are much more ready to take seriously seemingly wild speculations' (Hookway, 2003b, p. 189). But these observations only support the conclusion that collaborative research improves when team members adopt varied cognitive styles. In particular, they indicate that research teams benefit from including people who have a marked preference for their current viewpoint as well as people who are more ready to change their position. But such preference might not be indicative of dogmatism. Instead, it would seem to fit the intellectual virtue of firmness which is a disposition not to give up one's beliefs too soon in the face of counter-evidence (Roberts & Wood, 2007, ch. 7).[33] In short, arguments like Hookway's show that teams perform better when their members are diverse, but do not demonstrate that they benefit from the inclusion of intellectually vicious members.

In response it has been claimed that the required epistemic diversity within groups is best achieved when groups members exhibit less than virtuous motivations and dispositions. For example, Kitcher (1993) has argued that the credit motive is beneficial to scientific progress. Scientific communities where researchers are not solely motivated by a desire to discover the truth, but also want fame and honours do better at producing knowledge than otherwise equally positioned communities whose members do not have mixed motives. These results only obtain if scientists that are driven exclusively by a desire for knowledge are not altruistically prepared to sacrifice their acquisition of epistemic goods to the common good. These hypothetical scientists would thus fall short of what is required by intellectual humility since the latter involves disposition to accept auxiliary roles for the benefit of collective success. In addition, the desire to gain other people's esteem need not be vicious. On the contrary provided that one only wishes to be the recipient of admiration that is deserved, the credit motive is required by the virtue (closely linked to self-respect) of having a proper concern for being esteemed by other people (see Chapter 4).

Levy and Alfano (2020) provide even stronger arguments for the claim that group knowledge benefits from individual epistemic vice. First, they argue that dispositions to imitate blindly other people, to accept the beliefs of powerful individuals, and to conform with majority views are instrumental in the transmission of cultural practices that embody cumulative cultural knowledge. Yet these dispositions are indicative of intellectual servility. Second, they rely on research on group deliberation and especially on the wisdom of crowds (cf. Surowiecki, 2005)

---

[33] Cassam develops the same argument to show contra Kripke and Kuhn that dogmatism, as distinct from mere firmness, almost always obstructs rather than promotes knowledge (2019, pp. 112–113). Similar points could be made against Fantl's (2018) defence of forward looking dogmatism.

to argue that myside (confirmation) bias promotes the kind of beneficial epistemic diversity and independence required for group deliberation to outperform the deliberation of its expert members. These two arguments do not sit well along each other. The second suggests that, because of confirmation bias, individuals tend to stick with their pre-existing views even when these differ from received opinion. The first argument indicates instead that individuals are conformists who blindly defer to others.

Whilst I have no knock-down argument against these considerations, I have already indicated that a small bias in favour of one's pre-existing opinions is best thought in some circumstances as embodying the epistemic virtue of firmness rather than as an expression of dogmatism. It is thus plausible that the dispositions identified by Levy and Alfano that promote knowledge conducive group deliberations are not vicious after all. In response to their first argument, it is worth noting that those who blindly imitate and defer to others are primarily the young when they are inducted within existing cultural practices. A case can plausibly be made that their behaviour is not servile since it manifests the epistemic deference that novices appropriately show to experts. Levy and Alfano might object that this response is not wholly satisfactory, since it does not account for the uncritical and automatic nature of imitative behaviour that is crucial to cultural transmission. Perhaps, but it is unclear that imitation is wholly unreflective in adults who, if questioned, are likely to have some rationalizing explanation (however false) for their cultural practices. It is unreflective in young children, but this is to be expected as part of the process of habituation.

In conclusion there are good reasons to believe that the intellectual vices of inferiority and superiority are harmful to those who have them, to other epistemic agents who interact with them, and to the epistemic community as a whole. In addition, behaviours that are expressive of these vices are causally responsible for numerous moral and epistemic wrongs. These conclusions raise two further questions. The first concerns the responsibility for intellectual vice and is the topic of Chapter 8. The second, about strategies to reduce the harms and wrongs that flow from these vices, is addressed in Chapter 9.

8
Wrongs, Responsibility, Blame, and Oppression

The intellectual vices that are the topic of this book have many epistemically harmful consequences; they are also at the root of many wrongs inflicted on epistemic agents qua agents. But who is morally to blame for these harms and wrongs? Does the fault lie with the individuals who have developed intellectual vicious characters? Alternatively, should we largely excuse individuals who have acquired these character traits and point the finger at structural relations of social power that have played an important causal role in shaping people's epistemic sensibilities, cognitive styles, and intellectual character traits?

In this chapter I argue that individuals are often morally responsible in the sense of being accountable for their intellectual vices and derivatively for the epistemic conduct and doxastic states that stem from them. However, even though individuals are accountable in this way, it is often best if they are not subjected to blame in the form of anger or resentment directed at them by others. Prudentially, it might not be advisable to label people vicious since they might respond to this charge by becoming even worse. Morally, others who suffer from similar shortcomings might lack the required standing to blame individuals for vicious tendencies that are widely shared. Even though refraining from blaming the blameworthy might be the best thing to do, it does not follow that we must remain silent when faced with our own and others' tendencies towards intellectual vice. On the contrary, it is vitally important that we take responsibility for our shortcomings and that we encourage others to do the same. One of the reasons why taking responsibility matters is that it is crucial to self-respect which is essential to having the right measure of oneself.

Moral responsibility in the form of accountability is not however the only kind of responsibility that is of interest when attributing responsibility for intellectual vices and their products. The accountability responses of anger and resentment might be fitting reactions to some beliefs and behaviours that stem from intellectual vices, but other responses are equally at home including disdain, disapproval, and disesteem. These reactions are fitting because intellectual vices and their products are features of individuals' character that reflect badly on those who possess them. I follow Shoemaker (2015) in reserving the term 'attributability-responsibility' for the kind of responsibility agents have for those among their features that reflect on their character and thus warrant admiration when good or disdain when bad. I argue below that individuals are attributively responsible in a moral and epistemic sense for their character intellectual virtues and vices and for the activities and doxastic states that stem from them.

This chapter consists of three sections. Section 8.1 distinguishes different notions of moral and epistemic responsibility to argue that intellectual vices are attributable to the agents who have them. I defend the view that intellectually vicious individuals are not wholly answerable for their intellectual vices, but that they are usually accountable for them. Section 8.2 explains why often it is prudentially and morally advisable not to resent blameworthy individuals for their intellectual character vices, even though some expressions of disesteem might be fitting even in these cases. In Section 8.3, I argue that the intellectual character vices of superiority and inferiority are incompatible with the kind of self-respect that is essential for leading a truly flourishing life. I show how taking responsibility for these vices is essential to gaining the required self-respect.

8.1 Responsibilities for Belief, Ignorance, and Intellectual Vice

The view that intellectual vices include character traits is often described as responsibilism because its proponents have argued that epistemic agents are responsible for their beliefs and for their ignorance when these stem from their intellectual vices. In addition, agents would also be responsible for possessing and/ or exercising the vices themselves. In this regard, virtue responsibilism differs from virtue reliabilism which, since it identifies epistemic virtues with reliable cognitive faculties, does not need to be committed to the view that we are responsible for our beliefs and for the character traits from which they stem.[1] Hence, within the responsibilist framework responsibility is a necessary condition for intellectual vices. That is, intellectual deficits or shortcomings for which agents are not responsible are, by definition, not intellectual vices but something akin to a cognitive impairment.

The commitment of responsibilism to responsibility for vice has been taken by some of its opponents to show the inadequacy of the view. In particular, it has been argued that we are not responsible for our beliefs since we have no direct voluntary control over what we believe. We cannot believe something simply by deciding to do so. Thus, since responsibility is said to require direct voluntary control, and we do not have this kind of control over our beliefs, we cannot be responsible for the beliefs that we hold. In response some responsibilist virtue epistemologists have argued that we have this kind of control over many of our

---

[1] In reality the matter is more complex since reliabilist accounts of knowledge as an achievement often invoke notions of epistemic agency that bring suitability for attributions of responsibility in their trail. See for example, Greco (2010) and Sosa (2011).

beliefs.[2] Further, independently of whether we can voluntarily control what we believe, we can exercise control over the acquisition, or at least the exercise of character virtues and vices (Zagzebski, 1996, pp. 59–69). Zagzebski's defence of some form of doxastic voluntarism proceeds by comparing beliefs to acts. She relies on shared intuitions that we are responsible for a range of comportments including those that are carried out when drunk. She concludes that if responsibility requires voluntary control, then the notion of the voluntary must be sufficiently capacious to include drunken behaviour. It must also include habitual actions that are carried out unreflectively without the formulation of a clear intention, since we are often taken to be responsible for these. Once the range of activities for which we can be held to account is properly appreciated, Zagzebski argues, it becomes clear that believing is no less voluntary than many of these comportments.

Zagzebski's defence of responsibility for belief and intellectual vices stretches the notion of the voluntary beyond the most plausible interpretations of this notion. She is driven to this position because she never questions the assumption that we can only be responsible for what is within our voluntary control. It is precisely this assumption that has been repeatedly challenged in recent years. Although it is usually acknowledged that responsibility for belief presupposes that one believes freely, it is generally thought that this kind of doxastic freedom does not require direct voluntary control (McHugh, 2014). Instead, reasons responsiveness or reflective control would be sufficient for epistemic responsibility (McHugh, 2013).

In my opinion we can make the best progress in clarifying these issues if, at least temporarily, we set aside issues of control.[3] Instead, following an approach adopted in ethics by Shoemaker (2015), I wish to explore questions of responsibility by analysing responsibility-responses. These are reactive attitudes such as admiration, disdain, regret, pride, anger, blame, or praise. These emotions and their associated action tendencies are essential to the ways in which we hold each other responsible for actions, desires, judgements, and other personal qualities. In what follows, I first explain three kinds of responsibility responses, the notions of responsibility associated with each of them, and the conditions that agents must satisfy to be responsible in the required sense. My characterization of these three notions of responsibility and the defence of their distinctiveness are heavily indebted to Shoemaker's (2015) presentation of these issues. Armed with these

---

[2] The view that we have direct voluntary control over our beliefs is known as doxastic voluntarism. The standard case against it has been made by Alston (1989). Voluntarism has been defended in a qualified form by Weatherson (2008). See Peels (2017) for a more recent discussion of these issues.

[3] But note that I have argued in Chapter 2 that we have some control over epistemic activities. My point here is that we can best understand attributions of responsibility by bracketing questions of control, even though ultimately our responsibility responses might presuppose the presence of abilities that as a matter of fact can only be had if one can exercise some control.

distinctions, I address the questions of epistemic and moral responsibility for intellectual vices and for the epistemic activities and the doxastic states that flow from them. I argue that these bad-making features are attributable to epistemic agents even though agents are not fully answerable for them. In addition, in the many cases in which intellectual vices and their products are expressive of ill will or just a lack of due regard toward other epistemic agents, individuals are also morally responsible in the sense of being accountable for their bad behaving and believing. Finally, I argue that epistemic agents are also often responsible for their ignorance in so far as it is attributable to them and is an expression of a lack of regard for others' reasons and concerns.

My discussion of responsibility in terms of responsibility responses does not indicate a commitment to the view that being responsible is reducible to being held responsible in ways that accord with our practices of attributing responsibility to agents. For all I say in this chapter it is possible that what makes an attribution of responsibility correct is that they track independent facts about responsibility. I wish in this chapter to remain neutral on this metaphysical issue. My point is that much progress can be made even though we bracket this question and focus on common responsibility responses to intellectual vices and the bad believing that stems from them. By focusing on responsibility responses we can learn much about responsibility since these responses at least track facts about responsibility or might even constitute them.

Shoemaker (2015) identifies three distinct kinds of responsibility that are individuated by characteristic reactive attitudes.[4] These are: attributability, answerability, and accountability. Each of these is properly thought of as a kind of responsibility because the reactive attitudes that individuate them are, even though somewhat distinct, blaming, and praising responses. These attitudes include natural emotional reactions such as admiration, disdain, gratitude, anger, and resentment. Reactive attitudes are often said to be complex syndromes that include feelings, and possibly thoughts.[5] They are emotional evaluations of their targets that initiate action tendencies to blame, admire, punish, or reward. Understanding these reactive responses and the conditions for their fittingness, offers a basis for an account of the capacities agents must possess to count as responsible in each of the three distinctive senses of responsibility.

The responsibility-responses characteristic of attributability include positive and negative emotions such as awe, admiration or esteem, disdain, abhorrence, disesteem or revulsion. These reactive attitudes are evaluations of the character of their targets. We admire, esteem, or venerate individuals because of the quality of

---

[4] Strawson (2008) is the locus classicus for the notion of a reactive attitude.
[5] As I have implicitly suggested in my discussions of intellectual humility and of the vices of inferiority and superiority the emotional components of reactive attitudes might be identifiable with aspects of attitudes understood as summary evaluations.

their character traits. We disesteem, abhor, disdain or feel revolted by individuals who are of poor character. These aretaic evaluations are not mere gradings or appraisals. They are responsibility responses since they are ways of praising or blaming agents (Shoemaker, 2015, pp. 62–63). Admiring or esteeming someone is a way praising her. Disesteeming or showing disdain for a person are negative responses that are blame-like even though they do not involve punishment or resentment. For Shoemaker agents are attributable-responsible for features of their character which belong to what he describes as the deep self.[6]

For Shoemaker the deep self includes both authentic volitions that express what one truly cares about, and authoritative judgments that manifest one's evaluative stance about what one takes to be good and important. In short, the deep self includes those psychological qualities that embody the agent's deepest cares and commitments. The natural reaction to detecting personal features in other agents is admiration when they are evaluated as good or excellent, and disdain when one evaluates them as bad. Control is not what is at issue with attributability-responsibility. In Shoemaker's view, an agent is responsible in this sense only if she is capable of making commitments and having authentic cares. Further, she is only attributable-responsible for her deep self, and those among her beliefs, desires, and behaviours that stem from it.

The responsibility responses characteristic of answerability include positive and negative emotions such as approval, approbation, or pride, disdain, disapproval, disapprobation or regret. These reactive attitudes are evaluations of the judgement of their targets. We approve of people because of the quality of their judgment, and we are proud of the quality of our own. We disapprove of others when they display poor judgment, and we regret our own bad calls. Since approval and disapproval are ways of praising and blaming, answerability responses are responsibility responses. For Shoemaker agents are answerability responsible for the quality of their choices, beliefs, and judgements. That is for any of their propositional attitudes that the agent is capable of defending by supplying reasons in favour of them (as opposed to something else).

This form of responsibility is often defended by those who reject that voluntary control is required for responsibility. People are answerable-responsible for their beliefs, choices or actions if these reflect the quality of their reasons. Shoemaker attributes this account to Watson (2004) and to Scanlon (1998) noting that the latter thinks of it as attributability. He also notes that Watson and Scanlon take answerability to be the basis of attributability so that the deep self would only be expressed in authoritative judgments and would not also include our authentic cares.

---

[6] I take the deep self to be the part of a person's character that includes their authentic cares and authoritative judgments and other aspects of character that flow from them. Thus, honesty could be part of a person's deep self whilst a tendency to be neat might be part of her character without being part of her deep sense if neatness is not something she actually cares about.

Attributability, however, is neither necessary nor sufficient for answerability. Agents are answerable for their bad choices and beliefs even though these are out of character. An epistemic agent who is careless when forming a belief is the proper target of disapproval for his bad believing. However, it is possible that this error is an aberration from which one should not conclude that the agent in question is a carelessly bad thinker. If that is the case, the careless belief is not attributable to him. Thus, attributability is not necessary for answerability since we are answerable for features that are not attributable to us.

Attributability is also not sufficient for answerability since there are qualities of the deep self for which we are not answerable. For instance, a person might find that he cannot help but believe that his spouse is innocent of a crime for which she has been found guilty. He might be aware that he has no evidence for this belief, but he hangs on to it because believing otherwise feels like a betrayal. This agent is not answerable for this belief that does not stem from his judgment, and which he would not be prepared to rationally endorse. Nevertheless, this belief is expressive of what he stands for, and of his authentic volitions. It is a part of his deep self and for this reason, this epistemically deficient belief is attributable to him.

The responsibility responses characteristic of accountability include positive and negative emotions such as gratitude, gratification, and warm feelings, resentment, anger, and indignation. These reactive attitudes are evaluations of the quality of the regard or concern of their targets. We are angry with people whose actions show that they have given insufficient weight to our interests. We are grateful to those who show good will toward us. For Shoemaker agents are accountable when they have some capacity for empathetic understanding that involves appreciating how things look and feel from other people's perspective.

So defined accountability is a kind of responsibility that is not applicable to every domain. We tend not to resent, punish, or get angry at people for their poor aesthetic judgment, for instance. We also do not resent or punish people for their poor epistemic evaluations. There is a useful notion of epistemic blame that attaches to beliefs and forms of inquiry where the inquirer is at fault. These are cases where epistemic defects reflect badly on the agent. But, epistemic blame does not involve the kind of reactive attitudes that are characteristically accountability responses. We do not usually resent, punish, or even get angry at people who are careless, or closed-minded in their thinking. When we do, it is because we take them to be morally blameworthy for their bad believing. For example, a stranger might disapprove of students who are careless when thinking through the problems discussed in class. Their teacher, however, is warranted in being angry with them because she takes their carelessness to express a lack of due regard for the time and effort she has put in devising her lessons. The fact that epistemic blame is not expressed as resentment or anger (cf. Brown, 2018) strongly suggests that epistemic responsibility is not a matter of accountability (cf. Shoemaker, 2015, ch. 3).

These considerations go some way toward showing that accountability is distinct from answerability. Individuals are often answerable for their beliefs when these are the result of fallacious inference, but as I have claimed above they might not be accountable for them. Therefore, answerability is not sufficient for accountability. Answerability is also not necessary since individuals can be accountable for qualities for which they are not answerable. For instance, a person might behave in an insensitive manner by being loud when someone is trying to read or sleep, and thus show a lack of due regard for other people's reasons and interests, without even noticing that this is what she is doing. An individual who is oblivious to other people's point of view is not answerable for her behaviour because, since they would not be prepared to defend it, it is not an expression of the quality of her judgment. She is however accountable because it is an embodiment of her failure of empathetic understanding.

Attributability and accountability are also distinct. We hold people accountable and resent them for actions that are out of character and thus are not attributable to them. Thus, attributability is not necessary for accountability. It is also not sufficient since, for example, we disdain individuals who are gluttonous but do not resent them. These are qualities that are attributable to them because they are part of their deep self but for which they are not accountable since they are unrelated to the quality of their regard. This is why we are not inclined to be angry or resent people for their gluttony (unless it leads them to grab other people's share).

Having laid out these distinctions I am now in a position to assess whether agents are epistemically responsible for their intellectual vices and for the beliefs and epistemic activities that stem from them. I have already argued that responsibility accountability does not apply to the epistemic realm. Therefore, what we need to consider is whether intellectual vices are attributable to people and whether individuals are answerable for these psychological features.

It should be no surprise that intellectual character vices, and also vicious thinking styles, are attributable to agents since they are among the components of people's character or deep self. Indeed, we respond differently to others poor quality of believing depending on whether we take the shortcoming to be in or out of character. An example should illustrate the point. Alex is a careless thinker. She jumps to conclusions. She rarely examines the strength of the evidence for her views. Husseini is instead a conscientious thinker. He always examines arguments carefully. On a given occasion, Alex forms a belief on flimsy evidence as is her usual because of her careless ways. On that occasion, Husseini also carelessly forms this belief based on the same flimsy evidence. In his case this outcome is out of character. It happened because he was tired. In these circumstances we would respond to Alex by expressing our disesteem for her as an indication of our evaluation of her epistemically poor character. In response to Husseini, we are likely to express surprise and to mention his tiredness as an excuse. These different responses indicate that we blame Alex but not Husseini. We think that this instance of bad believing reflects badly on Alex and manifests her qualities as a bad believer. Our attitude to Husseini is different. We excuse him and think that this lapse is not indicative of who he is.

It might be objected that these attributability reactions are not fitting since epistemic agents are often unaware of their intellectual vices. Further, if these are pointed out to them, they might deny the accuracy of the attribution. Therefore, perhaps with the exception of epistemic malevolence, intellectual vices are not included in the evaluative stance reflectively endorsed by the agent herself. Individuals do not usually embrace their vices even when they are defining of who they are.

Nevertheless, in my view intellectual character vices are part of people's characters because they manifest agents' deepest cares. Such cares are embodied in the motivations that are essential aspects of these vices. For example, arrogant individuals are driven by the desire to feel good about themselves. The motivation for self-enhancement reflects one of their deepest cares. This is why arrogance is part of their character. Similarly both obsequious and vain individuals want above all to make a good impression on other people. It is the centrality of this motivation to their lives that explains why servility and vanity are aspects of their character.[7]

I have argued in Chapter 2 above that some intellectual vices are thinking styles and sensibilities rather than character traits. Arguably, not all sensibilities or thinking styles are attributable to epistemic agents who possess them since some are too shallow and restricted to narrow domains to figure as part of someone's character. That said, some sensibilities and thinking styles manifest themselves as insensitivity to morally relevant facts. These result in tendencies to be wilfully ignorant that often stem from deep motivations to protect the self or to be liked by other people. When these psychological qualities are the product of these self-defining motivations, they are attributable to the person who possesses them. Similarly, some thinking styles, such as being closed-minded because of high dispositional need for cognitive closure, can also be part of someone's character. The non-specific motivation to make one's mind up quickly is defining of the kind of person one is because it embodies what one cares about.

Given Shoemaker's (2015) account of answerability supplied above, individuals are surprisingly not wholly answerable for their intellectual vices of self-evaluation and for the epistemic activities and doxastic states that result from them. Answerability requires that one is able to provide reasons for one's beliefs and choices that justify them over some alternatives that one is also able to evaluate. This ability presupposes that one is able to notice the possibility of alternative

---

[7] The idea that mere attributability is sufficient to warrant a critical attitude toward a person is similar to Cassam's view that people can be criticized for traits that reflect badly on them even when they cannot be blamed for having these because they have no control over changing them (2019, pp. 133–135).

viewpoints or courses of action. These are abilities that are typically impaired in those who suffer from the intellectual vices of self-evaluation.[8] For example, closed-minded ways of thinking often reflect an inability to engage with alternative viewpoints. A closed-minded thinker is able to put forward reasons for his beliefs, but he is not capable of giving due weight to considerations that speak for alternative views. If this is right, agents are attributively responsible for their dogmatic and closed-minded bad believing but might not be answerable for it because they lack the capacity to appreciate reasons to believe otherwise.

One can make similar points adopting alternative accounts of responsibility as answerability such as that supplied by Smith (2012) who argues that individuals are responsible for those qualities that are expressive of their overall evaluative stance. Since dogmatic and closed-minded individuals do not endorse their closed-mindedness or dogmatism, these are not features that manifest people's evaluative stance.

It might be objected that intellectually vicious individuals are fully responsible for their neglect of points of view at variance with their own. After all, a person who ignores evidence that undermines her beliefs is answerable for her bad believing which reflects the poor quality of her judgment. I agree. But this example does not capture what is distinctive about the intellectual vices of self-appraisal. These vices, as I have argued in Chapter 7, cause failures of self-regulation and are at the root of extensive motivated processing of information. In these ways, these vices impair agents' abilities to engage with diverse points of view. It is this impairment that reduces the extent to which these agents are answerable-responsible for the believing that stems from their vices.

These considerations do not let intellectually vicious people completely off the hook. Firstly, these are agents who are on the whole capable to provide reasons for some of their beliefs and choices over some alternatives. Hence, they are answerable for these. Secondly, even in cases where intellectual vices impair their evaluative capacities, individuals typically retain some ability to consider alternatives. For instance, closed-minded people are rarely so closed-minded that they are completely unable to evaluate opinions and evidence contrary to their own. Hence, intellectually vicious individuals are to some extent answerable, even though their responsibility is reduced because their judgment is impaired.

It is perhaps noteworthy that this view entails that what excuses poor judgement is the current presence of intellectual vices rather than a history of epistemic deprivation in one's upbringing. The reason why the adult who was raised in a cult, who has been brainwashed or trained into becoming closed-minded, dogmatic or arrogant is not wholly answerable for his bad epistemic character is that his capacity for judgment is impaired, irrespectively of how this impairment has

---

[8] This might not apply to other intellectual vices. For example, epistemically malevolent individuals might be able to defend malevolence over benevolence.

come about. Individuals who owe their intellectual vices to a more mundane history of bad luck and lack of application are no more answerable for their bad believing than the person whose upbringing was seriously deficient. They might however differ with regard to their moral accountability for their vices and the beliefs that stem from them.

These conclusions run contrary to some recent prominent accounts about whether individuals are responsible for intellectual vices. One such account has been defended by Battaly (2016a) who describes it as personalism.[9] She takes this position to straddle reliabilism and responsibilism. In her view intellectual vices are personal qualities for which individuals are not responsible because they are not blameworthy for possessing them. Battaly's starting point are arguments that deny accountability for intellectual vices due to the fact that individuals lack the required effective control over the circumstances that led to their acquisition. That is, the intellectual characters we end up with are often largely due to environmental and interpersonal luck in one's upbringing. These are factors that are not within our control so that there is little we could have done as children to change them.

To this effect, Battaly primes our intuitions by presenting some hypothetical cases of people who have become dogmatic or closed-minded because they have been raised in very challenging circumstances such as being part of a cult or being indoctrinated by a community of extremists. Battaly notes that upon learning about their histories, we would refrain from blaming individuals who have suffered from such bad luck. She concludes that these cases are relevantly similar to the real example of Robert Harris that has been first discussed by Watson (2004). Harris was a brutal and heartless killer but not a psychopath, who suffered from horrendous abuse as a child. Watson and others have argued that as an abuse victim, Harris is not accountable for having turned into a morally vicious individual.

In my opinion these intuitions do not justify Battaly's conclusion that individuals are usually not responsible for possessing the intellectual vices that they have often acquired as children. In order to clarify the nature of our disagreement, some terminological points are in order. Battaly's initial presentation of personalism describes it as the view that intellectual vices can be personal qualities for which individuals are not blameworthy. However, in her answer to a possible

---

[9] More recently Battaly (2019) has argued that vice epistemology still lacks a serviceable account of responsibility since there is no single approach that explains responsibility for implicit biases (that she takes to be epistemic vices) without also attributing responsibility for all cognitive impairments. I believe that the approach adopted in this chapter can offer a response since it suggests that individuals are accountable for their implicit biases since these express the quality of their regard even though these same biases are not attributable to them. Importantly, individuals can also take responsibility for their implicit biases irrespective of whether they are criticizable for having them. However, I do not address head on the question of responsibility for implicit attitudes here. For a useful overview of responsibility for implicit bias, see Holroyd et al. (2017).

objection, Battaly (2016a, p. 113) acknowledges that personalism is compatible with responsibility for intellectual vice in what I have called, following Shoemaker (2015), the attributability sense. Robert Harris, irrespective of his upbringing, became a bad person. He is someone for whom disdain and even, perhaps, contempt are fitting. Similarly, the closed-minded individual who grew up in a cult is someone whom we do not admire. We disesteem him for his bad thinking, and may even feel disdain for him because of his closed-mindedness.

Given these points of agreement, I disagree with Battaly on two issues. First, attributability-responsibility is responsibility. When we disapprove of the dogmatic individual, even though we know about his challenging upbringing, our reaction is one of blame. Sure, we do not resent him or get angry, but disesteem is a blame response, rather than a mere negative grading, since it is a reaction that is intended to indicate that we distance ourselves from him and invite others to do the same. Hence, if to hold someone responsible is to blame him, attributability-responsibility is responsibility. Battaly wishes to remain neutral as to whether intellectual vices are attributable (2016a, p. 113), but the comparison with Harris, and our own intuitions about the cases presented by her, strongly indicate that we often take people to be attributable-responsible for their intellectual vices.

Second, terminological differences also mask another aspect of my disagreement with Battaly. There is a confusion in the literature in ethics over the meaning of 'attributability'. Some use it in the way I have described above, but others think of attributability as answerability. Battaly's use of Smith's use of the term (2008) strongly suggests that she belongs to this second camp. In that article, Smith defends the view that only what reflects an agent's evaluative stance, in the sense of being something one is able to defend over some alternatives, belongs to that person's deep self or character. In short, for Smith (and for Battaly) only that for which one is answerable is attributable. I disagree.

Intellectual vices make one less able to assess reasons and see alternative viewpoints. That is why individuals who have them are not fully answerable for possessing these vices or for the doxastic states and epistemic activities that flow from them. We manifest this judgement of diminished answerability in our responsibility responses. In order to see this point consider the following case. Both Alex and Husseini resist changing their mind about the safety of eating chlorinated chicken despite powerful evidence that their belief is false. Alex is notoriously closed-minded; she hardly ever changes her views irrespective of any new evidence that she might acquire. Husseini is instead a genuinely thoughtful guy but this time he has let prejudice govern his thinking. Provided one is aware of these facts, reactions to Alex and Husseini will differ. We disesteem Alex, wishing to distance ourselves from her. We do not try to reason with her or get her to see her mistake since we think that these attempts would be pointless. We feel frustrated by her precisely because we think there is no chance she will grasp the error of her ways. We disapprove of Husseini, and we might rebuke him. We think that someone like him should know better. That is, we take him to be answerable and that is why we reason with him. Our blaming responses to him are not of the distancing kind. Rather we approach him because we hope he will respond to our disapproval by re-evaluating his beliefs.[10]

In conclusion, Battaly uses 'attributability' to mean what I call 'answerability'. She argues that we might be responsible for intellectual vices in the sense that I label attributability. On this, terminological differences aside, I agree. I have also argued that we are not answerable for intellectual vices. Again, I suspect that Battaly would agree with the substance of the claim. However, I also think that keeping these two senses apart is crucial if we are to appreciate the varied nature of epistemic blame.

Finally, Battaly never makes it fully clear whether it is moral or epistemic responsibility that is at issue in her discussion. Be that as it may, as I have argued above, accountability never seems appropriate with regard to purely epistemic blame. That said, it is possible to be morally blameworthy for some of one's beliefs and other doxastic states. So the next question to ask is whether individuals are morally responsible for their intellectual vices and their products.

It is possible to be morally blameworthy for one's beliefs. Beliefs that are epistemically blameworthy and have the potential to cause harm or wrong to some people are plausible candidates.[11] I have argued in Chapter 7 that the intellectual character vices of inferiority and superiority are causally responsible for many epistemic harms and moral wrongs. Hence, it is useful to figure out whether agents are morally responsible for their intellectual vices. Given the framework I have been developing this question has three strands. First, one may ask whether agents are responsible in the attributability sense. Second, one may wish to know whether subjects are answerable. Finally, one might wonder whether they are accountable.

In my view agents are attributively responsible but not fully answerable for the same reasons provided above with regard to epistemic blame. This is not surprising since the criteria for attributability and answerability are the same in both the moral and the epistemic dimension. Hence, the outstanding question concerns accountability. Is blame in the form of anger and resentment ever fitting in response to agents who suffer from the vices of inferiority and superiority? The answer to this question appears positive. People often resent and are angry towards intellectually arrogant people because of their arrogance. Similar responses are natural reactions also to vanity and narcissism. People who possess the vices of inferiority are less

---

[10] Brown (2018) also runs together these two notions of blame as distancing that fits attributability and as disapproval that fits answerability. Epistemic blame can take both forms but only the former is wholly at home in cases of bad belief due to intellectual vice.

[11] These are not the only candidates. There might also be morally blameworthy but seemingly epistemically blameless or even epistemically justified belief (Gendler, 2011). The questions raised by this possibility have given rise to a fast growing literature. I set these worries aside here.

commonly the target of these reactive attitudes, especially when their character defects are perceived to stem from their difficult circumstances. That said, there are cases when individuals might be angry with timid people, for instance, because their timid silence has harmed the angry person or someone else she cares about. People might also resent servile individuals because their obsequiousness toward the powerful has made them complicit in the wrongs suffered by the less powerful. These responses indicate that, sometimes, we hold individuals who suffer from the intellectual vices of self-evaluation morally accountable for the harms and wrongs that flow from their vices.

The theory of accountability detailed above can explain why this is so. On this view people are accountable for their lack of due regard or empathetic understanding provided that they are capable of taking into account the needs and interests of other people. Arrogant, vain, and even narcissistic people are able to understand others' point of views, even though they often choose out of disregard not to exercise these capacities.[12] We hold them accountable because we think that their poor believing and behaviour expresses the poor quality of their regard for other people. Individuals who are arrogant do not care about how others feel or what they need. Vain and narcissistic people care about these things but in the wrong way. They might be charming but ultimately they only care to be liked and esteemed. Servile agents also care in the wrong way since they are only concerned with the opinion of the powerful. Finally, timid individuals are scared and thus fail to pay attention to others' needs. It is because accountability is a response to an evaluation of the quality of regard or empathic understanding, that individuals are accountable-responsible for their intellectual vices of superiority and inferiority.[13]

I wish to conclude this section with a few remarks about responsibility for ignorance. It is not easy to provide clear accounts of what makes one culpable for one's ignorance and of when ignorance is an excuse for bad behaviour and when it is not. Intuitively, one might think that culpable ignorance is never an excuse. Clearly, however, we cannot non-circularly explain what it takes for ignorance to be culpable by appealing to its inability to excuse the bad behaviour that flows from it, if we wish to appeal to culpability to explain why sometimes ignorance is no excuse. We can avoid this circularity by considering the agent's motivations for their bad behaviour. Individuals are morally blameworthy in the accountability sense when their action is expressive of a poor quality of regard for other people. Since it is possible for agents who are intuitively culpably ignorant when acting badly to lack any bad motives, there might be cases where even culpable ignorance excuses. Thus, it seems possible that a person who acts badly out of culpable ignorance, when intuitively she could and should have known better, might be partly excused for her bad behaviour because of her ignorance. For instance, a

---

[12] In this regard they differ from people who lack the ability to empathize with others.
[13] There might be exceptions such as when narcissism is a personality disorder.

person may kill someone when trying to save him by doing out of ignorance the wrong thing, when if she had paid attention at an earlier date, she would have known what to do (Smith, 2017). Her ignorance is intuitively culpable. She is epistemically blameworthy for her lack of knowledge in the sense of being answerable for it. Yet her ignorance excuses because her behaviour is in no way expressive of a lack of concern for the other person.

I have argued throughout that intellectually vicious individuals are often wilfully ignorant. I am now in a position to suggest that such ignorance does not excuse because it is itself an expression of poor quality of regard for other people. Hence, intellectually vicious individuals are accountable for their harmful behaviour even when such behaviour is a result of ignorance, provided that the ignorance itself is wilful and thus a manifestation of their lack of empathetic understanding.

Interestingly, however, wilful ignorance might not always be such that one could or should have known better. One of the most significant aspects of intellectual vices is that vicious individuals are often less able than others to consider alternative points of view or to pay attention to the right things when evidence is presented. Hence, there is a real sense in which they could not have known better (and therefore little point in thinking they should have). It is the same sense in which they are not wholly answerable for their bad believing. So it might well be that the wilful ignorance of those who are intellectually vicious is not culpable since they are not answerable for it, but nonetheless it fails to excuse them for their bad behaviour for which they are morally accountable. If this is right, there are cases of intuitively non-culpable ignorance that fails to excuse.[14]

8.2 Taking and Attributing Responsibility

So far I have argued that individuals are epistemically attributable-responsible for their intellectual character vices and for some of their sensibilities and thinking styles. Responses of disesteem or even contempt, indicating one's desire to differentiate or even distance oneself from those possessing these personal qualities, are often fitting.[15] I have also argued that the same individuals have only diminished answerability responsibility for these psychological features and for the bad believing that stems from them. If this is right, attitudes of reproach and

---

[14] I thus disagree with Calhoun (2016, p. ch. 7) assessment of the responsibilities of ordinary men who endorse the status quo in sexist society. I agree that they might be non-culpably ignorant because there is no clear sense in which they should have known better. But, because I do not think that their ignorance excuses, I don't think it follows that they are not responsible for their sexist behaviour.

[15] These might, however, be tempered by sympathy and understanding that especially harsh circumstances might have led some to develop character vices. Understanding might be especially fitting in relation to individuals whose vices of inferiority are in large part the outcome of hostile environmental circumstances.

disapproval are often not fitting since the personal qualities that they would target are not expressive of the evaluative stance reflectively endorsed by the agents who possess them. Arrogant individuals, for instance, do not necessarily approve of arrogance or see themselves as exemplifying that trait. These considerations lend support to the observation, whose consequences are discussed in Chapter 9, that trying to reason people out of their intellectual vices is likely to be a futile enterprise. Finally, I have also argued that people are morally accountable for their intellectual vices if these are expressive of a lack of due regard for other people's needs and interests. If this is right, anger and resentment are at least sometimes fitting responses to those who are vicious.

Granted that vicious individuals are often blameworthy in a manner that warrant resentment and other forms of severe censure, it remains an open question whether it is useful to blame the blameworthy. In what follows I argue that there frequently are prudential reasons that speak in favour of refraining from resenting or being angry with those who are intellectually vicious. I also defend the claim that many of us lack the moral standing required to blame the blameworthy. If so, there are additional moral reasons not to resent these individuals.[16]

I agree with Alfano (2013, pp. 94–96) that it is often inadvisable to call people vicious.[17] Experience tells us that labelling people arrogant, for example, is frequently counterproductive. Labelling people has significant consequences. Provided that the individuals so labelled understand the label and find its attribution to them plausible, their future behaviour becomes more consonant with the label. Labels, therefore, can work as self-fulfilling prophecies. Even though as far as I know there are no empirical studies of the effects of specifically labelling people as epistemically vicious, there is plenty of evidence that both negative and positive labels have these powers, when the labelled feature is thought to be fixed.[18]

Resenting people, punishing them, or showing anger towards them is not the same as calling them names. Expressing these negative reactions might be more effective than name calling. However, prudential considerations of another sort might nevertheless council caution about publicly expressing blame in this manner. I have argued that people are morally accountable-responsible for harms that flow from their intellectual vices. But it is exceedingly difficult to have sufficient evidence that the attribution of a vice to a person is accurate. Individuals might behave badly without being vicious if they lack the requisite bad motivations. Since people's motivations are hard to ascertain, attributions of vice might be misplaced.

---

[16] None of this imply that we should not stand up to arrogant bullies. It is often morally appropriate to hold them accountable for their actions. My concern here is with whether we should hold them responsible for their character traits.

[17] I am thus much more sceptical than Kidd (2016) about the utility of vice charging which as defined by him is essentially vice labelling.

[18] See Alfano (2013, pp. 88–96) for a discussion.

These two considerations suggest that, even though people are blameworthy for their vices in a way that would warrant resentment, calling them names and displaying this reaction might not always be effective responses. People respond negatively if they think others' resentment toward them is unwarranted. In addition, labelling people might contribute to worsening their behaviours. For all of these reasons, we must be extremely wary of blaming even the blameworthy for their intellectual vices.

One might accept these points but object that they only speak to the public expression of blame by means of verbal and non-verbal behaviours that convey one's attitude to its target. These considerations do not speak against one blaming another person in private whilst hiding one's reaction. This objection is well-taken, but only partly correct since the argument that it is hard to discern people's motivations speaks against attributing vices too quickly to people. If this is right, individuals often have reasons not to blame others for their traits even in private since it is hard to have sufficient evidence about people's characters. Further, there often are additional moral reasons not to resent others for their intellectual vices. Even though some individuals might be blameworthy, others might lack the requisite standing to blame them.[19]

The view that one must have earned an entitlement to be in a position to cast aspersion on others is captured in the pronouncement that those who live in glass houses shouldn't throw stones. There are at least two classes of cases in which it would not be morally appropriate for someone to blame someone else even though the person in question is blameworthy. First, individuals who are equally responsible would be hypocrites if they resented and punished others for faults that they share. Second, individuals who recognize that they do not have the fault in question only due to their good fortune are also not in a position to cast aspersions. If one acknowledges that, had one been in the same circumstances as the other person, one would have turned out the same way as this person, one should refrain from blaming. This tendency to believe that one is in no place to criticize someone for a defect that one would also have had it not been for one's good fortune explains the intuition that we should not, for example, blame for their dogmatism those who were raised in cults or extremely closed-minded communities. Battaly (2016a) is right to urge that we should not criticise individuals whose intellectual vices are strongly influenced by poor upbringing. But she is wrong to conclude that we should not blame them because they are not blameworthy. The intuition that we should refrain from blame in these cases is equally explained by the observation that we are no better than they are, merely luckier,

---

[19] Of course, there are also plenty of cases in which many people have the right standing because they do not share the fault of the blameworthy person and would not share it even if they had faced the same challenges.

and thus should be more generous, empathetic and forgiving in our interactions with these individuals.[20]

There exist, therefore, various reasons why we should not blame the blameworthy for their intellectual vices. Resenting them might prove counterproductive. Further, we might not have earned the entitlement to judge them thus. Given these conclusions, we might worry that intellectually vicious individuals are not held to account. We might fear that, unless other members of the community resent them, a message is sent that is tantamount to sanctioning harmful behaviours for which individuals are responsible. These, and similar concerns, have moved Calhoun (2016, ch. 7) to argue that in abnormal contexts the justification for engaging in blaming activities can be independent of the justification supporting attributions of responsibility. Hence, she concludes that it might be legitimate to blame the blameless in the service of delegitimizing unacceptable but widely accepted, or at least tolerated, behaviours. On the contrary, I have urged here against resentment or vice labelling directed at the blameworthy. Hence, it might appear that I propose that we implicitly legitimize intellectual vicious behaviour. In addition one might worry that refraining to criticize might actually promote some form of mutual absolution so that everyone feels okay about their faults since they are shared.[21]

I believe that these worries are misplaced. First, accountability responses are not the only kind of blaming attitudes one can adopt. What I have said here leaves space for the attribution of attributability responses. One way of expressing our praise for intellectual virtuous people is to express our admiration for them and to encourage others to share this attitude. Similarly, we might readily express our disesteem for people's character by distancing ourselves from them and enjoin others to do the same. Disesteem and disdain are responsibility responses that belong to the blame family but do not involve resentment or anger. Taking one's distance from other people is not the same as calling them names or resenting them. It might thus be less prone to backfire. Further, the expression of disesteem, unlike resentment, is at home even when one recognizes the same fault in oneself. Intuitively, it seems inappropriate to resent someone for doing something one is also guilty of doing. It does not seem equally inappropriate to disesteem someone for features for which one also disesteems oneself. This difference might lie in the fact that anger and resentment call for a response such as an apology from the person whom they address. Disesteem does not imply that the target of blame owes something to the person who is blaming them and thus the moral standing of the attributor is less important.

---

[20] Tognazzini and Coates (2018) offer a good introduction to discussions concerning which features of the blamers might make blaming on their part morally inappropriate.
[21] Thanks to Charlie Crerar for raising this concern.

Second, and perhaps more importantly, the most effective ways of tackling the intellectual vices of superiority and inferiority are at societal level rather than at the personal one. I have argued throughout that these vices are usually associated with occupying positions of domination or subordination in society. I have claimed, for instance, that the oppressed often develop the vices of timidity and servility in response to their oppression. If this is right, blaming them for their character vices would seem rather unjust. It is unfair, not because they are passive blameless victims of their circumstances, it is unfair because others are not better than them. Rather they are the winners of what Card (1996) has unforgettably labelled the 'unnatural lottery'. The most effective and morally appropriate response to this situation is to deal with the lottery itself by addressing structural matters of injustice.

There is, however, also space for some accountability responses in my account. In my view, accountability is something that we can develop by taking responsibility for our own intellectual vices. For example, circumstances might give a person an incentive to understand herself and, upon recognizing in herself some tendencies to servility or to arrogance, she might take responsibility for these aspects of her character. From this first personal point of view, there is no tension between acknowledging that our characters are often partly the result of contingent circumstances external to us, and undertaking to change or strengthen them in some ways. Taking responsibility for character does not presuppose that its formation is wholly up to us partly because this kind of responsibility is forward looking.

In her insightful discussion of these topics Card (1996) distinguishes backward looking attributions of responsibility to other people from forward looking undertaking of moral responsibility for whom one is and what one does. In her view, this first personal notion of responsibility includes three forward looking components: a managerial sense of understanding what is possible and deciding what to do; an answerability sense of making oneself answerable for one's choices; and a commitment sense of making oneself stand for something and following through with it (1996, p. 28).[22] Individuals whose circumstances have inflicted damage on their intellectual and moral characters can take responsibility for whom they have become by endeavouring to change their commitments, by finding ways of learning to become more answerable and by strengthening self-control so as to stick to the new choices that they have made.

Taking responsibility is a way of reclaiming agency so that one does not conceive of oneself as a victim of one's own circumstances. However, in order to be capable of taking responsibility one must possess a range of abilities. These include some degree of managerial control so that one is able to do what is required to act as one intends. But they also include the capacity to make

---

[22] Card describes these aspects of responsibility using a slightly different vocabulary. She also includes a backward looking credit dimension to taking responsibility.

commitments, to possess an evaluative stance and to develop an empathetic understanding of one's own and others' needs and interests. In short, only those who have the required capacities for accountability and attributability-responsibility and at least the potential to become answerable, are meaningfully able to take responsibility for who they are.

The importance of taking responsibility cannot be underestimated since doing so is a prerequisite to becoming someone who is worthy of having responsibilities. To be responsible in this sense is to be dependable, capable of good judgment and of empathetic understanding. Responsibility so understood is a virtue that for Card is akin to integrity (1996, pp. 24, 27). In my vocabulary taking responsibility is an essential part of the process of acquiring the measure of oneself and thus gaining secure self-esteem and acquiring self-respect since these attitudes to the self require the setting of standards which one lives up to.

8.3 Self-Esteem and Self-Respect

In this section I argue that those who suffer from the vices of inferiority and superiority show a lack of self-respect. I also show that taking responsibility for one's own intellectual vices is a way of acquiring self-respect. Self-respect so understood presupposes a modicum of intellectual humility conceived as the virtue of possessing the right measure of oneself.

A person has self-respect when she values her own worth. In order to value one's own worth a person must acknowledge, and have a positive attitude towards, her own value. In other words, she must recognise her good features, and value them as good. I follow Darwall (2006) and Dillon (2004, 2018) in acknowledging the existence of two broad kinds of self-respect: recognition and evaluative. Recognition respect involves recognizing one's own value qua entity with the status of being a person and thus both a moral and an epistemic agent. One might think of this kind of self-respect as an acknowledgment and a valuing of one's own dignity. So conceived, every person is equally worthy of recognition self-respect, even though some may not adequately respect themselves in this way.

Evaluative respect is the valuing of those features of the self that reflect well or badly on one's moral and intellectual character. Not all people are worthy of the same amount of evaluative self-respect. Those who exemplify virtues and other excellences are entitled to value themselves more highly than other people because of, and in proportion to, their possession of these features. People's evaluation of their good qualities might go wrong in a number of ways. People might under-estimate or overestimate the extent to which they exemplify individual virtues and vices, but they might also be wrong about which features are good to have and which are bad. It is thus possible for a person to have for herself an unwarranted amount of self-respect.

Philosophical opinions are divided on the relation of evaluative self-respect to self-esteem (Massey, 1995; Meyers, 1995). Some use the two terms more or less interchangeably to refer to individuals' evaluations of their qualities. So understood, evaluative self-respect, like high self-esteem, would be tantamount to having a good opinion of the worth of one's plans, ends, capacities, and character. Given this purely subjective conception of self-respect and self-esteem, it is possible for someone to respect himself even though the qualities and plans with which he identifies, and that are the basis of his self-respect, are morally unacceptable. This is the sense in which a gang member or mafia boss can have self-respect. They value their worth highly because they have commitments and characters that in their view match their values, even though what they value is morally bankrupt.

More frequently, philosophers differentiate self-respect from self-esteem. Self-respect, so understood, would differ from a positive attitude to the self or a good self-image. Rather, to have self-respect one must actually possess some good features and ground one's judgement of self-worth on these. Thus, the person who exudes self-confidence and appears to have a high opinion of himself might nevertheless lack in self-respect if he values the wrong things.

These two positions admit of an alternative in the form of a moderate subjectivist position that characterizes evaluative self-respect as high self-esteem based on evaluations of one's worth that are guided by the motivation to know oneself and based on values with which one identifies. This position is moderate because it presumes that self-respecting individuals must value knowing themselves whilst permitting that some of their other values be at variance with what is of moral significance. According to this view self-respect is self-esteem as a cluster of attitudes to the self and its qualities serving a knowledge function. That is to say, the self-respecting person is the individual who has confidence in her abilities and a good opinion of her qualities. These judgements and feelings are based on appraisals that are guided by the motivation to know oneself. For this reason, the person whose self-image is built from her honest attempt at self-understanding is likely in ordinary circumstances to have a fairly accurate view of her actual qualities. Such a person might arguably put the wrong values on some things. For example, she might place a lot of importance on physical attractiveness, and less value on friendliness. But provided that she has a positive attitude to herself based on those qualities of hers that she finds valuable, and provided her self-assessment is motivated by the desire to understand what she is like, such a person has self-respect. It would thus be possible for a person whose values are questionable to be self-respecting.[23]

---

[23] See Chapter 4 for my characterization of the virtue of pride that I understand as being closely related to self-respect.

On this conception, self-respect is not, however, a wholly subjective concept because it classifies as lacking in self-respect those who do not value self-knowledge but have high opinions of themselves that are based on evaluations motivated either by the need for self-enhancement or the need to be liked by others.[24] I have mentioned in Chapter 5 and 6 that these forms of self-esteem are unstable because they are self-deceptive. Now, I wish to add that they are undermining of self-respect as the ability to set for oneself values and plans that are consonant with self-knowledge and which one aspires to live up to.

The person who has a good opinion of herself because having that opinion makes her feel good about herself, would, if able to understand the motivations that guide her self-assessment, reappraise her opinion of herself and thus no longer hold herself in high esteem.[25] She would revise her views because she would discover that she does not value herself for her qualities, but instead values some qualities because she takes herself to possess them. Such realization would undermine one's positive assessment of these qualities since it is intended to measure them against allegedly independent standards. It is because this form of self-esteem floats free of the ability to have values by which one measures one's worth, that it is not a self-respecting self-esteem.

The motivation to be liked by others can also give rise to forms of high self-esteem that are not self-respecting. The person who discovers that her good opinion of herself is wholly dependent on others' attitudes to her qualities understands that her own valuation of her own worth is not determined by how she fares in relation to standards she has set for herself. Instead, she measures herself by how others judge her. This realization is undermining of self-esteem since it tantamount to acknowledging that one's values are not one's own.

In both incarnations these forms of self-esteem are not able to withstand scrutiny since understanding the true nature of one's valuations reveals that one's opinion of oneself is not determined by how one measures up to values that one has set or endorsed for oneself. In the first case, one would discover that one adjusts one's values to one's qualities rather than the other way round. In the second case, one would discover that one has not set the values by which one measures oneself. Either discovery is corrosive of valuations since they undermine the sense, which is essential to self-esteem as self-respect, that one lives by values that one has set for oneself.

The idea that only some forms of high self-esteem are forms of self-respect is consonant with recent psychological research on self-esteem which, as I mentioned in Chapter 5, suggests that only secure high self-esteem is associated

---

[24] There might be other ways in which high self-esteem is not a form of self-respect. I restrict to considering these because they are directly related to the vices of superiority.

[25] On the assumption that she takes herself to have set standards to which she wishes to adhere, rather wishing to set standards that match her features.

with good life outcomes, whilst defensive self-esteem is damaging those who possess it (Jordan et al., 2003; Schröder-Abé et al., 2007b). Defensive self-esteem, thus, lacks some of the important features of self-respect since the latter is generally thought to be intrinsically good, psychologically beneficial, and stable. These considerations do not establish that damaging forms of high self-esteem are those that could not be reflectively endorsed by the individuals who possess them. Nevertheless, they are highly suggestive given the established associations between defensive high self-esteem, general defensiveness, overconfidence, and excessive optimism about the popularity of one's opinions (Haddock & Gebauer, 2011; Jordan et al., 2005).

Given this understanding of the relation of self-esteem to self-respect. It is quite easy to see why the vices of superiority and inferiority entail lack of evaluative self-respect, or of recognition self-respect, or both. These character traits essentially involve a view of oneself that exhibits a failure to have one's own measure. This failure is not primarily a matter of mistaken beliefs about the nature and significance of one's qualities and abilities, even though such errors typically accompany these vices. These individuals demonstrate a lack of evaluative self-respect when they value themselves in a manner that would not withstand their scrutiny because these assessments are based on values that they do not reflectively endorse. Their estimations of their own features exhibit a lack of recognition self-respect when they undercut their very ability to set values for themselves that they can aspire to achieve.

The vices of inferiority are characterized by low self-esteem. Servile individuals lack evaluative self-respect because their evaluation of their own worth is sensitive to what works in gaining some social acceptance rather than to how they measure up to values that they would be prepared to endorse. Self-abasement is a worsening of servility since it entails thinking of oneself as wholly worthless. Insofar as self-abasement involves finding comfort in thinking of oneself as worthless, it is corrosive even of recognition self-respect, since self-abasing individuals are impaired in their ability to choose values or ideals for themselves. Timid individuals are also not self-respecting because their evaluation of their own worth is sensitive to what works in avoiding social rejection rather than to how they measure up to values that they would be prepared to endorse. Thus, they lack evaluative self-respect because they do not value their worth by values that they would endorse. Fatalism is a worsening of timidity because it entails a sense of hopelessness and despair. For this reason, fatalism also is tantamount to a loss of recognition self-respect since it involves seeing oneself as unable to set values by which to live.

The vices of superiority are characterized by unhealthy forms of high self-esteem. The person who suffer from superbia makes his self-esteem depend on his perceived superiority to others. What he values about himself is what makes him feel good about himself. As I have argued above this kind of high self-esteem is not self-respecting because it is not an assessment of one's own worth based on how one judges oneself to be measuring up to the values one endorses. The self-satisfied stance of the person with *superbia* would dissolve if he truly acknowledged that his self-appraisal is sensitive to the need for self-enhancement rather than being an assessment of how he measures up to what he values. Arrogance proper is a worsening of *superbia* that consists in taking oneself as the measure of value. Such a stance however does not withstand scrutiny, since it is impossible rationally to believe that a quality is good merely because one has it, whilst also believing that one is good because one has that good quality. In so far as arrogance undermines the ability to value, it deprives individuals of recognition self-respect.

Vain individuals also lack evaluative self-respect because, like servile people, they value what gains them social acceptance. Therefore, they do not value their own worth by values that they would endorse. Narcissism, as morbid self-infatuation, is similar to arrogance in some regards. Narcissists too set themselves as the standard by which to judge whether a property is admirable. Thus, narcissism, like arrogance, undermines the ability to value and is therefore corrosive of recognition self-respect. I have argued so far that the vices of superiority and inferiority exemplifies various forms of self-disrespect. It is for this reason above all that they are rightly classified as different ways in which one might fail to have the measure of oneself. Since these are failures that reflect badly on one, it makes sense to think of them as vices.

One way of addressing these shortcomings is to attempt to gain a measure of oneself. A first step in the right direction is taking responsibility for one's character vices. Taking this step is not easy, since these vices are stealthy (Cassam, 2015). Those who have them tend to lack the ability and the motivation to understand that they suffer from these shortcomings. Nevertheless, if an arrogant or a timid person comes to acknowledge that she has these vices and acquires the motivation to do something about it, she is thereby taking responsibility for her character vice.

Whilst it might be hard to achieve, the very act of taking responsibility and follow through with it is one way in which those who suffer from the vices of inferiority gain some self-esteem since it shows to the servile and self-abased that they are capable of the kind of autonomous activity in which they can take pride. It also shows to the timid and the fatalist that they are capable of initiative and thus are deserving of being esteemed. In addition, taking responsibility promotes the acquisition of other character traits that might help to reduce the grip of the vices of inferiority. For instance, assuming responsibility is a way to become more courageous and thus be less timid; more hopeful and therefore less fatalist; and have more integrity and hence less servile and the self-abasing.

Taking responsibility for their vices is also beneficial to those who suffer from the vices of superiority. It would allow those who are arrogant or suffer from *superbia* to become less defensive and thus to gain a sense of their self-worth or self-esteem that is more secure. It would help those who are vain to become more autonomous in their valuation of their own qualities. Similarly, it would assist the narcissist who is self-infatuated to develop integrity by measuring himself against values whose value is independent of his possession of them.

These considerations suggest that taking responsibility is instrumental to developing the measure of oneself. That is, taking responsibility is part of the process of becoming humble since humility is the virtue of having a sense of own's worth, strengths, and weaknesses, which is based on evaluations motivated by the desire for knowledge. This process is also, at least for those who suffer from the vices of superiority, a process of decentring, of acquiring the ability to see that they are not the measure of all value, that there are other ways of valuing things, other perspectives that they might need to consider in their reasoning. In this manner individuals are able to make themselves more answerable for their actions because they are able to consider reasons other than their own. They can also improve their empathetic understanding of how things look and feel from other perspectives and thus become agents who are more responsible in the sense of being more reliable, trustworthy, and empathic.

It might be argued that even though becoming humble might be of benefit to those who suffer from the vices of superiority, it is deleterious for those who already have low self-esteem and are beset with the negative effects of the vices of inferiority. This position has been defended by Dillon (forthcoming) who has argued that arrogance is a virtue of self-respect in resisting oppression. Humility, in so far as it is opposed to arrogance, would in these circumstances be a vice. In response, I would like to note that our disagreement is partly terminological.[26] What Dillon argues for convincingly is that subordinated individuals often behave out of self-respect in ways that others label 'arrogant'. I do not disagree. But I think that the application of the label is in these cases incorrect. These individuals are assertive but not arrogant. They exhibit pride but not self-conceit. The label 'arrogant' is applied to them in order to indicate that the speaker thinks that they are uppity and do not know their place. There is no arrogance in behaving in ways that are consonant with being deserving of equal recognition respect and in some instances high evaluative respect. Demanding such respect is compatible with humility and thus cannot be a manifestation of arrogance.[27] In addition, if—as I argued in this volume—humility is an attitude to the self of having the right measure of one's worth, it would seem that humility is something that everyone should strive to embody. Nevertheless, and in this I wholly agree with Dillon, we should be suspicious of calls for humility when they are addressed by the powerful to those who yield less power than they do.

---

[26] I have addressed the substantive parts of the disagreement in Chapter 5.

[27] Dillon and I also disagree about the meaning of humility since she believes it is best understood along traditional Christian lines as an attitude of taking oneself to be low and a disposition to self-abasement (Dillon, 2021).

In this section I have argued that taking responsibility for vice is one way of working to change one's attitudes. I have also claimed that due to the stealthiness of many vices people are unlikely to take even the first step toward improving their character. Fortunately, there are other interventions aimed at character improvement. Some of these are the topic of the next chapter where I address the prospects of reducing intellectual vices and promoting epistemic virtues.

9
Teaching Intellectual Virtues, Changing Attitudes

Not having the measure of one's own intellectual character because one is vain, arrogant, servile, or timid, I have argued in Chapter 7, is a cause of significant moral and epistemic harms. Further, it is the root of much wrongful behaviour that insults, diminishes, and is disrespectful to self and others. In this chapter I discuss some proposals that are designed to weaken vice or to inculcate and habituate the virtues, including intellectual humility, by means of education. Whilst I consider three possible strategies, I especially focus on exemplarism, since the idea that virtue can be learnt by emulating role models has recently gained much support, especially within the context of moral education (Croce & Vaccarezza, 2017; Kristjánsson, 2007, ch. 7; 2017).[1]

In my view, exemplarism is unlikely on its own to be a successful strategy when educating those people who are most in need to become more morally and intellectually virtuous. On the contrary, I show that those who are timid or servile will perceive exemplars as unattainable and respond by redoubling their low sense of self-worth. Individuals who are arrogant or vain will instead when faced by exemplars respond defensively. They will compare themselves positively to exemplars and thus learn nothing from the experience. Either way, those who are the furthest from virtue are unlikely to be helped by being presented with role models. Fortunately, there are alternative strategies for the cultivation of intellectual virtue in general, and humility in particular, that might prove more effective. In what follows, I detail one such alternative that—perhaps surprisingly—might prove effective. I propose that some version of self-affirmation, as a technique for affirming the self by affirming those values with which one identifies, might be effective in enhancing the self-esteem of those who are timid or servile, whilst rendering the self-esteem of those who are arrogant or vain more secure and therefore less fragile.

This chapter consists of three sections. In the first I discuss the prospects of two strategies for the cultivation of intellectual virtues. These are: explicit education

---

[1] My focus in this chapter is on interventions targeting individuals. It might ultimately be the case that these have limited efficacy. Actions intended to address social structures and reduce those inequalities that facilitate the institution of relations of domination and subordination might be harder to implement but have more significant long term effects.

and the repetition of virtuous activities. I conclude that both strategies encounter obstacles that make their success unlikely. The second section is dedicated to attempts to foster virtue by stimulating emulation when in the presence of role models or exemplars. I argue that despite its current popularity, and evidence of some success when educating cohorts of children, this strategy is unlikely on its own to be very effective for those who are most in need of virtue education. Finally, in the third section I describe self-affirmation techniques consisting in the affirmation of values. I compare this approach to a programme sketched by Webber (2016) for moral virtue education. Finally, I offer indirect empirical evidence that indicates that the self-affirmation strategy might be successful when trying to reduce the expression of vicious behaviour, and over time, might even lead to the development of more virtuous conduct.

9.1 Educating for Intellectual Virtue: Explicit Teaching and Repetition

The most explicit proposals for fostering intellectual virtue developed by virtue epistemologists have focused on the education of school children and college students in the classroom. This is no surprise since children and young adults are less set in their ways than older people. It would seem easier to mould the character of the youth than to change the character of adults whose habits might be hard to shift. In addition, virtue epistemologists are typically university teachers and as such they have naturally tried to develop strategies that they can apply in settings that are most pertinent to their work.

Following Aristotle, and borrowing a leaf out of books in moral character education, virtue epistemologists have typically advanced three broad strategies to foster the acquisition of intellectual character virtues. These are: learning from explicit instruction; providing opportunities for virtue habituation; and exposure to exemplars or role models (Baehr, 2013; Battaly, 2016b; Kristjánsson, 2007; Porter, 2016). In this section I evaluate the prospects for success of the first two strategies. In the next section I assess whether exemplarism is an effective means to virtue education.

The educationalist psychologist Ritchhart, a clear influence on both Baehr and Battaly, argues that the central aim of school education is to foster in children the right thinking dispositions (Ritchhart, 2002). Whilst he focuses on practising thinking routines as the main educational strategy for the development of intellectual character virtues, he also acknowledges the importance of explicit instruction about virtue concepts (Ritchhart, 2002, p. 48). The main purpose of this strategy is to teach the vocabulary appropriate to describe and understand the virtues and thus to enable students to recognize virtuous or vicious behaviour.

Ritchhart does not take this approach to occupy central stage in the acquisition of intellectual virtue and the transformation of character. The limitations of explicit instruction are well understood. Battaly, for instance, notes that learning about intellectual virtues so that one is able to recognize whether they are embodied in some activity might not prompt a person to become more virtuous (Battaly, 2016b, p. 179). In particular, imparting knowledge about the nature of the virtues offers by its own little incentive to put in the effort required to develop open-mindedness, inquisitiveness, or intellectual humility. Unless a person is already on the path to intellectual virtue, cares for the truth, and possesses sufficient self-control and motivation to stay the course, it is unlikely that this new knowledge would move her to leave her comfort zone and improve her intellectual character.

Intellectual humility in particular is especially unsuited to be fostered by means of explicit teaching. Humility, it would seem, is not something that can be best learnt by directly aiming to acquire it. The person who tries to become more humble needs to check her progress by evaluating whether she is becoming humbler and feel pleased with herself if she has, since in such a case she would have made progress toward her goal. Yet, there is something smug at feeling pleasure for one's own humility. Such behaviour would seem akin to what Alfano and Robinson (2014) have labelled 'humble bragging'. These considerations are far from conclusive but they suggest that the best means to acquire intellectual humility do not involve being told what it is and encouraged to pursue it (cf., Robinson & Alfano, 2016).[2]

This approach is even less likely to succeed if applied to those who have already developed intellectual vices. Explicit instruction can contribute to virtue development only if it is accompanied by the ability to recognize one's own present shortcomings, a hopeful attitude towards one's capacity to change, the motivation to address one's limitations, and finally the self-control necessary to enact and persevere in one's efforts to improve.[3] As I have argued in Chapter 7 these abilities are severely impaired in those who suffer from the vices of inferiority and superiority.

Individuals who are vain or arrogant are likely to overstate their achievements and underplay their limitations, whilst the opposite holds of those who are servile or timid. In addition, individuals who suffer from these vices are especially prone to motivated reasoning since biases are in some circumstances amplified by

---

[2] Paul Bloomfield in correspondence has pointed out that there might be differences between learning humility from scratch and learning to become more humble. Perhaps the child who is learning humility can be taught to aim directly at its acquisition. There are certainly important differences between these two cases but in either event there seems to be something un-humble with being pleased at one's progress towards humility.

[3] See Ahlstrom-Vij (2013) for a pessimistic assessment of humans' capacity for intellectual self-improvement.

attitude certainty and in others by uncertainty and low self-esteem (Clarkson et al., 2008; Sawicki et al., 2011; Wiersema et al., 2012). Thus, arrogant and vain individuals exemplify the closed-mindedness characteristic of those who are resistant to change because they are certain of the correctness of their views (McGregor et al., 2005). Servile and timid individuals who suffer from self-doubt might, if fearful, be prone to avoid examining unfamiliar information in detail, whilst, if sad or ashamed, might end up paying too much attention to new messages at the risk of becoming too easily persuadable (Gleicher & Petty, 1992; Phillips & Hine, 2016; Tiedens & Linton, 2001; Wood, 2000).

These results also indicate that individuals who suffer from the vices of inferiority and superiority are particularly bad at rationally updating their views in the light of newly available evidence. They are thus not moved, as they should, by reasons. They have reasons for some of their positions, but they are often unable to evaluate alternatives to them. It is precisely because their ability to make good judgments is impaired that, as I have argued in Chapter 8, these individuals are not fully answerable for their intellectual vices. These deficiencies of epistemic agency make people suffering from the vices of superiority and inferiority especially impervious to self-improvement by means of explicit education and exhortation.

Further, these individuals possess emotional orientations that are at odds with a hopeful attitude to self-improvement. Arrogant people are angry, vain individuals suffer from malicious envy. Those who are timid are fearful, whilst servile people are shame prone. The tendencies to chronic anger, envy, fear, or shame are not only incompatible with a hopeful disposition but also contribute to exacerbating attitude certainty and uncertainty and thus lead to biased beliefs (Crusius & Mussweiler, 2012; Smith & Ellsworth, 1985; Tiedens & Linton, 2001).

These same individuals also lack the motivation to improve since they are largely driven by the desire to self-enhance (when arrogant), to be esteemed (when vain), to avoid social exclusion (when timid) or to ingratiate (when servile). In every case people who suffer from vices of inferiority or superiority have motivations to behave in manners that do not contribute to fostering intellectual virtues. With the right incentives they might act in ways that mimic virtue but they fail to exemplify it. For instance, in a society that praises intellectual humility, vain individuals will try to behave in ways that are obstensively humble. However, because they want to be admired for their humility, they at best exemplify false modesty.

Finally, as I have also argued in Chapter 7 the vices of superiority and inferiority impair self-control. Self-regulatory failures are associated with defensive high self-esteem (Lambird & Mann, 2006), with vanity and narcissism (Ashton-James & Tracy, 2012), but also with low self-esteem (Phillips & Hine, 2016), fear (Baumeister & Heatherton, 1996) and shame (Gerber & Wheeler, 2009). These findings indicate that even if individuals afflicted with these vices were offered incentives that motivated them to change in their behaviour for the better, they would in any case lack the strength of will required to implement any change in their settled habits and routines.[4]

Habituation by means of repetition is another popular strategy for the acquisition of virtues, including intellectual virtues. This strategy was encouraged by Aristotle who argued that one becomes courageous, for example, by putting herself in situations that require its exercise (Aristotle, 1985, 1103b 15–20). Contemporary proponents of this approach suggest that educators create opportunities for the practice of virtues by bringing about their eliciting conditions. Thus, one would for example, stimulate open-mindedness in students by creating situations that call for open-minded responses (Battaly, 2016b).

This approach can be problematic. Habituation has at times being conceived as mindless repetition of the activities that are usually expressive of virtue.[5] So understood, habituation would be ill-suited for the acquisition of intellectual virtues since these are inconsistent with mindless repetition. Assuming that inquisitiveness, intellectual courage, autonomy, integrity, and critical thinking are intellectual virtues, asking children to engage unthinkingly in the repetition of any intellectual activity, is likely to inhibit rather than foster the acquisition of these virtues.

Alternatively, habituation might primarily involve creating opportunities for the exercise of virtue together with incentives to respond to these opportunities in the way in which a virtuous person would behave. This strategy, adopted by Battaly (2016b) and Baehr (2013), is not prima facie inconsistent with educating for intellectual virtue. However, it faces significant obstacles. To see why, we need to consider that some of the eliciting conditions of intellectual virtues are also eliciting condition of vice. One might respond to a set of challenging circumstances in the way in which an intellectually cowardly person would. Or, one might react as those who display courage would respond. More broadly, situations that offer opportunities to practice virtues also provide fertile ground to develop or cement vices.

An educator might stack the odds in favour of stimulating virtuous behaviours in students by providing suitable incentives such as grades and other virtue unrelated rewards. But this approach also has important downfalls since it relies on the presence in students of motivations that are at odds with intellectual virtues. Consider for instance, the paradoxical nature of encouraging students to behave in intellectually humble ways by giving them good grades. This strategy, it would seem, incentivises students to cultivate deception by encouraging them to

---

[4] This is not to deny that anticipating future shame is an incentive to exercise self-control (Patrick et al., 2009).

[5] Aristotle did not think of habituation as a mindless process. See Kristjánsson (2007) and Webber (2016).

behave in the ways characteristic of humility whilst satisfying desires that are likely to be at odds with this virtue. More broadly, although the issue is contested (Deci et al., 2001; Reiss, 2012), there is some empirical research suggesting that individuals find activities to be less valuable for their own sake when they are offered unrelated motives (such as a financial incentive) to carry them out, than they did before they were given any extrinsic reward (Deci & Ryan, 1985). If this research is not wholly misguided, the proposed strategy of offering students rewards for behaving in the same ways as virtuous individuals would act might be counterproductive since it would erode those motivations, such as the love of truth for its own sake, that are an essential component of the intellectual virtues.

The arguments developed in this section have strongly suggested that neither explicit teaching nor habituation, when this is conceived as incentivizing some behaviours and creating space for practicing them, are likely to foster intellectual virtues unless those who are being educated already possess suitable motivations. Rather, these strategies are likely to be ineffective, and sometimes counterproductive.

9.2 Exemplarism

Partly because the limitations of explicit teaching and practice as strategies of character formation are well-recognised, a different approach has recently gained extensive support. This approach, known as exemplarism, proposes that moral and intellectual virtues are fostered in young people and adults by exposing them to positive role models or exemplars (Zagzebski, 2017). Such exposure, by eliciting admiration, would prompt individuals to attempt to emulate the exemplars and thus promote self-improvement. In this section, I argue that this approach might be of some help to those who are already well-motivated and possess at least some aspects of virtue. It is however most likely on its own to be totally ineffective to assist those who are most in need of character change because of their entrenched tendencies to vice.

The use of role models has been a popular approach in the field of moral character education for a number of years. Unfortunately, as Kristjánsson (2007, ch. 7) bemoans, insufficient attention has been paid to how exposure to exemplars would be beneficial to students. It has been presumed that students would naturally imitate the role models in the manner of copycats. So understood education by fostering imitation of exemplars is open to a number of criticisms. For example, it inculcates in students slavishness and unthinkingness. These are morally problematic characteristics. If this is how exemplarism is meant to work, it is hard to see that it would have much to recommend for itself.

More recently, however, Zagzebski (2017) has proposed a different account of how exposure to positive exemplars is intended to induce improvement in those who are brought into contact with role models by means of fictional narratives or direct encounters. In her view the presence of exemplars elicits a positive response of admiration in those who are already receptive to the exemplars (Zagzebski, 2015). In turn admiration, after being subjected to critical reflection, triggers emulation that is an emotion responsible for a propensity to behave in the same manner as the exemplar would behave (Kristjánsson, 2017; Zagzebski, 2015, 2017). Whilst this approach to exemplarism addresses the worry that it merely fosters copycats, it is open to different criticisms. One is the concern that exemplarism is little more than hero worshipping (Kristjánsson, 2007, 2017). In response, Kristjánsson (2017) has argued that the target of admiration is not the role model but the admirable qualities, she or he instantiates. In other words, admiration is not a global emotion. A person admires someone for some of their qualities but not necessarily for others. The risk of hero worshipping can be avoided if individuals are encouraged to direct their attention to the esteemable properties of the role model rather than to the exemplar per se.

Another concern voiced by critics of exemplarism is that the exposure to exemplars might foster passivity or moral inertia rather than emulation (Kristjánsson, 2017, p. 24). Some individuals might think that they are unable to imitate the behaviour of the exemplar and thus react with despondency and sadness rather than admiration and emulation to the presence of the role model. Kristjánsson (2017, p. 31) suggests that attempting to emulate admirable qualities exemplified by role models might prove less daunting than trying to emulate exemplars. He accepts that this is an empirical claim for which he has at best only anecdotal evidence. A different answer has been supplied by Croce (2019). What might prove more effective than exposure to truly supra-human individuals is confrontation with role models that are perceived as attainable because they are not perfect, and relevant because they inhabit situations similar to one's own. This approach to addressing the problem of moral inertia is based on empirical evidence. Han et al. (2017) have found that exposure to attainable and relevant exemplars is more effective at promoting service engagement in students than being presented with stories of historic role models that are distant from the students' own experience.

In recent years exemplarism has been adopted as a viable strategy in intellectual character education following the example of moral education (Baehr, 2013, 2015; Battaly, 2016b; Croce, 2018). The approach would involve inspiring individuals to become more open-minded, more inquisitive, and intellectually humble by exposing them to attainable and relevant role models who are not perfect but exemplify to some significant degree the qualities typical of these intellectual virtues. Such exposure is intended to elicit admiration, and thus promote the emulation of these exemplars.

I have argued previously that this approach is, if adopted on its own, extremely unlikely to be effective for those individuals who are most in need of intellectual character transformation (Tanesini, 2016b, 2019). Exposure to exemplars might elicit spiteful envy or egoism rather than emulation in response to admirable exemplars.[6] This negative response in my view is precisely what is to be expected when individuals who already suffer from the vices of superiority are presented with positive exemplars. Exposure to role models might also elicit despondency in people who are beset from the vices of inferiority. Empirical research on social comparison judgements offers indirect support for these hypotheses.

Humans gauge their abilities by comparing themselves to other people. They also evaluate others' capacities by comparing them to oneself (Corcoran et al., 2011; Dunning & Hayes, 1996; Mussweiler & Rüter, 2003; Suls et al., 2020). These comparisons are often biased by motivations other than accuracy. When they feel threatened, individuals who are motivated to self-enhance tend to compare themselves to people they regard as less capable than they are by testing the hypothesis that they differ from these individuals (Vohs & Heatherton, 2004). However, if they are forced to compare themselves upward, as they would be when presented with a role model, they formulate the hypothesis that they are somewhat similar to the role model and engage in a search suited to confirm this hypothesis (Corcoran et al., 2011).[7] There is also evidence that these individuals are especially prone to malicious envy when engaging in social comparisons with people who are clearly superior to them (Smallets et al., 2016).

These results strongly suggest that exposure to role models is largely ineffective and possibly counter-productive when trying to eradicate the vices of superiority. Individuals whose high self-esteem is defensive or who display narcissistic propensities tend to think of themselves as already similar to attainable and relevant exemplars. They are thus not going to be motivated to change and emulate the role models. Further, if exposed with ideal exemplars that are clearly superior, arrogant, and narcissistic individuals experience malicious envy. They do not admire the good qualities of the role model and wish to acquire them; instead they either denigrate the value of these features and/or desire to bring down the role models and deprive them of their admirable qualities.[8] Either way, exposure to exemplars does not lead to self-improvement. It might even contribute to worsening the situation since it offers opportunities to experience malicious envy and thus to cement one's propensity to vice.

The evidence from studies of social comparison judgments also supports the suspicion that exposure to exemplars, especially if these are genuinely admirable, induces despondency and despair in those who suffer from the vices of inferiority. These individuals tend spontaneously to compare themselves for differences to people whom they judge to be superior to them. Such upward comparisons often

---

[6] This possibility is also acknowledged by Zagzebski (2015).
[7] I do not mean to imply that such an hypothesis is consciously formulated. Nevertheless, such hypothesis in the form of a directional question guides their evaluations. Because of asymmetries of error costs the evidential search is biased in favour of evidence supporting the working hypothesis.
[8] See Protasi (2016) for a taxonomy of different kinds of envy.

make people feel worse about themselves (Corcoran et al., 2011). Because they are demotivating, exposure to exemplars is counterproductive for those that suffer from the vices of inferiority.

The arguments developed so far indicate that by itself exposure to exemplars, be they attainable or ideal, is unlikely to help those most in need of intellectual character education. However, empirical research on social comparison judgements also shows that the presentation of role models can be effective in some circumstances. Individuals whose upward social comparisons are motivated by the desire to improve themselves might benefit by comparing themselves to role models. Typically this occurs only when the exemplar is perceived as attainable (Corcoran et al., 2011, pp. 124–125). In these cases, it is likely that social comparison judgments prompt benign envy (rather than admiration) of the exemplars. Envy is benign or, in Protasi's (2016) vocabulary, emulative when it is directed at a good perceived to be attainable. This kind of envy motivates self-improvement because it stimulates one to become more similar to the role model with whom one affiliates.

Empirical research on envy and social comparison judgments further supports the suspicion that only those who are already on the way to virtue find exposure to exemplars beneficial. Smallets et al. (2016), for instance, found that individuals with defensive high self-esteem are especially prone to malicious envy (either spiteful because it denigrates the exemplar for a quality one feels one cannot get or aggressive because it wishes to deprive the exemplar of the feature one feels one can obtain for oneself). These are individuals who, if the accounts I provided in Chapter 5 and 6 are correct, suffer from the vices of superiority. The same study also found that it is individuals with high secure self-esteem that respond to upward comparisons with benign envy (Smallets et al., 2016). Given the account of intellectual humility supplied in Chapter 4, this results indicates that it is people who already somewhat virtuous that can take advantage of upward comparisons to improve themselves.[9] This option is also unavailable to individuals who suffer from the vices of inferiority since their low self-esteem and self-deprecation is exacerbated by their upward social comparisons. They, nevertheless, engage in these activities because this behaviour makes them more likeable in the eyes of their peers (Vohs & Heatherton, 2004).

In conclusion, the arguments in this section show that although exposure to exemplars has a useful place in intellectual character education, it is only likely to be effective for people who are already motivated to improve. It is, by itself, of no

---

[9] To my mind it is wholly unclear whether emulative envy is at all different from emulation triggered by admiration. If these two emotions are largely the same, then the envy model proposed by Sullivan and Alfano (2019) is not a genuine alternative to the admiration model. Sullivan and Alfano think of the model in terms of envy triggering competitive ambition. It is true that the agonistic model is incompatible with the emulative one, but the sort of envy that triggers agonism is aggressive envy and not benign envy as Sullivan and Alfano claim.

help in the case of individuals who because of their vices are motivated either to self-enhance or to be socially accepted and liked.

9.3 Self-Affirmation

The main obstacle to self-improvement, if the discussion so far is roughly correct, is motivational.[10] Individuals who do not have the measure of themselves have strong motivations to self-enhance, to seek others' approval, or to avoid social exclusion, that prevent them from learning from exemplars or benefit from explicit education about virtue. This observation indicates that interventions that might weaken the hold of these motivations should be effective in making these individuals more receptive to activities designed to effect their character transformation. In this section I describe one intervention along these lines: self-affirmation.

Techniques involving self-affirmation can be varied. They do not involve telling oneself that one is great or the best. Rather, they are interventions that direct people to reflect on the values that are most central to them as people (McQueen & Klein, 2006; Steele, 1988). This process is intended to help subjects understand better which values they endorse and the reasons why these are important to them. Individuals might be asked to elaborate by themselves a list of values or to choose them from a catalogue developed by others. They might also be asked to write a paragraph or so justifying their choices. Affirmation of the self via affirmation of the values one holds dear is intended to make one's sense of self-worth more secure and less vulnerable to threats. There is substantial empirical evidence that these interventions are effective in reducing defensiveness (Sherman & Cohen, 2002; Sherman & Cohen, 2006). If, as I argued here and in Chapters 5 and 7, defensiveness is the motivation that biases the self-assessments carried out by arrogant individuals, any intervention that reduces this motivation should help to make these people more open to change. This speculation is supported by evidence that self-affirmed individuals become more accepting of higher quality information (Sherman & Cohen, 2002; Sherman & Hartson, 2011).

Research focusing on the use of affirmation of the self through reflection on values to promote self-improvement and academic performance has shown it to be effective and to have long lasting beneficial consequences (Cohen & Sherman, 2014). Provided the intervention is timed properly self-affirmation can become self-sustaining and trigger a changed enduring perception of one's own situation (Cohen & Sherman, 2014).

---

[10] The proposals for self-improvement presented in the final chapter of Cassam (2019) are also dependent of already possessing some motivation to improve.

The mechanisms that make self-affirmation effective are not well-understood. There is, however, reason to believe that it promotes a more expansive understanding of oneself and of what one cares about (Critcher & Dunning, 2015). In turn this more capacious self-understanding makes one's sense of self-worth more capable of withstanding possible threats, by coming to see oneself as more complex and multifaceted than one previously thought but also less dependent on external sources and thus less susceptible to being threatened.

Self-affirmation can help individuals suffering from defensive high self-esteem to be less self-defensive (Haddock & Gebauer, 2011). It might thus be extremely effective in targeting their motivations and thus make them more open to self-improvement. It is possible that some of the beneficial effects of self-affirmation are dependent on the values that are reflectively endorsed. If this is the case, there is reason to prefer interventions where subjects are presented with lists of values favouring openness to change (e.g., freedom and creativity) and self-transcendence (e.g., generosity) (Schwartz et al., 2012). Left alone these individuals whose self-esteem is defensive might choose values of self-enhancement such as power that are unlikely to be effective in making them less sensitive to threats.

The idea that self-affirmation might be an effective intervention in the reduction of arrogant behaviour might seem wholly counter-intuitive. One might think that arrogant people need to be chastised or taken down a peg, rather than having their sense of self-worth affirmed. However, if the account of arrogance developed in this book is correct, this character vice is a defensive response to underlying insecurities. The effectiveness of an intervention that strengthens people's self-respect by helping them to make their self-esteem depend on their reflections on values rather than on their fear of threats should therefore not be surprising.

One might object to the suggestion that self-affirmation techniques are added to the arsenal of strategies available for the promotion of character education, by noting that teachers might be unable to tell which students would benefit from it. It might indeed be impossible to tell at first sight which individuals are extremely defensive. Yet self-affirmation works best when it is deployed early on as a preliminary to other approaches. Fortunately, the fact that we cannot look into others' hearts and minds to figure out their true character traits is not an obstacle in this instance.

One of the advantages of self-affirmation is that its administration is beneficial to all rather than merely to those who are driven to defensiveness because of a desire for self-enhancement. In particular self-affirmation techniques are well known to buffer individuals against the negative effects on performance, including performance in intellectual tasks, of stereotype threat (Sherman & Hartson, 2011; Steele, 2010). Given the links between the vices of inferiority and membership in stereotyped and subordinated groups, it would seem that one and the same technique might serve to relieve the fear characteristic of those who suffer from intellectual timidity as well as the defensiveness of those who suffer from intellectual arrogance.

Clearly self-affirmation is unlikely to be a panacea for the reduction of vice and the cultivation of virtue, but because it affects motivation, it is a different strategy from those advocated by many proponents of character education such as explicit education, exposure to exemplars and the creation of opportunities to practise virtue. I conclude this section by comparing self-affirmation to the intervention described by Webber (2016) as a positive programme for moral improvement. There are similarities between our proposals since Webber recommends embedding one's values such as generosity in one's cognition and behaviour primarily by engaging in critical reflection on one's behaviour in relation to the demands of values (2016, p. 150). However, Webber thinks of this process as one of strengthening one's attitudes in the face of situational challenges. In this regard, our approaches differ. I have argued in Chapter 5 and 7 that those who suffer from the vices of superiority have strong attitudes that are often defensive. Their shortcomings cannot be addressed by strengthening their attitudes even further, what they need instead is a change of attitude. Attitude strengthening is also not particularly helpful to individuals suffering from the vices of inferiority since the root of their vice does not lie in the weakness of their attitudes but in the functions that these attitudes serve. That said, the convergence between my proposal and Webber's is significant since we both argue that the cultivation of virtue require targeted interventions designed to bring about attitude change.

I have argued that the main barrier posed by vice to the acquisition of virtue is motivational. I have proposed that we can overcome this obstacle by helping individuals to become less defensive and less fearful of social exclusion. This approach recommends encouraging people to focus on what they value. Focusing on personal values and how these are reflected in one's own behaviour can be seen as a means to educate for humility. The humble person has the measure of herself because her self-assessments are not biased by egocentric motivations of ego-defence or of social-adjustment. On the contrary she evaluates herself by the measure of her values. Value affirmation promotes this stance to oneself because it contributes to making one's sense of self-worth depend on how one measures up to values one would reflectively endorse.

To conclude, in this book I have demonstrated the explanatory power of accounts of some intellectual character vices and virtues in terms of attitudes. I have relied on the attitudinal framework to offer rich descriptions of eight vices and three virtues and to highlight their motivational and emotional aspects. I have shown that individuals are epistemically responsible for intellectual vices because these are attributable to them. They are also morally accountable for these character traits, even though others are rarely in a position to blame them for these shortcomings. Finally, I have offered an intervention designed to reduce these vices and promote the cultivation of humility.

References

Abramson, L., Metalsky, G., and Alloy, L. (1989). Hopelessness depression: A theory-based subtype of depression. *Psychological Review, 96*, 358–372. doi:10.1037/0033-295X.96.2.358.

Ackerman, R. A., Witt, E. A., Donnellan, M. B., Trzesniewski, K. H., Robins, R. W., and Kashy, D. A. (2011). What does the narcissistic personality inventory really measure? *Assessment, 18*(1), 67–87. doi:10.1177/1073191110382845.

Ahlstrom-Vij, K. (2013). Why we cannot rely on ouselves for epistemic improvement. *Philosophical Issues, 23*(Epistemic Agency), 276–296. doi:10.1111/phis.12014.

Aikin, S. F., and Clanton, C. J. (2010). Developing group-deliberative virtues. *Journal of Applied Philosophy, 27*(4), 409–424. doi:10.1111/j.1468-5930.2010.00494.x.

Ajzen, I. (2005). *Attitudes, Personality and Behavior* (2nd ed.). Maidenhead: Open University Press.

Alfano, M. (2012). Expanding the situationist challenge to responsibilist virtue epistemology. *The Philosophical Quarterly, 62*(247), 223–249. doi:10.1111/j.1467-9213.2011.00016.x.

Alfano, M. (2013). *Character as Moral Fiction*. Cambridge: Cambridge University Press.

Alfano, M. (2017). Epistemic situationism: An extended prolepsis. In A. Fairweather and M. Alfano (eds), *Epistemic Situationism* (pp. 44–61). Oxford: Oxford University Press.

Alfano, M. (2018). A plague on both your houses: Virtue theory after situationism and repligate. *Teoria, 38*(2), 115–122. doi:10.4454/teoria.v38i2.

Alfano, M., and Robinson, B. (2014). Bragging. *Thought: A Journal of Philosophy, 3*(4), 263–272. doi:10.1002/tht3.141.

Alfano, M., Iurino, K., Stey, P., Robinson, B., Christen, M., Yu, F., and Lapsley, D. (2017). Development and validation of a multi-dimensional measure of intellectual humility. *PLoS ONE, 12*(8), e0182950. doi:10.1371/journal.pone.0182950.

Alighieri, D. (1994). *La Commedia Secondo L'Antica Vulgata*, (G. Petrocchi ed. 2 riv ed.). Firenze: Casa editrice Le lettere.

Alston, W. P. (1989). *Epistemic Justification: Essays in the Theory of Knowledge*. Ithaca: Cornell University Press.

Alvarez, M. (2016). Reasons for action: Justification, motivation, explanation. In E. N. Zalta (Ed.), *Stanford Encyclopedia of Philosophy* (Winter 2016 ed.). Retrieved from https://plato.stanford.edu/archives/win2016/entries/reasons-just-vs-expl/.

Annas, J. (2011). *Intelligent Virtue*. Oxford: Oxford University Press.

Arango-Muñoz, S., and Michaelian, K. (2014). Epistemic feelings, epistemic emotions: Review and introduction to the focus section. *Philosophical Inquiries, 2*(1), 97–122. doi:10.4454/philinq.v2i1.79.

Aristotle. (1985). *Nichomachean Ethics* (T. Irwin, Trans.). Indianapolis and Cambridge: Hackett Publishing Company.

Aristotle. (2007). *On Rhetoric: A Theory of Civic Discourse* (G. A. Kennedy, Trans. 2nd ed.). New York and Oxford: Oxford University Press.

Ashton-James, C. E., and Tracy, J. L. (2012). Pride and prejudice: How feelings about the self influence judgments of others. *Personality and Social Psychology Bulletin, 38*(4), 466–476. doi:10.1177/0146167211429449.

Axtell, G. (2008). Expanding epistemology: A responsibilist approach. *Philosophical Papers*, 37(1), 51–87.
Baehr, J. (2010). Epistemic malevolence. *Metaphilosophy*, 41(1–2), 189–213. doi:10.1111/j.1467-9973.2009.01623.x.
Baehr, J. (2011). *The Inquiring Mind: On Intellectual Virtues and Virtue Epistemology*. Oxford: Oxford University Press.
Baehr, J. (2013). Educating for intellectual virtues: From theory to practice. *Journal of Philosophy of Education*, 47(2), 248–262. doi:10.1111/1467-9752.12023.
Baehr, J. (2015). *Cultivating Good Minds: A Philosophical and Practical Guide to Educating for Intellectual Virtues*. Retrieved from http://intellectualvirtues.org/why-should-weeducate-for-intellectual-virtues-2-2.
Baehr, J. (2016). The four dimensions of an intellectual virtue. In C. Mi, M. Slote, and E. Sosa (Eds.), *Moral and Intellectual Virtues in Western and Chinese Philosophy* (pp. 86–98). New York and London: Routledge.
Baier, A. (1994). *Moral Prejudices: Essays on Ethics*. Cambridge, Mass. and London: Harvard University Press.
Banaji, M. R., and Heiphetz, L. (2010). Attitudes. In S. T. Fiske, D. T. Gilbert, and G. Lindzey (eds), *Handbook of Social Psychology* (5th ed., Vol. 1, pp. 353–393). Hoboken, NJ: John Wiley & Sons.
Baron, R. S. (2000). Arousal, capacity, and intense indoctrination. *Personality and Social Psychology Review*, 4(3), 238–254. doi:10.1207/S15327957PSPR0403_3.
Bartky, S. L. (1990). *Femininity and Domination: Studies in the Phenomenology of Oppression*. London: Routledge.
Battaly, H. (2014). Varieties of epistemic vice. In J. Matheson and R. Vitz (eds), *The Ethics of Belief: Individual and Social* (pp. 51–76). Oxford: Oxford University Press.
Battaly, H. (2015). *Virtue*. Cambridge: Polity Press.
Battaly, H. (2016a). Epistemic virtue and vice: Reliabilism, responsibilism, and personalism. In C. Mi, M. Slote, and E. Sosa (eds), *Moral and Intellectual Virtues in Western and Chinese Philosophy* (pp. 99–120). New York and London: Routledge.
Battaly, H. (2016b). Responsibilist virtues in reliabilist classrooms. In J. S. Baehr (ed.), *Intellectual Virtues and Education: Essays in Applied Virtue Epistemology* (pp. 163–183). New York and London: Routledge.
Battaly, H. (2017). Testimonial injustice, epistemic vice, and vice epistemology. In I. J. Kidd, J. Medina, and G. J. Pohlhaus (eds), *The Routledge Handbook of Epistemic Injustice* (pp. 223–231). London and New York: Routledge.
Battaly, H. (2018a). Can closed-mindedness be an intellectual virtue? *Philosophy: Royal Institute of Philosophy Supplement*, 84, 23–45. doi:10.1017/s135824611800053x.
Battaly, H. (2018b). Closed-mindedness as an intellectual vice. In C. Kelp and J. Greco (eds), *Virtue Theoretic Epistemology* (pp. 15–41). Cambridge: Cambridge University Press.
Battaly, H. (2019). Vice epistemology has a responsibility problem. *Philosophical Issues*, 29(1), 24–36. doi:10.1111/phis.12138.
Baumeister, R. F., and Heatherton, T. F. (1996). Self-regulation failure: An overview. *Psychological Inquiry*, 7(1), 1–15. doi:10.1207/s15327965pli0701_1.
Baumeister, R. F., and Vohs, K. D. (2001). Narcissism as addiction to esteem. *Psychological Inquiry*, 12(4), 2016–2210. doi:https://www.jstor.org/stable/1449473.
Baumeister, R. F., Gailliot, M., DeWall, C. N., and Oaten, M. (2006). Self-regulation and personality: How interventions increase regulatory success, and how depletion moderates the effects of traits on behavior. *Journal of Personality*, 74(6), 1773–1801. doi:10.1111/j.1467-6494.2006.00428.x.

Baumeister, R. F., Smart, L., and Boden, J. M. (1996). Relation of threatened egotism to violence and aggression: The dark side of high self-esteem. *Psychological Review, 103*, 5–33. doi:10.1037/0033-295X.103.1.5.

Bell, D. W., and Esses, V. M. (2002). Ambivalence and response amplification: A motivational perspective. *Personality and Social Psychology Bulletin, 28*(8), 1143–1152. doi:10.1177/01461672022811012.

Bell, M. (2013). *Hard Feelings: The Moral Psychology of Contempt*. New York: Oxford University Press.

Berlin, I. (2013). *The Hedgehog and the Fox* (H. Hardy ed. 2nd ed.). Princeton and Oxford: Princeton University Press.

Bishop, M., and Trout, J. D. (2005). The pathologies of standard analytic epistemology. *Noûs, 39*(4), 696–714. doi:10.1111/j.0029-4624.2005.00545.x.

Bommarito, N. (2013). Modesty as a virtue of attention. *Philosophical Review, 122*(1), 93–117. doi:10.1215/00318108-1728723.

Bosson, J. K., Brown, R. P., Zeigler-Hill, V., and Swann, W. B. (2003). Self-enhancement tendencies among people with high explicit self-esteem: The moderating role of implicit self-esteem. *Self and Identity, 2*(3), 169–187. doi:10.1080/15298860309029.

Bosson, J. K., Swann, W. B., and Pennebaker, J. W. (2000). Stalking the perfect measure of implicit self-esteem: The blind men and the elephant revisited? *Journal of Personality and Social Psychology, 79*, 631–643.

Brady, M. S. (2013). *Emotional Insight: The Epistemic Role of Emotional Experience*. New York: Oxford University Press.

Brady, M. S. (2017). The Appropriateness of Pride. In A. J. Carter and E. C. Gordon (eds), *The Moral Psychology of Pride* (pp. 13–30). London and New York: Rowman and Littlefield.

Brannon, L. A., Tagler, M. J., and Eagly, A. H. (2007). The moderating role of attitude strength in selective exposure to information. *Journal of Experimental Social Psychology, 43*(4), 611–617. doi:10.1016/j.jesp.2006.05.001.

Brennan, G., and Pettit, P. (2004). *The Economy of Esteem: An Essay on Civil and Political Society*. Oxford and New York: Oxford University Press.

Brown, J. (2018). What is epistemic blame? *Noûs, 54*(2), 389–407. doi:10.1111/nous.12270.

Brownstein, M. (2016). Implicit bias. In E. N. Zalta (ed.), *The Stanford Encyclopedia of Philosophy* (Spring 2016 Edition). Retrieved from http://plato.stanford.edu/archives/spr2016/entries/implicit-bias/.

Bruner, J., and O'Connor, C. (2017). Power, bargaining, and collaboration. In T. Boyer, C. Mayo-Wilson, and M. Weisberg (eds), *Scientific Collaboration and Collective Knowledge* (pp. 135–157). New York: Oxford University Press.

Bushman, B. J., and Baumeister, R. F. (1998). Threatened egotism, narcissism, self-esteem, and direct and displaced aggression: Does self-love or self-hate lead to violence? *Journal of Personality and Social Psychology, 75*(1), 219–229. doi:10.1037/0022-3514.75.1.219.

Byerly, T. R. (2020). *Intellectual Dependability: A Virtue Theory of the Epistemic and Educational Ideal*. London: Routledge.

Cacioppo, J. T., and Petty, R. E. (1982). The need for cognition. *Journal of Personality and Social Psychology, 42*, 116–131. doi:10.1037/0022-3514.42.1.116.

Cacioppo, J. T., Petty, R. E., Feinstein, J. A., and Jarvis, W. B. G. (1996). Dispositional differences in cognitive motivation: The life and times of individuals varying in need for cognition. *Psychological Bulletin, 119*(2), 197–253. doi:10.1037/0033-2909.119.2.197.

Cacioppo, J. T., Petty, R. E., Kao, C. F., and Rodriguez, R. (1986). Central and peripheral routes to persuasion: An individual difference perspective. *Journal of Personality and Social Psychology, 51*, 1032–1043. doi:10.1037/0022-3514.51.5.1032.

Calhoun, C. (2016). *Moral Aims: Essays on the Importance of Getting It Right and Practicing Morality with Others*. New York: Oxford University Press.

Campbell, W. K., and Foster, J. D. (2007). The narcissistic self: Background, the extended agency model, and ongoing controversies. In C. Sedikides and S. Spencer (eds), *The Self* (pp. 115–138). Hove: Psychology.

Campbell, W. K., Bosson, J. K., Goheen, T. W., Lakey, C. E., and Kernis, M. H. (2007). Do narcissists dislike themselves 'deep down inside'? *Psychological Science, 18*(3), 227–229. doi:10.1111/j.1467-9280.2007.01880.x.

Campbell, W. K., Reeder, G. D., Sedikides, C., and Elliot, A. J. (2000). Narcissism and comparative self-enhancement strategies. *Journal of Research in Personality, 34*(3), 329–347. doi:10.1006/jrpe.2000.2282.

Card, C. (1996). *The Unnatural Lottery: Character and Moral Luck*. Philadelphia: Temple University Press.

Carruthers, P. (2017). Are epistemic emotions metacognitive? *Philosophical Psychology, 30*(1–2), 58–78. doi:10.1080/09515089.2016.1262536.

Cassam, Q. (2015). Stealthy vices. *Social Epistemology Review and Reply Collective, 4*(10), 19–25. doi: http://wp.me/p1Bfg0-2na.

Cassam, Q. (2016). Vice epistemology. *The Monist, 99*(2), 159–180. doi:10.1093/monist/onv034.

Cassam, Q. (2019). *Vices of the Mind*. Oxford: Oxford University Press.

Césaire, A. (1972). *Discourse on Colonialism* (J. Pinkham, Trans.). New York: Monthly Review Press.

Cheatham, L., and Tormala, Z. L. (2015). Attitude certainty and attitudinal advocacy: The unique roles of clarity and correctness. *Personality and Social Psychology Bulletin, 41*(11), 1537–1550. doi:10.1177/0146167215601406.

Chen, S., Duckworth, K., and Chaiken, S. (1999). Motivated heuristic and systematic processing. *Psychological Inquiry, 10*(1), 44–49. doi:10.1207/s15327965pli1001_6.

Chen, S., Shechter, D., and Chaiken, S. (1996). Getting at the truth or getting along: Accuracy—versus impression motivated heuristic and systematic processing. *Journal of Personality and Social Psychology, 71*(2), 262–275. doi:10.1037/0022-3514.71.2.262.

Church, I. M. (2016). The doxastic account of intellectual humility. *Logos and Episteme, 7*(4), 413–433. doi:10.5840/logos-episteme20167441.

Cichocka, A., Marchlewska, M., and Golec de Zavala, A. (2016). Does self-love or self-hate predict conspiracy beliefs? Narcissism, self-esteem, and the endorsement of conspiracy theories. *Social Psychological and Personality Science, 7*(2), 157–166. doi:10.1177/1948550615616170.

Clarkson, J. J., Tormala, Z. L., DeSensi, V. L., and Christian Wheeler, S. (2009). Does attitude certainty beget self-certainty? *Journal of Experimental Social Psychology, 45*(2), 436–439. doi:10.1016/j.jesp.2008.10.004.

Clarkson, J. J., Tormala, Z. L., and Rucker, D. D. (2008). A new look at the consequences of attitude certainty: the amplification hypothesis. *Journal of Personality and Social Psychology, 95*(4), 810–825. doi:10.1037/a0013192.

Clarkson, J. J., Tormala, Z. L., and Rucker, D. D. (2011). Cognitive and affective matching effects in persuasion: An amplification perspective. *Personality and Social Psychology Bulletin, 37*(11), 1415–1427. doi:10.1177/0146167211413394.

Coady, D. (2010). Two concepts of epistemic injustice. *Episteme*, 7(2), 101–113. doi:10.3366/E1742360010000845.

Coady, D. (2017). Epistemic injustice as distributive injustice. In I. J. Kidd, J. Medina, and G. J. Pohlhaus (eds), *The Routledge Handbook of Epistemic Injustice* (pp. 61–68). London and New York: Routledge.

Cobb, A. D. (2019). Hope for intellectual humility. *Episteme*, 16(1), 56–72. doi:10.1017/epi.2017.18.

Cohen, G. L., and Sherman, D. K. (2014). The psychology of change: Self-affirmation and social psychological intervention. *Annual Review of Psychology*, 65, 333–371. doi:10.1146/annurev-psych-010213-115137.

Collins, P. H. (1991). *Black Feminist Thought: Knowledge, Consciousness, and the Politics of Empowerment* (2nd ed.). New York: Routledge.

Cooper, J. (2008). *Cognitive Dissonance: Fifty Years of a Classic Theory*. Los Angeles, Calif. and London: SAGE.

Corcoran, K., Crusius, J., and Mussweiler, T. (2011). Social comparison: Motives, standards, and mechanisms. In D. Chadee (ed.), *Theories in Social Psychology* (pp. 119–139). Oxford: Wiley Blackwell.

Crerar, C. (2017). Motivational approaches to intellectual vice. *Australasian Journal of Philosophy*, 96(4), 753–766. doi:10.1080/00048402.2017.1394334.

Critcher, C. R., and Dunning, D. (2015). Self-affirmations provide a broader perspective on self-threat. *Personality and Social Psycholology Bulletin*, 41(1), 3–18. doi:10.1177/0146167214554956.

Croce, M. (2018). Il potenziale educativo degli esemplari intellettuali. *Etica and Politica/Ethics and Politics*, 2, 143–162. doi:http://hdl.handle.net/10077/22331.

Croce, M. (2019). Exemplarism in moral education: Problems with applicability and indoctrination. *Journal of Moral Education*, 48(3), 291–302. doi:10.1080/03057240.2019.1579086.

Croce, M., and Vaccarezza, M. S. (2017). Educating through exemplars: Alternative paths to virtue. *Theory and Research in Education*, 15(1), 5–19. doi:10.1177/1477878517695903.

Crusius, J., and Lange, J. (2014). What catches the envious eye? Attentional biases within malicious and benign envy. *Journal of Experimental Social Psychology*, 55, 1–11. doi:10.1016/j.jesp.2014.05.007.

Crusius, J., and Mussweiler, T. (2012). When people want what others have: The impulsive side of envious desire. *Emotion*, 12(1), 142–153. doi:10.1037/a0023523.

Cunningham, W. A., Preacher, K. J., and Banaji, M. R. (2001). Implicit attitude measures: Consistency, stability and convergent validity. *Psychological Science*, 12(2), 163–170. doi:10.1111/1467-9280.00328.

Darwall, S. L. (2006). *The Second-Person Standpoint: Morality, Respect, and Accountability*. Cambridge, Mass.: Harvard University Press.

DeBono, K. G. (1987). Investigating the social-adjustive and value-expressive functions of attitudes: Implications for persuasion processes. *Journal of Personality and Social Psychology*, 52, 279–287.

Deci, E. L., and Ryan, R. M. (1985). *Intrinsic Motivation and Self-determination in Human Behavior*. New York: Plenum.

Deci, E. L., Koestner, R., and Ryan, R. M. (2001). Extrinsic rewards and intrinsic motivation in education: Reconsidered once again. *Review of Educational Research*, 71(1), 1–27. doi:10.3102/00346543071001001.

Deonna, J. A., Rodogno, R., and Teroni, F. (2011). *In Defense of Shame: The Faces of an Emotion*. Oxford: Oxford University Press.

Dillon, R. S. (2004). Kant on arrogance and self-respect. In C. Calhoun (ed.), *Setting the Moral Compass: Essays by Women Philosophers* (pp. 191–216). Oxford and New York: Oxford University Press.

Dillon, R. S. (2007). Arrogance, self-respect and personhood. *Journal of Consciousness Studies*, 14(5–6), 101–126.

Dillon, R. S. (2018). Respect. *The Stanford Encyclopedia of Philosophy (Spring 2018 Edition).* Retrieved from http://plato.stanford.edu/archives/fall2015/entries/respect/.

Dillon, R. S. (2021). Humility and self-respect: Kantian and feminist perspectives. In M. Alfano, M. P. Lynch, and A. Tanesini (eds), *The Routledge Handbook on the Philosophy of Humility* (pp. 59–71). New York and London: Routledge.

Dillon, R. S. (forthcoming). Self-respect, arrogance, and power: A feminist analysis. In R. Dean and O. Sensen (eds), *Respect.* New York: Oxford University Press.

Dokic, J. (2012). Seeds of self-knowledge: Noetic feelings and metacognition. In M. J. Beran, J. L. Brandl, J. Perner, and J. Proust (eds), *Foundations of Metacognition* (pp. 716–761). Oxford: Oxford University Press.

Dolezal, L. (2015). *The Body and Shame: Phenomenology, Feminism, and the Socially Shaped Body.* Lanham, Boulder, New York, London: Lexington Books.

Doris, J. M. (2002). *Lack of Character: Personality and Moral Behavior.* Cambridge: Cambridge University Press.

Driver, J. (1989). The virtues of ignorance. *The Journal of Philosophy*, 86(7), 373–384. doi:10.2307/2027146.

Driver, J. (1999). Modesty and ignorance. *Ethics*, 109(4), 827–834. doi:10.1086/233947.

Driver, J. (2001). *Uneasy Virtue.* Cambridge: Cambridge University Press.

Driver, J. (2016). Minimal virtue. *The Monist*, 99(2), 97–111. doi:10.1093/monist/onv032.

Du Bois, W. E. B. (1990). *The Souls of Black Folk* (1st Vintage Books/Library of America ed.). New York: Vintage Books/Library of America.

Dunning, D., and Hayes, A. F. (1996). Evidence for egocentric comparison in social judgment. *Journal of Personality and Social Psychology*, 71, 213–229. doi:10.1037/0022-3514.71.2.213.

Dweck, C. S. (2006). *Mindset: The New Psychology of Success* (1st ed.). New York: Random House.

Eagly, A. H., Kulesa, P., Chen, S., and Chaiken, S. (2001). Do attitudes affect memory? Tests of the congeniality hypothesis. *Current Directions in Psychological Science*, 10(1), 5–9. doi:10.1111/1467-8721.00102.

Elster, J. (1983). *Sour Grapes: Studies in the Subversion of Rationality.* Cambridge: Cambridge University Press.

Emmons, R. A. (1984). Factor analysis and construct validity of the narcissistic personality inventory. *Journal of Personality Assessment*, 48(3), 291–300. doi:10.1207/s15327752jpa4803_11.

Evans, J. S. (2008). Dual-processing accounts of reasoning, judgment, and social cognition. *Annual Review of Psychology*, 59, 255–278. doi:10.1146/annurev.psych.59.103006.093629.

Fanon, F. (1986). *Black Skin, White Masks* (C. L. Markmann, Trans.). London: Pluto Press.

Fantl, J. (2018). *The Limitations of the Open Mind.* Oxford: Oxford University Press.

Fazio, R. H. (1990). Multiple processes by which attitudes guide behavior: The MODE model as an integrative framework. In M. P. Zanna (ed.), *Avances in Experimental Social Psychology* (Vol. 23, pp. 75–109). San Diego, CA: Academic Press.

Fazio, R. H. (2000). Accessible attitudes as tools for object appraisal: Their costs and benefits. In G. R. Maio and J. M. Olson (eds), *Why We Evaluate: Functions of Attitudes* (pp. 1–36). Mahwah, N.J. and London: Lawrence Erlbaum.

Fazio, R. H., and Olson, M. A. (2007). Attitudes: Foundations, functions and consequences. In M. A. Hogg and J. Cooper (eds), *The SAGE Handbook of Social Psychology* (Concise Student ed. pp. 139–160). London: SAGE.

Fazio, R. H., Jackson, J. R., Dunton, B. C., and Williams, C. J. (1995). Variability in automatic activation as an unobtrusive measure of racial attitudes: A bona fide pipeline? *Journal of Personality and Social Psychology*, 69, 1013–1027. doi:10.1037/0022-3514.69.6.1013.

Fazio, R. H., Sanbonmatsu, D. M., Powell, M. C., and Kardes, F. R. (1986). On the automatic activation of attitudes. *Journal of Personality and Social Psychology*, 50(2), 229–238. doi:10.1037//0022-3514.50.2.229.

Feinberg, J. (1984). *The Moral Limits of the Criminal Law: Harm to Others* (Vol. 1). New York: Oxford University Press.

Fischer, P. (2011). Selective exposure, decision uncertainty, and cognitive economy: A new theoretical perspective on confirmatory information search. *Social and Personality Psychology Compass*, 5(10), 751–762. doi:10.1111/j.1751-9004.2011.00386.x.

Frankfurt, H. G. (2005). *On Bullshit*. Princeton and Oxford: Princeton University Press.

Fricker, M. (2007). *Epistemic Injustice: Power and the Ethics of Knowing*. Oxford: Oxford University Press.

Frye, M. (1983). *Politics of Reality: Essays in Feminist Theory*. Berkeley: Crossing Press.

Galligan, P. (2016). Shame, publicity, and self-esteem. *Ratio*, 29(1), 57–72. doi:10.1111/rati.12078.

Garcia, J. L. A. (2006). Being unimpressed with ourselves: Reconceiving humility. *Philosophia*, 34(4), 417–435. doi:10.1007/s11406-006-9032-x.

Gawronski, B., and Bodenhausen, G. V. (2006). Associative and propositional processes in evaluation: An integrative review of implicit and explicit attitude change. *Psychological Bulletin*, 132(5), 692–731. doi:10.1037/0033-2909.132.5.692.

Gendler, T. S. (2011). On the epistemic costs of implicit bias. *Philosophical Studies*, 156(1), 33–63. doi:10.1007/s11098-011-9801-7.

Gerber, J., and Wheeler, L. (2009). On being rejected a meta-analysis of experimental research on rejection. *Perspectives on Psychological Science*, 4(5), 468–488. doi:10.1111/j.1745-6924.2009.01158.x.

Gleicher, F., and Petty, R. E. (1992). Expectations of reassurance influence the nature of fear-stimulated attitude change. *Journal of Experimental Social Psychology*(28), 86–100. doi:10.1016/0022-1031(92)90033-G.

Goffman, E. (1959). *The Presentation of Self in Everyday Life*. London: Penguin.

Greco, J. (2010). *Achieving Knowledge: A Virtue-Theoretic Account of Epistemic Normativity*. Cambridge: Cambridge University Press.

Greenwald, A. G., McGhee, D. E., and Schwartz, J. L. K. (1998). Measuring individual differences in implicit cognition: The Implicit Association Test. *Journal of Personality and Social Psychology*, 74, 1464–1480. doi:10.1037/0022-3514.74.6.1464.

Gregg, A. P., and Sedikides, C. (2010). Narcissistic fragility: Rethinking its links to explicit and implicit self-esteem. *Self and Identity*, 9(2), 142–161. doi:10.1080/15298860902815451.

Haddock, G., and Gebauer, J. E. (2011). Defensive self-esteem impacts attention, attitude strength, and self-affirmation processes. *Journal of Experimental Social Psychology*, 47(6), 1276–1284. doi:10.1016/j.jesp.2011.05.020.

Hahn, A., Judd, C. M., Hirsh, H. K., and Blair, I. V. (2014). Awareness of implicit attitudes. *Journal of Experimental Psychology: General*, 143(3), 1369–1392. doi:10.1037/a0035028.

Hahn, U., and Harris, A. J. L. (2014). What does it mean to be biased? *Psychology of Learning and Motivation*, 61, 41–102. doi:10.1016/b978-0-12-800283-4.00002-2.

Han, H., Kim, J., Jeong, C., and Cohen, G. L. (2017). Attainable and relevant moral exemplars are more effective than extraordinary exemplars in promoting voluntary service engagement. *Frontiers in Psychology, 8*(283). doi:10.3389/fpsyg.2017.00283.

Harman, G. (2000). The nonexistence of character traits. *Proceedings of the Aristotelian Society, 100,* 223–226. doi:0.1111/j.0066-7372.2003.00013.x.

Hazlett, A. (2012). Higher-order epistemic attitudes and intellectual humility. *Episteme, 9*(3), 205–223. doi:10.1017/epi.2012.11.

Hazlett, A. (2017). Intellectual pride. In A. J. Carter and E. C. Gordon (eds), *The Moral Psychology of Pride* (pp. 79–97). London and New York: Rowman & Littlefield.

Healy, K. (2016 April, 28). how rude. *Kieran Healy Blog*. Retrieved from https://kieranhealy.org/blog/archives/2016/04/28/how-rude/

Hill, S. E., DelPriore, D. J., and Vaughan, P. W. (2011). The cognitive consequences of envy: Attention, memory, and self-regulatory depletion. *Journal of Personality and Social Psychology, 101*(4), 653–666. doi:10.1037/a0023904.

Holroyd, J., Scaife, R., and Stafford, T. (2017). Responsibility for implicit bias. *Philosophy Compass, 12*(3), e12410. doi:10.1111/phc3.12410.

Holton, R. (2001). III—What is the role of the self in self-deception? *Proceedings of the Aristotelian Society, 101*(1), 53–69. doi:10.1111/j.0066-7372.2003.00021.x.

Hookway, C. (2002). Emotions and epistemic evaluations. In P. Carruthers, S. P. Stich, and M. Siegal (eds), *The Cognitive Basis of Science* (pp. 251–262). Cambridge: Cambridge University Press.

Hookway, C. (2003a). Affective states and epistemic immediacy. *Metaphilosophy, 34*(1–2), 78–96. doi:10.1111/1467-9973.00261.

Hookway, C. (2003b). How to be a virtue epistemologist. In M. R. DePaul and L. T. Zagzebski (eds), *Intellectual Virtue: Perspectives from Ethics and Epistemology* (pp. 183–202). Oxford: Clarendon Press.

Hookway, C. (2008). Epistemic immediacy, doubt and anxiety: On a role for affective states in epistemic evaluation. In G. Brun, U. Doguoglu, and D. Kuenzle (eds), *Epistemology and Emotions* (pp. 51–65). Aldershot: Ashgate.

Hursthouse, R. (2001). *On Virtue Ethics*. Oxford: Oxford University Press.

Imhoff, R., and Lamberty, P. K. (2017). Too special to be duped: Need for uniqueness motivates conspiracy beliefs. *European Journal of Social Psychology, 47,* 724–734. doi:10.1002/ejsp.2265.

John, O. P., and Robins, R. W. (1994). Accuracy and bias in self-perception: Individual differences in self-enhancement and the role of narcissism. *Journal of Personality and Social Psychology, 66*(1), 206–219. doi:10.1037/0022-3514.66.1.206.

Jones, K. (2004). Trust and terror. In P. DesAutels and M. U. Walker (eds), *Moral Psychology: Feminist Ethics and Social Theory* (pp. 3–18). Lanham: Rowman & Littlefield Publishers.

Jones, K. (2012). The politics of intellectual self-trust. *Social Epistemology, 26*(2), 237–252. doi:10.1080/02691728.2011.652215.

Jordan, C. H., Logel, C., Spencer, S. J., Zanna, M. P., Wood, J. V., and Holmes, J. G. (2013). Responsive low self-esteem: Low explicit self-esteem, implicit self-esteem, and reactions to performance outcomes. *Journal of Social and Clinical Psychology, 32*(7), 703–732. doi:10.1521/jscp.2013.32.7.703.

Jordan, C. H., Spencer, S. J., and Zanna, M. P. (2005). Types of high self-esteem and prejudice: How implicit self-esteem relates to ethnic discrimination among high explicit self-esteem individuals. *Personality and Social Psychology Bulletin, 31*(5), 693–702. doi:10.1177/0146167204271580.

Jordan, C. H., Spencer, S. J., Zanna, M. P., Hoshino-Browne, E., and Correll, J. (2003). Secure and defensive high self-esteem. *Journal of Personality and Social Psycholology*, 85(5), 969–978. doi:10.1037/0022-3514.85.5.969.

Jost, J. T., Glaser, J., Kruglanski, A. W., and Sulloway, F. J. (2003). Political conservatism as motivated social cognition. *Psychological Bulletin*, 129(3), 339–375. doi:10.1037/0033-2909.129.3.339.

Kahneman, D. (2012). *Thinking, Fast and Slow*. London: Penguin.

Karmarkar, U. R., and Tormala, Z. L. (2010). Believe me, I have no idea what I'm talking about: The effects of source certainty on consumer involvement and persuasion. *Journal of Consumer Research*, 36(6), 1033–1049. doi:10.1086/648381.

Katz, D. (1960). The functional approach to the study of attitudes. *Public Opinion Quarterly*, 24(2), 163–204. doi:10.1086/266945.

Kidd, I. J. (2016). Charging others with epistemic vice. *The Monist*, 99(2), 181–197. doi:10.1093/monist/onv035.

Kidd, I. J. (2017a). Capital epistemic vices. *Social Epistemology Review and Reply Collective*, 6(8), 11–16.

Kidd, I. J. (2017b). Cranks, pluralists, and epistemic vices. *Social Epistemology Review and Reply Collective*, 6(7), 7–9.

Kidd, I. J. (2019). Epistemic corruption and education. *Episteme*, 16(2), 220–235. doi:10.1017/epi.2018.3.

Kieran, M. (2017). Creativity, vanity, narcissism. In B. Gaut and M. Kieran (eds), *Creativity and Philosophy* (pp. 74–92). London: Routledge.

Kitcher, P. (1993). *The Advancement of Science: Science without Legend, Objectivity without Illusions*: Oxford University Press.

Knobloch-Westerwick, S., and Meng, J. (2009). Looking the other way: Selective exposure to attitude-consistent and counterattitudinal political information. *Communication Research*, 36(3), 426–448. doi:10.1177/0093650209333030.

Kornblith, H. (2012). *On Reflection*. Oxford: Oxford University Press.

Kristjánsson, K. (2001). Pridefulness. *Journal of Value Inquiry*, 35(2), 165–178. doi:0.1023/A:1010314507529.

Kristjánsson, K. (2006). Emulation and the use of role models in moral education. *Journal of Moral Education*, 35(1), 37–49. doi:10.1080/03057240500495278.

Kristjánsson, K. (2007). *Aristotle, Emotions, and Education*. Aldershot and Burlington, VT: Ashgate.

Kristjánsson, K. (2014). Is shame an ugly emotion? Four discourses—two contrasting interpretations for moral education. *Studies in Philosophy and Education*, 33(5), 495–511. doi:10.1007/s11217-013-9399-7.

Kristjánsson, K. (2017). Emotions targeting moral exemplarity: Making sense of the logical geography of admiration, emulation and elevation. *Theory and Research in Education*, 15(1), 20–37. doi:10.1177/1477878517695679.

Kruglanski, A. W. (2004). *The Psychology of Closed Mindedness*. Hove: Psychology Press.

Kruglanski, A. W., Webster, D. M., and Klem, A. (1993). Motivated resistance and openness to persuasion in the presence or absence of prior information. *Journal of Personality and Social Psychology*, 65, 861–876. doi:10.1037//0022-3514.65.5.861.

Krumrei-Mancuso, E. J. (2017). Intellectual humility and prosocial values: Direct and mediated effects. *The Journal of Positive Psychology*, 12(1), 13–28. doi:10.1080/17439760.2016.1167938.

Kunda, Z. (1990). The case for motivated reasoning. *Psychological Bulletin*, 108(3), 480–498. doi:10.1037/0033-2909.108.3.480.

Lackey, J. (2018). The duty to object. *Philosophy and Phenomenological Research, 101*(1), 35–60. doi:10.1111/phpr.12563.

Lakin, J. L., Jefferis, V. E., Cheng, C. M., and Chartrand, T. L. (2003). The Chamaleon effect as social glue: Evidence for the evolutionary significance of nonconscious mimicry. *Journal of Nonverbal Behavior, 27*(3), 145–162. doi:10.1023/A:1025389814290.

Lambird, K. H., and Mann, T. (2006). When do ego threats lead to self-regulation failure? Negative consequences of defensive high self-esteem. *Personality and Social Psychology Bulletin, 32*(9), 1177–1187. doi:10.1177/0146167206289408.

Lavine, H., and Snyder, M. (1996). Cognitive processing and the functional matching effect in persuasion: The mediating role of subjective perceptions of message quality. *Journal of Experimental Social Psychology, 32*(6), 580–604. doi:10.1006/jesp.1996.0026.

Le Morvan, P., and Peels, R. (2016). The nature of ignorance: Two views. In R. Peels and M. Blaauw (eds.), *The Epistemic Dimensions of Ignorance* (pp. 12–32). Cambridge: Cambridge University Press.

Leary, M. R., and Baumeister, R. F. (2000). The nature and function of self-esteem: Sociometer theory. In *Advances in Experimental Social Psychology* (Vol. 32, pp. 1–62) Cambridge. Mass.: Academic Press.

Leary, M. R., Diebels, K. J., Davisson, E. K., Jongman-Sereno, K. P., Isherwood, J. C., Raimi, K. T., ... Hoyle, R. H. (2017). Cognitive and interpersonal features of intellectual humility. *Personality and Social Psychology Bulletin, 43*(6), 793–813. doi:10.1177/0146167217697695.

LeBel, E. P. (2010). Attitude accessibility as a moderator of implicit and explicit self-esteem correspondence. *Self and Identity, 9*(2), 195–208. doi:10.1080/15298860902979166.

Levy, N. (2015). Neither fish nor fowl: Implicit attitudes as patchy endorsements. *Noûs, 49*(4), 800–823. doi:10.1111/nous.12074.

Levy, N., and Alfano, M. (2020). Knowledge from vice: Deeply social epistemology. *Mind, 129*(515), 887–915. doi:10.1093/mind/fzz017.

London, B., Downey, G., Romero-Canyas, R., Rattan, A., and Tyson, D. (2012). Gender-based rejection sensitivity and academic self-silencing in women. *Journal of Personality and Social Psychology, 102*(5), 961–979. doi:10.1037/a0026615.

Lugones, M. (2003). *Pilgrimages/Peregrinajes: Theorizing Coalition against Multiple Oppressions*. Lanham; Boulder; New York and Oxford: Rowman & Littlefield.

Lupien, S. P., Seery, M. D., and Almonte, J. L. (2010). Discrepant and congruent high self-esteem: Behavioral self-handicapping as a preemptive defensive strategy. *Journal of Experimental Social Psychology, 46*, 1105–1108. doi:10.1016/j.jesp.2010.05.022.

Lynch, M. P. (2018). Epistemic arrogance and the value of political dissent. In C. R. Johnson (Ed.), *Voicing Dissent: The Ethics and Epistemology of Making Disagreement Public* (pp. 129–139). New York and London: Routledge.

Lynch, M. P. (2019). *Know-It-All Society: Truth and Arrogance in Political Culture*. New York and London: Liverlight Publishing Corporation.

Machery, E. (2016). De-Freuding implicit attitudes. In M. S. Brownstein and J. M. Saul (eds), *Implicit Bias and Philosophy: Metaphysics and Epistemology* (Vol. 1, pp. 104–129). Oxford: Oxford University Press.

Maheswaran, D., and Chaiken, S. (1991). Promoting systematic processing in low-motivation settings: Effect of incongruent information on processing and judgment. *Journal of Personality and Social Psychology., 61*(1), 13–25. doi:10.1037/0022-3514.61.1.13.

Maibom, H. L. (2010). The Descent of Shame. *Philosophy and Phenomenological Research, 80*, 566–594. doi:10.1111/j.1933-1592.2010.00341.x.

Maio, G. R., and Haddock, G. (2004). Theories of Attitudes: Creating a Witches Brew. In G. Haddock and G. R. Maio (eds), *Contemporary Perspectives on the Psychology of Attitudes* (pp. 425–453). Hove: Psychology.
Maio, G. R., and Haddock, G. (2007). Attitude Change. In A. W. Kruglanski and E. T. Higgins (eds), *Social Psychology: Handbook of Basic Principles* (2nd ed., pp. 565–586). New York: Guilford Press.
Maio, G. R., and Haddock, G. (2015). *The Psychology of Attitudes and Attitude Change* (2nd ed.). London: SAGE.
Maio, G. R., and Olson, J. M. (2000a). Emergent Themes and Potential Approaches to Attitude Function: The Function-Structure Model of Attitudes. In G. R. Maio and J. M. Olson (eds), *Why We Evaluate: Functions of Attitudes* (pp. 417–442). Mahwah, N.J. and London: Lawrence Erlbaum.
Maio, G. R., and Olson, J. M. (eds) (2000b). *Why We Evaluate: Functions of Attitudes*. Mahwah, NJ: Lawrence Erlbaum Associates.
Maio, G. R., Esses, V. M., Arnold, K. H., and Olson, J. M. (2004). The function-structure model of attitudes: Incorporanting the need for affect. In G. Haddock and G. R. Maio (eds), *Contemporary Perspectives on the Psychology of Attitudes* (pp. 9–33). Hove: Psychology.
Mandelbaum, E. (2014). Thinking is believing. *Inquiry*, 57(1), 55–96. doi:10.1080/0020174x.2014.858417.
Marchlewska, M., Cichocka, A., and Kossowska, M. (2018). Addicted to answers: Need for cognitive closure and the endorsement of conspiracy beliefs. *European Journal of Social Psychology*, 48(2), 109–117. doi:10.1002/ejsp.2308.
Marsh, K. L., and Julka, D. L. (2000). A motivational approach to experimental tests of attitude functions theory. In G. R. Maio and E. T. Olson (eds), *Why We Evaluate: Functions of Attitudes* (pp. 271–294). Mahwah, NJ: Lawrence Erlbaum Associates.
Martin, A. M. (2014). *How We Hope: A Moral Psychology*. Princeton: Princeton University Press.
Massey, S. J. (1995). Is self-respect a moral or a psychological concept? In R. S. Dillon (ed.), *Dignity, Character, and Self-Respect* (pp. 198–217). New York and London: Routledge.
Mathews, A., and MacLeod, C. (1994). Cognitive approaches to emotion and emotional disorders. *Annual Review of Psychology*, 45, 25–50.
McDowell, J. H. (1994). *Mind and World*. Cambridge, Mass and London: Harvard University Press.
McGeer, V. (2004). The art of good hope. *The Annals of the American Academy of Political and Social Science*, 592, 100–127.
McGregor, I. (2003). Defensive zeal: Compensatory conviction about attitudes, values, goals, groups, and self-definitions in the face of personal uncertainty. In S. J. Spencer, S. Fein, M. P. Zanna, and J. M. Olson (eds), *Ontario Symposium on Personality and Social Psychology. Motivated Social Perception: The Ontario Symposium, Vol. 9)* (pp. 73–92). Mahwah, NJ, US: Lawrence Erlbaum Associates Publishers.
McGregor, I., and Marigold, D. C. (2003). Defensive zeal and the uncertain self: What makes you so sure? *Journal of Personality and Social Psychology*, 85(5), 838–852.
McGregor, I., Nail, P. R., Marigold, D. C., and Kang, S. J. (2005). Defensive pride and consensus: Strength in imaginary numbers. *Journal of Personality and Social Psychology*, 89(6), 978–996. doi:10.1037/0022-3514.89.6.978.
McHugh, C. (2013). Epistemic responsibility and doxastic agency. *Philosophical Issues*, 23 (Epistemic Agency), 132–157. doi:10.1111/phis.12007.

McHugh, C. (2014). Exercising doxastic freedom. *Philosophy and Phenomenological Research, 88*(1), 1–37. doi:10.1111/j.1933-1592.2011.00531.x.

McQueen, A., and Klein, W. M. P. (2006). Experimental manipulations of self-affirmation: A systematic review. *Self and Identity, 5*(4), 289–354. doi:10.1080/15298860600805325.

Medina, J. (2013). *The Epistemology of Resistance: Gender and Racial Oppression, Epistemic Injustice, and Resistant Imaginations*. Oxford and New York: Oxford University Press.

Medina, J. (2016). Ignorance and racial insensitivity In R. Peels and M. Blaauw (eds), *The Epistemic Dimensions of Ignorance* (pp. 178–201). Cambridge: Cambridge University Press.

Mele, A. R. (2001). *Self-deception Unmasked*. Princeton: Princeton University Press.

Mendoza-Denton, R., Downey, G., Davis, A., Purdie, V. J., and Pietrzak, J. (2002). Sensitivity to status-based rejection: Implications for African American students' college experience. *Journal of Personality and Social Psychology, 83*(4), 896–916. doi:10.1037//0022-3514.83.4.896.

Mercier, H., and Sperber, D. (2017). *The Enigma of Reason*. Cambridge (MA): Harvard University Press.

Meyers, D. T. (1995). Self-respect and autonomy. In R. S. Dillon (ed.), *Dignity, Character, and Self-Respect* (pp. 218–248). New York and London: Routledge.

Miller, C. B. (2013). *Moral Character: An Empirical Theory*. Oxford: Oxford University Press.

Miller, C. B. (2014). *Character and Moral Psychology*. Oxford: Oxford University Press.

Mills, C. W. (2007). White ignorance. In S. Sullivan and N. Tuana (eds), *Race and Epistemologies of Ignorance* (pp. 13–38). Albany: State University of New York Press.

Montmarquet, J. A. (1993). *Epistemic Virtue and Doxastic Responsibility*. Lanham, Md.: Rowman & Littlefield Publishers.

Moody-Adams, M. (1995). Race, class, and the social construction of self-respect In R. S. Dillon (ed.), *Dignity, Character, and Self-Respect* (pp. 271–289). New York and London: Routledge.

Moore, D. A., and Schatz, D. (2017). The three faces of overconfidence. *Social and Personality Psychology Compass, 11*(8), 1–12. doi:10.1111/spc3.12331.

Morgan-Knapp, C. (2019). Comparative pride. *The Philosophical Quarterly, 69*(275), 315–331. doi:10.1093/pq/pqy050.

Morton, A. (2010). *Epistemic Emotions*. Oxford: Oxford University Press.

Morton, A. (ed.) (2017). *Pride Versus Self-Respect*. London and New York: Rowman & Littlefield.

Mussweiler, T. (2020). How social comparison affects the self: The selective accessibility mechanism. In J. Suls, R. L. Collins, and L. Wheeler (eds), *Social Comparison, Judgment, and Behavior* (pp. 32–51). Oxford: Oxford University Press.

Mussweiler, T., and Rüter, K. (2003). What friends are for! The use of routine standards in social comparison. *Journal of Personality and Social Psychology, 85*, 467–481. doi:10.1037/0022-3514.85.3.467.

Nadelhoffer, T., and Wright, J. C. (2017). The twin dimensions of the virtue of humility: Low self-focus and high other-focus. In W. Sinnott-Armstrong and C. B. Miller (eds), *Moral Psychology: Virtues and Vices* (Vol. 5, pp. 309–371). Cambridge: MIT Press.

Nagel, J. (2010). Epistemic anxiety and adaptive invariantisms. *Philosophical Perspectives (Epistemology), 24*, 407–435. doi:10.1111/j.1520-8583.2010.00198.x.

Nussbaum, M. C. (2016). *Anger and Forgiveness: Resentment, Forgiveness, Justice*. New York: Oxford University Press.

Nuyen, A. T. (1999). Vanity. *The Southern Journal of Philosophy, 37*(4), 613–627. doi:10.1111/j.2041-6962.1999.tb00885.x.

Okin, S. M. (1996). Feminism, moral development, and the virtues. In R. Crisp (ed.), *How Should One Live?* (pp. 211–229). Oxford: Clarendon Press.

Olin, L., and Doris, J. M. (2014). Vicious minds. *Philosophical Studies, 168*(3), 665–692. doi:10.1007/s11098-013-0153-3.

Olson, D. (2015). A case for epistemic agency. *Logos and Episteme, 6*(4), 449–474. doi:10.5840/logos-episteme20156435.

Olson, M. A., Fazio, R. H., and Hermann, A. D. (2007). Reporting tendencies underlie discrepancies between implicit and explicit measures of self-esteem. *Psychological Science, 18*(4), 287–291.

Patrick, V. M., Chun, H. H., and Macinnis, D. J. (2009). Affective forecasting and self-control: Why anticipating pride wins over anticipating shame in a self-regulation context. *Journal of Consumer Psychology, 19*(3), 537–545. doi:10.1016/j.jcps.2009.05.006.

Peels, R. (2017). *Responsible Belief: A Theory in Ethics and Epistemology*. New York: Oxford University Press.

Petrocelli, J. V., Tormala, Z. L., and Rucker, D. D. (2007). Unpacking attitude certainty: Attitude clarity and attitude correctness. *Journal of Personality and Social Psychology, 92*(1), 30–41. doi:10.1037/0022-3514.92.1.30.

Pettigrove, G. (2012). Meekness and 'moral' anger. *Ethics, 122*, 341–370. doi:10.1086/663230.

Petty, R. E., and Cacioppo, J. T. (1986). The elaboration likelihood model of persuasion. In L. Berkowitz (ed.), *Advances in Experimental Social Psychology* (Vol. 19, pp. 123–205). Orlando, FL: Academic Press.

Petty, R. E., and Wegener, D. T. (1998). Attitude change: Multiple roles for persuasion variables. In D. Gilbert, S. Fiske, and L. Gardner (eds), *The Handbook of Social Psychology* (4 ed., pp. 323–390). New York: McGraw-Hill.

Petty, R. E., Briñol, P., Tormala, Z. L., and Wegener, D. T. (2007). The role of metacognition in social judgment. In A. W. Kruglanski and E. T. Higgins (eds), *Social Psychology: Handbook of Basic Principles* (2nd ed., pp. 254–284). New York: Guilford Press.

Petty, R. E., Wheeler, C. S., and Bizer, G. Y. (2000). Attitude functions and persuasion: An elaboration likelihood approach to matched versus mismatched messages. In G. R. Maio and J. M. Olson (eds), *Why We Evaluate: Functions of Attitudes* (pp. 133–162). Mahwah, NJ: Lawrence Erlbaum Associates.

Phillips, W. J., and Hine, D. W. (2016). En route to depression: Self-esteem discrepancies and habitual rumination. *Journal of Personality, 84*(1), 79–90. doi:10.1111/jopy.12141.

Pornpitakpan, C. (2004). The persuasiveness of source credibility: A critical review of five decades' evidence. *Journal of Applied Social Psychology, 34*(2), 243–281. doi:10.1111/j.1559-1816.2004.tb02547.x.

Porter, S. L. (2016). A therapeutic approach to intellectual virtue formation in the classroom. In J. S. Baehr (ed.), *Intellectual Virtues and Education: Essays in Applied Virtue Epistemology* (pp. 221–239). New York and London: Routledge.

Priest, M. (2017). Intellectual humility: An interpersonal theory. *Ergo, an Open Access Journal of Philosophy, 4*(20180709). doi:10.3998/ergo.12405314.0004.016.

Protasi, S. (2016). Varieties of envy. *Philosophical Psychology, 29*(4), 535–549. doi:10.1080/09515089.2015.1115475.

Proust, J. (2008). Epistemic agency and metacognition: An externalist view. *Proceedings of the Aristotelian Society (Hardback), 108*(1pt3), 241–268. doi:10.1111/j.1467-9264.2008.00245.x.

Proust, J. (2013). *The Philosophy of Metacognition: Mental Agency and Self-Awareness*. Oxford: Oxford University Press.

Raskin, R. N., and Terry, H. (1988). A principle components analysis of the Narcissistic Personality Inventory and further evidence of its construct validity. *Journal of Personality and Social Psychology, 54*, 890–902.

Ratcliffe, M. (2008). *Feelings of Being: Phenomenology, Psychiatry, and the Sense of Reality*. Oxford and New York: Oxford University Press.

Rees, C. F., and Webber, J. (2014). Constancy, fidelity and integrity. In S. Van Hooft (ed.), *The Handbook of Virtue Ethics* (pp. 399–408). Durham: Acumen Press.

Reiss, S. (2012). Intrinsic and extrinsic motivation. *Teaching of Psychology, 39*(2), 152–156. doi:10.1177/0098628312437704.

Rheinschmidt, M. L., and Mendoza-Denton, R. (2014). Social class and academic achievement in college: The interplay of rejection sensitivity and entity beliefs. *Journal of Personality and Social Psychology, 107*(1), 101–121. doi:10.1037/a0036553.

Riggs, W. (2010). Open-mindedness. *Metaphilosophy, 41*(1–2), 172–188. doi:10.1111/j.1467-9973.2009.01625.x.

Ritchhart, R. (2002). *Intellectual Character: What It Is, Why It Matters, and How to Get It* (1st ed.). San Francisco: Jossey-Bass.

Roberts, R. (2016). Humility and gratitude. In D. Carr (ed.), *Perspectives on Gratitude: An Interdisciplinary Approach* (pp. 57–69). Abingdon and New York: Routledge.

Roberts, R. C., and West, R. (2015). Natural epistemic defects and corrective virtues. *Synthese, 192*(8), 2557–2576. doi:10.1007/s11229-015-0669-5.

Roberts, R. C., and West, R. (2017). Jesus and the virtues of pride. In A. J. Carter and E. C. Gordon (eds.), *The Moral Psychology of Pride* (pp. 99–121). London and New York: Rowman & Littlefield.

Roberts, R. C., and Wood, W. J. (2003). Humility and epistemic goods. In M. R. DePaul and L. T. Zagzebski (eds), *Intellectual Virtue: Perspectives from Ethics and Epistemology* (pp. 257–279). Oxford: Clarendon.

Roberts, R. C., and Wood, W. J. (2007). *Intellectual Virtues: An Essay in Regulative Epistemology*. New York: Oxford University Press.

Robinson, B., and Alfano, M. (2016). I know you are, but what am I? Anti-individualism in the development of intellectual humility and Wu-Wei. *Logos and Episteme, 7*(4), 435–459. doi:10.5840/logos-episteme20167442.

Roets, A., Kruglanski, A. W., Kossowska, M., Pierro, A., Hong, Y.-y., James, M. O., and Mark, P. Z. (2015). The motivated gatekeeper of our minds: New directions in need for closure theory and research. *Advances in Experimental Social Psychology, 52*, 221–283. doi:10.1016/bs.aesp.2015.01.001.

Romero-Canyas, R., Downey, G., Reddy, K. S., Rodriguez, S., Cavanaugh, T. J., and Pelayo, R. (2010). Paying to belong: When does rejection trigger ingratiation? *Journal of Personality and Social Psychology, 99*(5), 802–823. doi:10.1037/a0020013.

Roskos-Ewoldsen, D. R., and Fazio, R. H. (1992). On the orienting value of attitudes: Attitude accessibility as a determinant of an object's attraction of visual attention. *Journal of Personality and Social Psychology, 63*(2), 198–211. doi:10.1037/0022-3514.63.2.198.

Rudolph, A., Schröder-Abé, M., Riketta, M., and Schütz, A. (2010). Easier when done than said! *Zeitschrift für Psychologie/Journal of Psychology, 218*(1), 12–19. doi:10.1027/0044-3409/a000003.

Sawicki, V., Wegener, D. T., Clark, J. K., Fabrigar, L. R., Smith, S. M., and Bengal, S. T. (2011). Seeking confirmation in times of doubt. *Social Psychological and Personality Science, 2*(5), 540–546. doi:10.1177/1948550611400212.

Sawicki, V., Wegener, D. T., Clark, J. K., Fabrigar, L. R., Smith, S. M., and Durso, G. R. (2013). Feeling conflicted and seeking information: When ambivalence enhances and diminishes selective exposure to attitude-consistent information. *Personality and Social Psychology Bulletin, 39*(6), 735–747. doi:10.1177/0146167213481388.

Scanlon, T. M. (1998). *What We Owe to Each Other*. Cambridge (Mass) and London: The Belknap Press of Harvard University Press.

Schlenker, B. R., and Pontari, B. A. (2000). The strategic control of information: Impression management and self-presentation in daily life. In A. Tesser, R. B. Felson, and J. M. Suls (Eds.), *Psychological Perspectives on Self and Identity* (pp. 199–232). Washington: American Psychological Association.

Schröder-Abé, M., Rudolph, A., and Schütz, A. (2007a). High implicit self-esteem is not necessarily advantageous: discrepancies between explicit and implicit self-esteem and their relationship with anger expression and psychological health. *European Journal of Personality, 21*(3), 319–339. doi:10.1002/per.626.

Schröder-Abé, M., Rudolph, A., Wiesner, A., and Schütz, A. (2007b). Self-esteem discrepancies and defensive reactions to social feedback. *International Journal of Psychology, 42*(3), 174–183. doi:10.1080/00207590601068134.

Schwartz, S. H., Cieciuch, J., Vecchione, M., Davidov, E., Fischer, R., Beierlein, C., ... Konty, M. (2012). Refining the theory of basic individual values. *Journal of Personality and Social Psychology, 103*(4), 663–688.

Scott-Kakures, D. (2000). Motivated believing: Wishful and unwelcome. *Noûs, 34*(3), 348–375. doi:10.1111/0029-4624.00215.

Sherman, D. K., and Cohen, G. L. (2002). Accepting threatening information: Self-affirmation and the reduction of defensive biases. *Current Directions in Psychological Science, 11*(4), 119–123. doi:10.1111/1467-8721.00182.

Sherman, D. K., and Cohen, G. L. (2006). The psychology of self-defense: Self-affirmation theory. In *Advances in Experimental Social Psychology* (Vol. 38, pp. 183–242) Cambridge, Mass.: Academic Press.

Sherman, D. K., and Hartson, K. A. (2011). Reconciling self-protection with self-improvement: Self-affirmation theory. In M. D. Alicke and C. Sedikides (eds.), *Handbook of Self-Enhancement and Self-Protection* (pp. 128–151). New York: The Guilford Press.

Shoemaker, D. (2015). *Responsibility from the Margins* (1st ed.). Oxford: Oxford University Press.

Smallets, S., Streamer, L., Kondrak, C. L., and Seery, M. D. (2016). Bringing you down versus bringing me up: Discrepant versus congruent high explicit self-esteem differentially predict malicious and benign envy. *Personality and Individual Differences, 94*, 173–179. doi:10.1016/j.paid.2016.01.007.

Smith, A. M. (2008). Control, responsibility, and moral assessment. *Philosophical Studies, 138*(3), 367–392. doi:10.1007/s11098-006-9048-x.

Smith, A. M. (2012). Attributability, answerability, and accountability: In defense of a unified account. *Ethics, 122*(3), 575–589. doi:10.1086/664752.

Smith, C. A., and Ellsworth, P. C. (1985). Patterns of cognitive appraisal in emotion. *Journal of Personality and Social Psychology, 48*(4), 813–838. doi:10.1037/0022-3514.48.4.813.

Smith, H. M. (2017). Tracing cases of culpable ignorance. In R. Peels (ed.), *Perspectives on Ignorance from Moral and Social Philosophy* (pp. 95–119). New York and London: Routledge.

Smith, S. M., Fabrigar, L. R., Macdougall, B. L., and Wiesenthal, N. L. (2008). The role of amount, cognitive elaboration, and structural consistency of attitude-relevant knowledge in the formation of attitude certainty. *European Journal of Social Psychology, 38*(2), 280–295. doi:10.1002/ejsp.447.

Snow, N. (2013). Hope as an intellectual virtue. In M. W. Austin (Ed.), *Virtues in Action: New Essays in Applied Virtue Ethics* (pp. 152–170). New York: Palgrave Macmillan Publishing.

Snow, N. E. (1995). Humility. *The Journal of Value Inquiry, 29*(2), 203–216. doi:10.1007/bf01079834.

Snow, N. E. (2010). *Virtue as Social Intelligence: An Empirically Grounded Theory.* New York: Routledge.

Snow, N. E., Wright, J. C., and Warren, M. T. (2019). Virtue measurement: Theory and applications. *Ethical Theory and Moral Practice, 23*(2), 277–293. doi:10.1007/s10677-019-10050-6.

Snyder, M. (1974). Self-monitoring of expressive behavior. *Journal of Personality and Social Psychology, 30*(4), 526–557. doi:10.1037/h0037039.

Snyder, M., and DeBono, K. G. (1989). Understanding the functions of attitudes: Lessons from personality and social behavior. In A. R. Pratkanis, S. J. Breckler, and A. G. Greenwald (eds), *Attitude Structure and Function* (pp. 339–359). Hillsdale, NJ: Lawrence Erlbaum Associates.

Sosa, E. (2007). *A Virtue Epistemology. Apt Belief and Reflective Knowledge, Vol. I.* Oxford: Clarendon Press.

Sosa, E. (2009). *Reflective Knowledge: Apt Belief and Reflective Knowledge, Volume 2.* Oxford: Clarendon Press.

Sosa, E. (2011). *Knowing Full Well.* Princeton and Oxford: Princeton University Press.

Soyarslan, S. (2018). From humility to envy: Questioning the usefulness of sad passions as a means towards virtue in Spinoza's Ethics. *European Journal of Philosophy, 28*(1), 33–47. doi:10.1111/ejop.12422.

Spelman, E. V. (1990). *Inessential Woman: Problems of Exclusion in Feminist Thought.* London: Women's Press.

Spinoza, B. d. (1985). *The Collected Works of Spinoza* (E. Curley, trans. Vol. 1). Princeton: Princeton University Press.

Steele, C. (2010). *Whistling Vivaldi and Other Clues to How Stereotypes Affect Us.* New York and London: W. W. Norton.

Steele, C. M. (1988). The psychology of self-affirmation: Sustaining the integrity of the self. In L. Berkowitz (ed.), *Advances in Experimental Social Psychology Volume 21* (pp. 261–302). Cambridge, Mass.: Academic Press.

Stichter, M. (2016). Practical skills and practical wisdom in virtue. *Australasian Journal of Philosophy, 94*(3), 435–448. doi:10.1080/00048402.2015.1074257.

Stocker, M., and Hegeman, E. (1996). *Valuing Emotions.* Cambridge: Cambridge University Press.

Strawson, P. F. (2008). *Freedom and Resentment and Other Essays.* London: Routledge.

Sullivan, E., and Alfano, M. (2019). Negative epistemic exemplars. In B. R. Sherman and S. Gouen (eds), *Overcoming Epistemic Injustice: Social and Psychological Perspectives* (pp. 17–31). London and New York: Rowman & Littlefield.

Sullivan, S., and Tuana, N. (eds). (2007). *Race and Epistemologies of Ignorance*. Albany: State University of New York Press.

Suls, J., Collins, R. L., and Wheeler, L. (eds). (2020). *Social Comparison, Judgment, and Behavior*. Oxford: Oxford University Press.

Surowiecki, J. (2005). *The Wisdom of Crowds*. New York: Anchor Books.

Swank, C. (2000). Epistemic vice. In G. Axtell (ed.), *Knowledge, Belief, and Character: Readings in Virtue Epistemology* (pp. 195–204). Lanham: Rowman & Littlefield.

Tanesini, A. (2016a). I—'Calm down, dear': Intellectual arrogance, silencing and ignorance. *Aristotelian Society Supplementary Volume, 90*(1), 71–92. doi:10.1093/arisup/akw011.

Tanesini, A. (2016b). Teaching virtue: Changing attitudes. *Logos and Episteme, 7*(4), 503–527. doi:10.5840/logos-episteme20167445.

Tanesini, A. (2018a). Arrogance, anger and debate. *Symposion: Theoretical and Applied Inquiries in Philosophy and Social Sciences, 5*(2) (Special issue on Skeptical Problems in Political Epistemology, edited by Scott Aikin and Tempest Henning), 213–227. doi:10.5840/symposion20185217.

Tanesini, A. (2018b). Caring for esteem and intellectual reputation: Some epistemic benefits and harms. *Royal Institute of Philosophy Supplement, 84*, 47–67. doi:10.1017/s1358246118000541.

Tanesini, A. (2018c). Epistemic vice and motivation. *Metaphilosophy, 49*(3), 350–367. doi:10.1111/meta.12301.

Tanesini, A. (2018d). Intellectual humility as attitude. *Philosophy and Phenomenological Research, 96*(2), 399–420. doi:10.1111/phpr.12326.

Tanesini, A. (2018e). Intellectual servility and timidity. *Journal of Philosophical Research, 43*, 21–41. doi:10.5840/jpr201872120.

Tanesini, A. (2019). Reducing arrogance in public debate. In J. Arthur (ed.), *Virtues in the Public Sphere* (pp. 28–38). London: Routledge.

Tanesini, A. (2020). Virtuous and vicious intellectual self-trust. In K. Dormandy (ed.), *Trust in Epistemology* (pp. 218–238). New York and London: Routledge.

Tanesini, A. (forthcoming). Attitude psychology and virtue epistemology: A new framework. In N. Ballantyne and D. Dunning (eds), *Reason, Bias, and Inquiry: New Perspectives from the Crossroads of Epistemology and Psychology*. New York: Oxford University Press.

Taylor, G. (1985). *Pride, Shame, and Guilt: Emotions of Self-Assessment*. New York: Oxford University Press.

Taylor, G. (2006). *Deadly Vices*. Oxford: Clarendon Press.

Tessman, L. (2005). *Burdened Virtues: Virtue Ethics for Liberatory Struggles*. New York and Oxford: Oxford University Press.

Tiberius, V., and Walker, J. D. C. (1998). Arrogance. *American Philosophical Quarterly, 35*(4), 379–390. doi:https://www.jstor.org/stable/20009945.

Tiedens, L. Z., and Linton, S. (2001). Judgment under emotional certainty and uncertainty: The effects of specific emotions on information processing. *Journal of Personality and Social Psychology, 81*(6), 973–988. doi:10.1037/0022-3514.81.6.973.

Timpe, K. (2008). Moral character. *Internet Encyclopedia of Philosophy*. Retrieved from http://www.iep.utm.edu/moral-ch/

Tognazzini, N., and Coates, D. J. (2018). Blame. In E. N. Zalta (ed.), *The Stanford Encyclopedia of Philosophy* (Fall 2018 ed., pp. 1–42). Retrieved from https://plato.stanford.edu/archives/fall2018/entries/blame/.

Tormala, Z. L. (2016). The role of certainty (and uncertainty) in attitudes and persuasion. *Current Opinion in Psychology, 10*, 6–11. doi:10.1016/j.copsyc.2015.10.017.

Tormala, Z. L., and Rucker, D. D. (2007). Attitude certainty: A review of past findings and emerging perspectives. *Social and Personality Psychology Compass*, 1(1), 469–492. doi:10.1111/j.1751-9004.2007.00025.x.

Tracy, J. L., and Robins, R. W. (2007). Emerging insights into the nature and function of pride. *Current Directions in Psychological Science*, 16(3), 147–150. doi:10.1111/j.1467-8721.2007.00493.x.

Tracy, J. L., Cheng, J. T., Robins, R. W., and Trzesniewski, K. H. (2009). Authentic and hubristic pride: The affective core of self-esteem and narcissism. *Self and Identity*, 8(2–3), 196–213. doi:10.1080/15298860802505053.

Tuana, N. (2006). The speculum of ignorance: The women's health movement and epistemologies of ignorance. *Hypatia*, 21(3), 1–19. doi:10.1111/j.1527-2001.2006.tb01110.x.

Van Boven, L., Judd, C. M., and Sherman, D. K. (2012). Political polarization projection: Social projection of partisan attitude extremity and attitudinal processes. *Journal of Personality and Social Psychology*, 103(1), 84–100. doi:10.1037/a0028145.

van de Ven, N., Zeelenberg, M., and Pieters, R. (2009). Leveling up and down: The experiences of benign and malicious envy. *Emotion*, 9(3), 419–429. doi:10.1037/a0015669.

van Harreveld, F., van der Pligt, J., and de Liver, Y. N. (2009). The agony of ambivalence and ways to resolve it: Introducing the MAID model. *Personality and Social Psychology Review*, 13(1), 45–61. doi:10.1177/1088868308324518.

Vater, A., Schröder-Abé, M., Schütz, A., Lammers, C.-H., and Roepke, S. (2010). Discrepancies between explicit and implicit self-esteem are linked to symptom severity in borderline personality disorder. *Journal of Behavior Therapy and Experimental Psychiatry*, 41(4), 357–364. doi:10.1016/j.jbtep.2010.03.007.

Vohs, K. D., Baumeister, R. F., and Ciarocco, N. J. (2005). Self-regulation and self-presentation: regulatory resource depletion impairs impression management and effortful self-presentation depletes regulatory resources. *Journal of Personality and Social Psychology*, 88(4), 632–657. doi:10.1037/0022-3514.88.4.632.

Vohs, K. D., and Heatherton, T. F. (2001). Self-esteem and threats to self: Implications for self-construals and interpersonal perceptions. *Journal of Personality and Social Psychology* 81(6), 1103–1118. doi:10.1037/0022-3514.81.6.1103.

Vohs, K. D., and Heatherton, T. F. (2004). Ego threat elicits different social comparison processes among high and low self-esteem people: Implications for interpersonal perceptions. *Social Cognition*, 22(1), 168–191. doi:10.1521/soco.22.1.168.30983.

Von Wright, G. H. (1963). *The Varieties of Goodness*. London: Routledge & Kegan Paul.

Vonk, R. (2002). Self-serving interpretations of flattery: Why ingratiation works. *Journal of Personality and Social Psychology*, 82(4), 515–526. doi:10.1037/0022-3514.82.4.515.

Watson, G. (2004). *Agency and Answerability: Selected Essays*. Oxford: Clarendon Press.

Watt, S. E., Maio, G. R., Haddock, G., and Johnson, B. T. (2008). Attitude functions in persuasion: Matching, involvement, self-affirmation, and hierarchy. In W. D. Crano and R. Prislin (eds.), *Attitudes and Attitude Change* (pp. 189–211). New York: Psychology Press.

Weatherson, B. (2008). Deontology and Descartes' demon. *Journal of Philosophy*, 105(9 (Epistemic Norms)), 540–569. doi:10.5840/jphil2008105932.

Webber, J. (2015). Character, attitude and disposition. *European Journal of Philosophy*, 23(4), 1082–1096. doi:10.1111/ejop.12028.

Webber, J. (2016). Instilling virtue. In A. Masala and J. Webber (eds), *From Personality to Virtue: Essays on the Philosophy of Character* (pp. 134–154). Oxford: Oxford University Press.

Webster, D. M., and Kruglanski, A. W. (1994). Individual differences in need for cognitive closure. *Journal of Personality and Social Psychology,* 67(6), 1049–1062. doi:10.1037/0022-3514.67.6.1049.
Wheeler, L., and Suls, J. (2020). A history of social comparison. In J. Suls, R. L. Collins, and L. Wheeler (eds), *Social Comparison, Judgment, and Behavior* (pp. 5–31). Oxford: Oxford University Press.
Whitcomb, D., Battaly, H., Baehr, J., and Howard-Snyder, D. (2017). Intellectual humility: Owning our limitations. *Philosophy and Phenomenological Research,* 94(3), 509–539. doi:10.1111/phpr.12228.
White, P. H., Sanbonmatsu, D. M., and Croyle, R. T. (2002). Test of socially motivated underachievement: 'Letting up' for others. *Journal of Experimental Social Psychology,* 38(2), 162–169. doi:10.1006/jesp.2001.1495.
Wiersema, D. V., Van der Pligt, J., and Van Harreveld, F. (2010). Motivated memory: Memory for attitude-relevant information as a function of self-esteem. *Social Cognition,* 28(2), 219–239. doi:10.1521/soco.2010.28.2.219.
Wiersema, D. V., van Harreveld, F., and van der Pligt, J. (2012). Shut your eyes and think of something else: Self-esteem and avoidance when dealing with counter-attitudinal information. *Social Cognition,* 30, 323–334. doi:10.1521/soco.2012.30.3.323.
Wilson, A. T. (2016). Modesty as kindness. *Ratio,* 29(1), 73–88. doi:10.1111/rati.12045.
Wollstonecraft, M. (1992). *A Vindication of the Rights of Woman: With Strictures on Political and Moral Subjects* (W. a. I. b. M. Brody ed.). London: Penguin Books.
Wood, J. V., Giordano-Beech, M., Taylor, K. L., Michela, J. L., and Gaus, V. (1994). Strategies of social comparison among people with low self-esteem: Self-protection and self-enhancement. *Journal of Personality and Social Psychology,* 67(4), 713–731. doi:10.1037//0022-3514.67.4.713.
Wood, W. (2000). Attitude change: Persuasion and social influence. *Annual Review of Psychology,* 51(1), 539–570. doi:10.1146/annurev.psych.51.1.539.
Wu, K., Li, C., and Johnson, D. E. (2011). Role of self-esteem in the relationship between stress and ingratiation. *Psychological Reports,* 108(1), 239–251. doi:10.2466/07.09.20.PR0.108.1.239-251.
Zagzebski, L. T. (1996). *Virtues of the Mind: An Inquiry into the Nature of Virtue and the Ethical Foundations of Knowledge.* Cambridge: Cambridge University Press.
Zagzebski, L. T. (2010). Exemplarist virtue theory. *Metaphilosophy,* 41(1–2), 41–57. doi:10.1111/j.1467-9973.2009.01627.x.
Zagzebski, L. T. (2012). *Epistemic Authority: A Theory of Trust, Authority, and Autonomy in Belief.* Oxford and New York: Oxford University Press.
Zagzebski, L. T. (2015). I-admiration and the admirable. *Aristotelian Society Supplementary Volume,* 89(1), 205–221. doi:10.1111/j.1467-8349.2015.00250.x.
Zagzebski, L. T. (2017). *Exemplarist Moral Theory.* New York, NY: Oxford University Press.
Zeigler-Hill, V., and Terry, C. (2007). Perfectionism and explicit self-esteem: The moderating role of implicit self-esteem. *Self and Identity,* 6(2–3), 137–153. doi:10.1080/15298860601118850.
Zunick, P. V., Teeny, J. D., and Fazio, R. H. (2017). Are some attitudes more self-defining than others? Assessing self-related attitude functions and their consequences. *Personality and Social Psychology Bulletin,* 43(8), 1136–1149. doi:10.1177/0146167217705121.

Index

For the benefit of digital users, indexed terms that span two pages (e.g., 52–53) may, on occasion, appear on only one of those pages.

Abramson, L. 133n.26
Acceptance of limitations 12, 15, 73–4, 79–84, 121n.6, 134
  as distinct from modesty 81
Ackerman, R. A. 127–8
Admiration 7, 14–15, 87n.22, 91, 102, 102n.22, 110, 117, 120–9, 121n.7, 155, 160, 163, 166, 168–72, 177–8, 184, 190, 196, 198–201, 201n.9
Ahlstrom-Vij, K. 35n.40, 36–7, 195n.3
Aikin, S. F. 127n.15
Ajzen, I. 67–8
Alfano, M. 7n.9, 48n.2, 62n.27, 64, 64n.29, 79n.9, 166–7, 182, 182n.18, 195, 201n.9
Alighieri, D. 98n.8
Alston, W. P. 170n.2
Alvarez, M. 42
Anger 16, 37–8, 47–8, 66–7, 98–103, 112–13, 113n.43, 115, 150, 154, 171, 173–4, 184, 196
Annas, J. 46, 61n.26, 62, 64–5
APE 60n.22
Arango-Muñoz, S. 24n.10
Aristotle 84n.17, 94, 96, 102, 102n.21, 121n.8, 194, 197, 197n.5
Arrogance 12–15, 34, 43–4, 61n.25, 62–3, 66–7, 87–9, 96–8, 106–10, 128, 147, 149–50, 152, 156–62, 181–2, 189–90, 195–7
  And humiliation 161–2
  And intimidation 161–2
  And pride 86
  And superbia 106–7, 109
  As hyper-autonomy 106, 109
  As self-reliance 106
  As virtue 110, 191
Ashton-James, C. E. 83–5, 87–8, 147–8, 151, 196–7
Asymmetry of error costs 13n.23, 55–7, 65–6, 82n.15, 105, 114n.48, 131n.24, 142–3, 145, 147–8, 200n.7
Attention 7, 24–9, 32, 36, 39–40, 46, 61, 64–5, 83–4, 94, 131–2

Attitudes 11, 46, 48, 204
  Ambivalent 52–3, 57–8, 146–7
  And situational influences 52–3, 68
  As associative states 50–2
  As constructs 50
  As causal bases of virtues and vices 48–9, 61, 67–9
  As reason-responsive 51–2, 64–5
  Content 48–52
  Function 48–51, 53–8, 65–6
  See also Function matching effects
    Defensive 15–16, 54–6, 62–6, 97–9, 103, 119–20, 131–2, 136, 142–4, 146, 188
    Instrumental 54–5
    Knowledge 54, 63–4, 73–4, 77–9, 81–2, 88, 187
    Object appraisal 54
    Social adjustive 15–16, 54–7, 63–4, 97–8, 114–21, 125–6, 129, 136, 142–4, 146, 156–7, 188
    Value expressive 54, 57, 59, 62–3, 73–4, 78–9, 81–2, 88
  Measurement 59–61, 63
    Dissociation 60–1, 60n.21
    Explicit measures 59
    Implicit measures 59, 68, 103n.24
    See also Evaluative Priming and Implicit Association Test
  Object 48–51
  Structure 48–9, 52–3
  Strength 48–51, 58–9, 146, 204
    Accessibility 49–50, 52–3, 58, 63, 65, 78–9, 103, 103n.25, 104–5
    Centrality 49–50, 59, 63
    Certainty 59, 67, 105, 146–50, 159–60, 195–6
    Extremity 49–50, 58, 148
Austen, J. 106
Axtell, G. 26n.16

Baehr, J. 8, 31n.28, 35n.39, 46n.64, 47, 47n.65, 97n.3, 194–5, 197, 199
Baier, A. 152n.17
Banaji, M. R. 51

INDEX 225

Baron, R. S. 130, 149
Bartky, S. L. 3n.5, 9-10, 114n.47, 117
Battaly, H. 7n.9, 32nn.31-32, 40-1, 40n.46, 41n.50, 61n.25, 164-5, 177-9, 183-4, 194-5, 197, 199
Baumeister, R. F. 63-4, 102n.22, 134n.28, 150-1, 151nn.13,14, 155-6, 163, 196-7
Baxter, D. 96n.1
Bell, D. W. 52-3
Bell, M. 14n.25, 96, 106
Berlin, I. 30n.25
Bishop, M. 10
Blame 16-17, 38-9, 170-3, 177-9, 181-6
  Standing 16-17, 168, 182-4
Bloomfield, P. 4n.6, 45n.62, 116nn.53,54, 195n.2
Bodenhausen, G. V. 60n.22
Bommarito, N. 65, 65n.31, 74-5, 77
Bosson, J. K. 60n.21, 103, 103n.24, 147-8
'Boomerang vision' 106
Brady, M. S. 27-8, 84-5, 91n.27
Brannon, L. A. 58, 105
Brennan, G. 90n.26
Brown, J. 173, 179n.10
Brownstein, M. 60n.22, 61n.24
Bruner, J. 93n.29
Bushman, B. J. 102n.22
Byerly, T. R. 34n.37

Cacioppo, J. T. 31, 53-4, 63-4, 83, 83n.16, 144, 159-60
Calhoun, C. 181n.14, 184
Campbell, W. K. 93, 101n.20, 127-9, 127n.18, 155-6, 161-3
Card, C. 3n.5, 40n.48, 112, 185, 185n.22, 186
Carruthers, P. 24n.10
Carter, J. A. 99n.12
Cassam, Q. 3, 7n.9, 22n.4, 26-7, 29n.24, 30n.25, 32n.32, 39-42, 43n.57, 44-5, 100n.16, 141-2, 151, 156-8, 164-5, 166n.33, 175n.7, 190, 202n.10
Césaire, A. 112
Chaiken, S. 145n.6, 148
Character 46, 61-2, 171-2, 175
Character traits, see Vices and Virtues
Cheatham, L. 159-60
Chen, S. 53-4, 55n.15, 63-4, 143-4, 149n.10
Church, I. M. 79
Cichocka, A. 152
Clanton, C. J. 127n.15
Closed-mindedness 32n.32, 58, 65, 105, 109-10, 141, 149-50, 168-77, 183-4, 195-6
  As a virtue 164-5
Clarkson, J. J. 34, 59, 105, 146-7, 154, 195-6
Coady, D. 93n.29

Coates, D. J. 184n.20
Cobb, A. D. 79n.10, 80-1, 131n.25
Cognitive Affective Personality System (CAPS) 48n.2
Cognitive bias 7-8, 13n.23, 142, 166-7
Cognitive closure, need for 30-2, 34n.34, 58, 62-3, 105, 149-50, 152, 175
Cognitive dissonance 114-15, 131, 158-9, 162-3
Cognitive impairments 38-9
Cognition, need for 29, 63-4, 82-3, 83n.16
Cohen, G. L. 17, 105, 202
Collins, P. H. 111n.37
Congeniality effect 143-4, 150
Consistency, cross-situation 46
Contempt 16, 66-7, 106, 154
Cooper, J. 114n.49, 130n.22, 162-3
Corcoran, K. 4, 88-9, 108-9, 200-1
Crerar, C. 8n.10, 40-1, 43, 184n.21
Critcher, C. R. 203
Croce, M. 193, 199
Crusius, J. 150, 196
Cunningham, W. A. 60n.21

Darwall, S. L. 186
DeBono, K. G. 145n.5, 146
Deci, E. L. 197-8
Defensive high self-esteem see self-esteem
Deonna, J. A. 84n.17, 111-12, 112nn.39,40
Depressive attributional style 111, 115, 156
Dillon, R. S. 85, 87n.22, 96, 107n.32, 110, 186, 191, 191n.27
Directional question 13n.23, 55-7, 105, 114n.48, 145, 200n.7
Dogmatism 2, 7-9, 26-7, 30-1, 35, 43, 81, 105, 109-10, 141, 149-50, 164-7, 176-7, 183-4
Dokic, J. 24n.10, 33-4
Dolezal, L. 111, 112n.40
Doris, J. M. 7n.9, 39, 48n.2, 64
Double-consciousness 112, 117-18
Doxastic voluntarism 169-70
Driver, J. 48n.1, 74-5, 75n.2
Du Bois, W. E. B. 3-4, 112, 115
Dunning, D. 200, 203
Dweck, Carol S. 1-2, 83n.16, 130, 133

Eagly, A. H. 143n.4
Eccentricities 38-9
Education 17, 193
  Explicit teaching 194-7
  Habituation 197-8
Elaboration Likelihood Model (ELM) 53-4, 56n.16, 144, 159-60
Ellsworth, P. C. 149n.9, 150, 196

Elster, J. 94
Emmons, R. A. 127n.17, 128n.19, 129
Emotion 16, 47, 61, 66–7, 82–3, 146, 149–50
Emulation 13, 95, 123, 193, 198–9
Envy 47, 66–7, 95, 123–5, 150, 200–1
   Benign 95, 123, 201
   Malicious 123, 150, 155, 196, 200–1
   Spiteful 16, 45n.63, 47, 66–7, 102, 120–1, 123–5, 127, 151, 155, 161, 199–201
Epistemic activities 23–6, 32–4
Epistemic agency 35–40
Epistemic anxiety 153–6
Epistemic evaluations 23–6
   Cognitive and affective 23–6
   First and second order 23–5
Epistemic feelings 24–6, 31–4, 37–8, 47, 59, 67, 130, 147–8, 152–4
   Of certainty/uncertainty 31, 34, 37, 47, 59, 67, 147–9, 152–4
   Of confidence 86, 147–8, 152, 154
   Of doubt 24–6, 31, 37, 47, 130, 149, 151–6
Epistemic injustice 161–2
Esses, V. M. 52–3
Esteem/Disesteem 73–4, 90–4, 112–13, 120–2, 124, 129–30, 161–3, 166, 168–9, 171–2, 184, 190, 196
Evaluative Priming 59, 59n.20
Evans, J. S. 144
Exemplarism 17, 193–4, 198–202
Explanation, mere 42

Fanon, F. 9–10, 112
Fantl, J. 32n.32, 165n.32, 166n.33
Fatalism 1–3, 5, 12, 14–15, 66–7, 86–7, 119–20, 133–7, 156, 189–90
Fazio, R. H. 51, 54, 58, 59n.20, 60, 63, 78–9, 150n.11
Fear 16, 24–5, 37–8, 66–7, 129–35, 149–51, 156, 195–7
Feinberg, J. 160–1
Fischer, P. 143n.3
Fixed Mindset 1–2, 82–3, 83n.16, 130, 133, 135
Foolishness 45
Foster, J. D. 101n.20, 127–8, 127n.18, 155–6, 161–3
Frankfurt, H. G. 3n.4
Fricker, M. 9n.13, 27, 39–40, 95, 161–2
Frye, M. 106n.29
Function matching effects 53–4, 56n.16, 68–9, 143–5

Galileo 42–4
Galligan, P. 111
Garcia, J. L. A. 74–5, 77

Gawronski, B. 60n.22
Gebauer, J. E. 17, 56, 63–5, 97–8, 103, 128, 148, 188–9, 203
Gendler, T. S. 179n.11
Generosity 83, 87, 126, 128–9, 203
Gerber, J. 151, 155–6, 196–7
Gleicher, F. 149, 195–6
Goffman, E. 2–3, 21n.1
Gratitude 77n.6, 171
Greco, J. 27n.18, 169n.1
Greenwald, A. G. 59n.20
Gregg, A. P. 128, 147

Haddock, G. 11, 17, 50–3, 50n.7, 52n.9, 54n.14, 55–7, 59, 63–6, 64n.30, 82, 97–8, 103, 128, 143–5, 148, 150, 188–9, 203
Hahn, A. 60n.23
Hahn, U. 143n.1
Han, H. 17, 199
Harman, G. 48n.2
Harms 16, 141
   And wrongs 160–4
   To epistemic community 164–7
   To others 159–67
   To self 141–59
Harris, A. J. L. 143n.1
Harris, R. 177–8
Hartson, K. A. 202–3
Haughtiness, see Superbia
Hayes, A. F. 200
Hazlett, A. 79, 86n.21, 88n.25
Healy, K. 99n.12
Heatherton, T. F. 108–9, 114–16, 151, 151n.13, 156, 196–7, 200–1
Hegeman, E. 101–2
Heiphetz, L. 51
Heuristics 37, 53–4, 144–5, 149
Heuristics Systematic Model (HSM) 53–4, 55n.15, 56n.16, 144, 159–60
Hill, S. E. 150–1
Hine, D. W. 151, 195–7
Holroyd, J. 177n.9
Holton, R. 158
Hookway, C. 8, 9n.12, 22nn.4–5, 24–7, 25n.12, 166
Hopefulness 6, 16, 79–81, 82n.14, 95, 133–4, 190, 195
Hopelessness 1–2, 16, 66–7, 80–1, 133–5, 156, 189
Hume, D. 120n.5
Humility or Intellectual Humility 6–7, 12–13, 43–4, 65n.31, 73–84, 130–1, 191, 195, 197–9, 201
   And Intellectual humility 11, 15

As interpersonal virtue 76–7
Ignorance-based accounts 74–6
Knowledge-based accounts 79–80
Low self-focus accounts 77
Hursthouse, R. 66–7

Ignorance 7–8, 28–9, 62–3, 74–5, 101n.18, 105, 109–10, 152, 159–60, 170–1, 175, 180–1
Imhoff, R. 31, 126n.14, 152
Information Processing 24–6, 24n.10, 26n.14, 34, 36–40, 45, 53–4, 54n.12, 58, 60, 105, 142–51, 153
Implicit Association Test (IAT) 59, 59n.20, 97–8
Implicit Bias 57–61, 177n.9
  See also Attitudes, Implicit measures
Ingratiation 14–16, 62–3, 110, 112–17, 124n.12, 132, 162–3
Inquiry 23–6
  Effective and responsible 22–3

John, O. P. 147
Jones, K. 153, 156n.23
Jordan, C. H. 103, 117–18, 117n.56, 136, 147–8, 188–9
Jost, J. T. 31n.27, 105
Julka, D. L. 54

Kahneman, D. 30n.26, 144
Karmarkar, U. R. 159n.27
Katz, D. 54
Kidd, I. J. 7n.9, 149–50, 162, 182n.17
Kieran, M. 120n.5
Kitcher, P. 9n.12, 166
Klein, W. M. P. 202
Knobloch-Westerwick, S. 146–7
Kornblith, H. 35n.40
Kripke, S. 166n.33
Kristjánsson, K. 84n.17, 85, 95, 112n.39, 123, 193–4, 197n.5, 198–9
Kruglanski, A. W. 30, 105, 149–50
Krumrei-Mancuso, E. J. 77n.6
Kuhn, T. 166n.33
Kunda, Z. 5n.8, 13n.23, 55, 142

Lackey, J. 163n.29
Lakin, J. L. 63–4
Lamberty, P. K. 31, 126n.14, 152
Lambird, K. H. 150–1, 196–7
Lange, J. 150
Lavine, H. 145
Laziness 67, 109–10

Le Morvan, P. 7n.9
Leary, M. R. 34n.36, 79n.9, 82n.15, 83n.16, 134n.28, 151n.14
LeBel, E. P. 103n.25
Levy, N. 26n.14, 166–7
Linton, S. 148–50, 195–6
London, B. 132
Love
  Of truth 43–4, 76–8, 80–1, 134, 166, 195
  See also self-love
Lugones, M. 106
Lupien, S. P. 108, 150–1
Lynch, M. P. 99, 107

Machery, E. 67–9, 68n.35
MacLeod, C. 149, 156
Maheswaran, D. 145n.6, 148
Maibom, H. L. 111
Maio, G. R. 11, 50–9, 50n.7, 52n.9, 54n.14, 63–6, 64n.30, 82, 108, 143–5, 150
Mandelbaum, E. 153–4
Mann, T. 150–1, 196–7
Marchlewska, M. 152
Marigold, D. C. 105, 147, 154, 156, 158–9
Marsh, K. L. 54
Martin, A. M. 133–4
Massey, S. J. 187
Mathews, A. 149, 156
McDowell, J. H. 39–40
McGeer, V. 134
McGregor, I. 101n.20, 103, 105, 128, 147–8, 154, 156, 158–9, 195–6
McHugh, C. 170
McQueen, A. 202
Medina, J. 2n.2, 3n.5, 14n.25, 27, 96, 101n.18, 107n.31, 109–10, 158n.25
Mele, A. R. 157
Mendoza-Denton, R. 135, 135n.29
Meng, J. 146–7
Mercier, H. 30n.26
Meyers, D. T. 187
Michaelian, K. 24n.10
Miller, C. B. 26n.16, 46, 48n.2, 61n.26, 62
Mills, C. W. 7n.9, 24n.10
MODE 60
Modesty 12, 15, 65, 73–9, 85
  as distinct from acceptance of limitations 81
Montmarquet, J. A. 47n.65
Moody-Adams, M. 96–7
Moore, D. A. 147n.8
Morgan-Knapp, C. 84–5, 89
Morrison, T. 110
Morton, A. 24–5, 85

Motivated cognition 5, 13n.23, 45, 64–5, 141–50, 156–8, 176, 195–6
   Accuracy motive 12, 54, 80, 82n.15, 83, 88–9, 142
   Ego-defence 12, 13n.23, 14–15, 55–6, 64–5, add from ch 5 134–6, 141–3, 157
   Social acceptance 12, 14–15, 55–7 add ch 5 and ch 6, 135–6, 141
Motivation 40–6, 53–5, 93, 119–20, 195–8
   And character traits 34–5, 45–7, 141, 174–7
   And motives 43n.56, 47
   And sensibilities 28–9, 45–6, 174–7
   And thinking styles 31–2, 45–6, 141, 174–7
Mussweiler, T. 88–9, 108–9, 196, 200

Nadelhoffer, T. 76n.5, 77, 83
Nagel, J. 153–4
Narcissism 3–6, 12–15, 61n.25, 66–7, 93, 102n.22, 117, 119–20, 126–9, 147, 149–52, 155–6, 159–63, 175–80, 190–1
   Conflation with arrogance 101–2, 126–9
Narcissistic Personality Inventory 125n.13, 127–9
Nussbaum, M. C. 101–2
Nuyen, N. T. 121n.7, 126

Obsequiousness, *see* Servility
Observant, being 26–8, 36, 40–1, 46, 74, 86, 119–20
O'Connor, C. 93n.29
Okin, S. M. 10n.14
Olin, L. 7n.9, 39
Olson, D. 35n.40
Olson, J. M. 53–8, 108
Olson, M. A. 51, 103, 103n.24
Open-mindedness 7–8, 32–4, 37–9, 43, 79, 79n.9, 83, 164–5, 165n.32, 195, 197, 199
Oppression 3n.5, 9–10, 100n.15, 110, 113n.43, 158n.25, 161n.28, 185, 191

Patrick, V. M. 156n.22, 197n.4
Peels, R. 7n.9, 170n.2
Personalism 177–9
Persuasion 53–4, 54n.13, 58, 63–4, 64n.30, 68–9, 82, 105, 142–9, 159–60
Petrocelli, J. V. 59
Pettigrove, G. 150n.12
Pettit, P. 90n.26
Petty, R. E. 53–4, 59, 63–4, 67, 83, 83n.16, 144–5, 147–9, 159–60, 195–6
Phillips, W. J. 151, 195–7
Pontari, B. A. 124n.12
Pornpitakpan, C. 159–60
Porter, S. L. 194

Prejudice 9, 26–7, 29–32, 87, 93, 100, 103, 142, 147–50, 178–9
Pride 7, 12–13, 15, 73–5, 78, 84–9
   And modesty 86–9
   As character trait 85–6
   As emotion 84–7
   Authentic pride 87
   Comparative pride 89
   Hubristic pride 87, 100
Proper concern for esteem 12–13, 15, 73–4, 89–95, 166
Priest, M. 76, 76n.5
Protasi, S. 95, 109n.35, 123, 161, 200n.8, 201
Proust, J. 23n.8, 24n.10, 25n.12, 26n.15, 33–4

Racism 28–9
Raskin, R. N. 125n.13, 127–8
Ratcliffe, M. 66–7, 103
Rationalization 42–5, 65
Reactive attitudes 170–1
Rees, C. F. 48n.3, 67
Reiss, S. 197–8
Responsibility 16–17, 40, 163, 168,
   Attributability 16–17, 38–40, 168–81
   Attributing responsibility 181–5
   Answerability 16–17, 38, 168–81
   Accountability 16–17, 40, 168–81
   Taking responsibility 40, 168, 185–6, 190–1
Reputation 91–2, 92n.28, 121–2
Rheinschmidt, M. L. 135
Riggs, W. 33–4, 39
Ritchart, R. 194–5
Roberts, R. C. 8n.11, 39, 61n.25, 75n.3, 86, 98n.9, 100n.14, 101n.17, 106, 166
Robins, R. W. 87, 100, 147
Robinson, B. 195
Roets, A. 30–1
Romero-Canyas, R. 112n.42, 115–16, 150, 162–3
Roskos-Ewoldsen, D. R. 150n.11
Rucker, D. D. 59, 146–8
Rudolph, A. 115
Rüter, K. 88–9, 200
Ryan, R. M. 197–8

Sawicki, V. 146–8, 195–6
Scanlon, T. M. 172
Schatz 147n.8, 152n.15
Schlenker, B. R. 124n.12
Schröder-Abé, M. 97–8, 103, 111, 115, 115n.52, 128, 156, 188–9
Schwartz, S. H. 203
Scott-Kakures, D. 13n.23, 29n.22, 55, 142
Sedikides, C. 128, 147
Selective exposure effect 143–4, 146–50, 152

Self-abasement 3–6, 12, 14–15, 66–7, 75, 86–7, 96–8, 113n.45, 116–18, 127n.17, 152, 155–6, 189
  As heteronomy 116–17, 117n.55
Self-affirmation 17, 104n.26, 193–4, 202–4
Self-certainty 34
Self-concept *see* self-esteem
Self-confidence 115, 129–30, 149–50
Self-control 34–40, 141–2, 150–5, 176, 185–6, 195–7, 197n.4
Self-enhancement 5, 44, 65–6, 103, 156–8, 175, 189–90, 203
Self-esteem 61–2, 73, 84, 87, 89–90, 97–8, 119–20, 186–92
  Damaged self-esteem 97–8, 115–18, 117n.56, 136, 151
  Defensive high self-esteem 15, 63–4, 87–8, 97–8, 101n.20, 102–5, 107–9, 128–9, 142, 147–8, 150–1, 188–9, 196–7, 200–1, 203
  Discrepant self-esteem 61, 97–8, 103n.25, 158–9
  Low self-esteem 103n.24, 111, 112n.42, 113–15, 130–2, 134–6, 146, 150, 156, 189, 195–7, 201
  Secure high self-esteem 87–8, 102, 188–9, 201
Self-deception 28–9, 44–6, 65, 141, 156–9, 188
Self-knowledge 93, 131, 141–2, 156–8
Self-infatuation *see* self-love, morbid
Self-love 66–7, 85, 102,
  Self-love, morbid 1, 3–6, 16, 67, 119, 126, 136, 155, 190–1
Self-monitoring 56–7, 63–4, 115–16, 125–6, 129, 155–6
Self-respect 7, 85–7, 87n.22, 94–5, 110, 166, 168–9, 186–92
Self-silence 129–32, 162–3
Self-sabotage 108, 150–1
Self-satisfaction 2–5, 87
Self-trust 129–30, 141–2, 152–6, 161
Servility 7, 12, 14–15, 62–3, 66–7, 96–8, 110–16, 149–51, 155–7, 160, 163, 166–7, 175, 179–80, 185, 189, 195–7
Shame 5–6, 16, 47, 66–7, 84–5, 84n.17, 111–12, 149–50, 155–6, 195–7
  And shame-proness 111–13, 117, 196
Sherman, D. K. 17, 105, 202–3
Shoemaker, D. 168–73, 175–8
Situationism 48n.2, 62–4
Smallets, S. 109, 200–1
Smith, A. M. 176, 178
Smith, C. A. 149n.9, 150, 196
Smith, H. M. 180–1
Smith, S. M. 59

Snow, N. E. 46, 48n.2, 64–5, 79, 81n.12, 133–4
Snyder, M. 63–4, 115–16, 125, 145–6, 155–6
Social comparison judgment 4–6, 73–4, 88–9, 95, 108–9, 115–16, 193, 199–201
  Motivation to improve 12–13, 73–4, 82, 85–9, 95, 120–1, 201
  Motivation to self-enhance 108–9, 196, 200
  Motivation to ingratiate 115–16, 196
Social epistemology 7–11
  Autonomous 8
  Ameliorative 10, 22–3
Social psychology 10, 48
Sosa, E. 8, 27n.18, 169n.1
Soyarslan, S. 80–1
Spelman, E. V. 106
Sperber, D. 30n.26
Spinoza, B. 98n.8, 113n.44
Steele, C. M. 202–3
Stability, temporal 46, 61–4
Stichter, M. 28n.19
Stocker, M. 101–2
Strawson, P. F. 171n.4
Sullivan, E. 201n.9
Sullivan, S. 28n.20
Suls, J. 109n.34, 135n.30, 200
Surowiecki, J. 166–7
Swank, C. 11–12
Superbia 12, 14–15, 48, 66–7, 96–106, 109, 147, 189–90
  And Hubristic pride 100

Tanesini, A 14nn.24,26, 39n.45, 41n.51, 43n.57, 49n.4, 79n.11, 84n.18, 90n.26, 92n.28, 101n.19, 106n.29, 110n.36, 120n.4, 129n.21, 152n.16, 199–200
Taylor, G. 84–5, 111, 124
Terry, C. 151
Terry, H. 125n.13, 127–8
Tessman, L. 3n.5, 10n.15, 84n.17, 100n.15, 112, 113n.43
Thatcher, D. 130
Thatcher, T. 129n.21
Tiberius, V. 123n.11
Tiedens, L. Z. 148–50, 195–6
Timidity 12, 14–15, 66–7, 93, 95, 119–20, 129–33, 149–50, 156, 160, 162–3, 179–80, 185, 189–90, 195–7
  And courage 130–1
Timpe, K. 68n.34
Tognazzini, N. 184n.20
Tormala, Z. L. 59, 146–8, 159–60, 159n.27
Tracy, J. L. 83–5, 87–8, 100, 147–8, 151, 196–7

Trout, J. D. 10
Tuana, N. 7n.9, 27, 28n.20

Uniqueness, need for 31, 126n.14, 127, 152

Vaccarezza, M. S. 193
Van Boven, L. 148
van de Ven, N. 123n.9
Van Harreveld, F. 151
Vanity 3, 7, 13–15, 66–7, 93, 95, 102, 119–26, 147, 151, 155, 160–1, 163, 175, 179–80, 190–1, 195–7
  And servility 124–5
  And superbia 124–5
Vater, A. 115
Vice 7–9, 11–12, 26–35
  Motivational account 40–6
  Character traits 32–5, 37–8, 45–6, 62–3, 83
  Sensibilities 27–9, 35–6, 45–6, 62–3, 65, 83–4, 119–20, 133–4, 152
  Stealthiness 44–5, 156–7, 157n.24, 190, 192
  Thinking styles 29–32, 36–7, 45–6, 62–3, 83, 119–20, 133–4, 152
Vices of inferiority 14, 96–8, 119–20, 141–3, 189, 199–201, 203
Vices of superiority 13–14, 96–8, 119–20, 141–2, 189–90, 199–201, 203
  Relations among them 14–15
Virtues
  As correctives 39–40
  As dispositions 67–9
  As intelligent 46, 61, 64–5
  As part of character 46
  As cross-situationally consistent 46, 61–4, 79n.11, 121
  As temporally stable 46, 121
  And motivation 61, 65–6, 79n.11
  Intellectual and Moral 11–12

Virtue reliabilism 8
Virtue responsibilism 8
Vohs, K. D. 108–9, 114–16, 155–6, 163, 200–1
Von Wright, G. H. 9
Vonk, R. 163

Walker, J. D. C. 123n.11
Watson, G. 172, 177
Watt, S. E. 56–7, 63–5, 82, 104n.26, 115–16, 125–6, 143
Weatherson, B. 170n.2
Webber, J. 11n.19, 48n.3, 54n.13, 67, 67n.33, 114n.49, 193–4, 197n.5, 204
Webster, D. M. 30
Wegener, D. T. 159–60
West, R. 39, 61n.25, 98n.9
Wheeler, L. 109n.34, 135n.30, 151, 155–6, 196–7
Whitcomb, D. 79, 113n.44
White, P. H. 114
Wiersema, D. V. 150, 195–6
Wilson, A. T. 76
Whole Trait Theory 48n.2
Wollstonecraft, M. 116n.54
Wood, J. V. 134–5
Wood, W. 114n.49, 131, 149, 195–6
Wood, W. J. 8n.11, 61n.25, 75n.3, 86, 100n.14, 101n.17, 106, 166
Wright, J. C. 76n.5, 77, 83
Wrongs 160–4
Wu, K. 112n.42, 132, 162–3

Zagzebski, L. T. 8, 17, 41n.49, 43n.56, 47, 80–1, 91, 107n.30, 117n.55, 121n.8, 153n.19, 169–70, 198–9, 200n.6
Zeigler-Hill, V. 151
Zunick, P. 59